THE VOLCANO

- ADAM WRAY -

THE VOLCANO

My Life - Proof of God's Existence?

- ADAM WRAY -

PUBLISHING

Publisher: Man of the Earth Publishing LLC

Web: AdamWrayTheVolcano.com

ISBN: 979-8-9863777-0-4

- Disclaimers -

This book contains detailed means of suicidal actions. Do not attempt what is described. Neither the publisher nor the author condone such acts and they will not be held liable in the event any self-inflicted harm results directly or indirectly from reading this book.

For the sake of privacy, fictional names are used in this book. Some characteristics have been altered, some dialogue has been recreated, and some events have been simplified. Otherwise, everything you are about to read really happened according to my memory.

There is no actual volcano in this book.

△

The Volcano
Adam Wray

- Table of Contents -

Movement A - EARTH
1 —— Atmosphere i ———————————————————— 1
2 —— Budding ———————————————————————— 3
3 —— The Attempt ———————————————————— 13
4 —— Fern ——————————————————————————— 17
5 —— Falling Leaves ——————————————————— 23
6 —— Crop Circles ————————————————————— 59
7 —— Relationships ———————————————————— 71
8 —— Atmosphere ii ———————————————————— 103

Movement B - GABRIELLE
9 —— Warming Up ———————————————————— 109
10 — Dates ——————————————————————————— 113
11 — Her Story ————————————————————————— 133
12 — More Dates ———————————————————————— 137
13 — My Sneak ——————————————————————— 159
14 — Engagement ————————————————————— 169

Movement C - THE VOLCANO
15 — Lightning ——————————————————————— 187
16 — Letters ———————————————————————— 193
17 — Projects ——————————————————————— 233
18 — New News ——————————————————————— 255
19 — Beautiful Notes ——————————————————— 263
20 — Bright Light ————————————————————— 273

Movement A
EARTH

- Chapter 1 -
Atmosphere i

How can one be so selfish as to be sad? How can one not appreciate their life and the world that was given to us for free? Why would one think this gift is imperfect and desire to alter it in some way? What if you gave me a gift and I threw it down and stomped on it? We have an entire world of opportunity at the fleshy end of our fingertips, why waste it? We should be grateful for every breath we take. As I take a deep breath and gaze at the humbling scope of mass clouds in the sky, I realize God's love for me, and I am happy today.

It wasn't always so easy for me to look up into a spectrum of atmosphere on a regular drive home from work and have such a wave of contentment and satisfaction like today. At this ripened age of 31, I have conquered a trip of tribulations and trials. I have battled social anxiety, depression, and spiritual doubt. Sure, not everything has gone as planned, but I have something you don't have. I have proof of God's existence, and I have decided to share my story with history.

- Chapter 2 -
Budding

It was the mid-eighties, short shorts, weird colors, *poofy* hair, denim, and giant sunglasses. At Applegate apartments in Frederick, Maryland there was a little community pool. This was a fun place for Jacqueline (Alexander) and her girlfriend to relax and eye down the *hella* bodacious hunks. One particular shiny day Jackie leaned over to her friend and said "see that man over there, I am going to marry him one day." Who is he, are you wondering? The girls didn't even know yet who he was. Jackie proceeded to ogle and smile at him. Built like the former semi-pro athlete he was and displaying his moves on the diving board, he had a little bit of extra confidence. As he got out of the water and slicked back his dark and dense Seinfeld hair, he noticed Jackie noticing him. As suave as he can be, he approached Jackie. She was your quintessential blond with an almost Marilyn Monroe vibe minus excessive glam. Jackie's giant and beautiful yet mischievous smile equipped with perfect teeth naturally drew the attention of the man in question. "So, I see you're looking at me," he said.

One year later I was born (May 17, 1985).

The man was my father, Diamond Adams. Jackie would change her name to "Mom," but hadn't changed her name to "Adams" quite yet. Dad was awarded the opportunity to pick out my first name: "Ray." Mom chose "Diamond" to be my middle name. So, there I was, "Ray Diamond Adams," bright tailed and bushy eyed. Yeah, I am backwards but it's suiting because I really did come out facing the wrong way. Being different is a theme that would continue for much of my life.

I don't really remember the first few years of my life as babies are pretty brainless. There have been allegations and/or hints that my dad wasn't exactly ready to be a family man. Apparently, I am an "I'll pull out" baby, and my sister Amili, who came around two years later was a "broken condom" baby. How do I know this? Well my mother is quite open, and it is something that would later become a source of contention between us. But I digress. I do have a few fond memories of the first four years of my life in Frederick. In many of those memories I was running. I remember running down the hall, running from the pool to the ice cream truck, and running from the police after I pulled the fire alarm when there wasn't any fire! Ok I didn't run from the police but I was scared to death that the firemen were going to take me to jail. It was peer pressure from my sister, I was four and she was two, how did she convince me to pull that alarm? How did I even reach it? Amili also got me in trouble with the old rolled-down-sock lady who lived below us. Amili and I both had rambunctious spells and made noise that bothered said old lady. I remember her blaming me for the noise that Amili may have had the upper hand in producing. The most memorable thing about Applegate apartments was that pool where my parents met. I remember being afraid of the black line that separated the shallow end from the deep. Could it swallow me up? With my father, I remember taking long walks behind and around the pool towards a billboard adjacent to the highway. This is one of the greatest and most innocent memories I have; I am proud of it.

The whole family, including my older brother Zach (Thompson - from Jackie's first marriage) up and moved to Hagerstown, Maryland in 1990 to be closer to the rest of the Alexander family (Mom's side). I also have an even older brother named Ralph (Thompson) but he was already an adult at this time. We called my mom's parents "Nana," and "Pappy." They lived in Hagerstown but we still only saw them every once in a while. They were a horse family; they owned horses and rode them frequently. I rode on one myself at a young age, but it was never something I really got into the way my mother, aunts, and uncles did.

Mom and Dad eventually did marry. They left the house one day dressed up and said "we're going to go change Mommy's last name."

As a child, all I wanted to do was draw and create. My favorite thing to draw was always some *Teenage Mutant Ninja Turtles.* I was also already into cars and would make up my own makes and models. I loved Lincoln Logs and Legos. I was never into much physical activity or interaction with other people. I was timid around strangers and preferred staying home. Pre-K was eschewed and my first day of kindergarten was a horrifying affair that's buried itself in my memory. I don't recall being detached from my mother at any previous point of my life; Mom was a stay-at-homer. When she dropped me off in the classroom and tried to flee, I freaked out. I latched on to her and started screaming "no, no, no!" As I was weeping, Mom bent down and assured me that she would come back for me soon. I eventually calmed down but this is an example of my already prominent social anxiety.

My personality traits or lack thereof drew attention from in-class counselor, Mrs. Rice. I don't know if maybe they suspected autism or something but I was pulled aside and was given special assignments and some kind of an examination. I recall passing the brain teaser test where I had to draw particular shapes inside of other shapes and other problem-solving quizzes. Mrs. Rice was impressed with my innovative skills. All while doing this, I took heed to what was going on in the regular class, so I think I at least proved that I had a high level of intelligence. Through the years at the elementary school I would continue to impress with my artistic abilities and every one of my art class projects ended up on display in the hallways. I remained reserved and shy.

One day in first grade I think it was, I remember really needing to go pee. I was simply too scared to raise my hand and ask to use the bathroom, So I just peed myself. I got slapped in the face for peeing myself. I remember Mom finding out by smelling me and an argument set off as a result. It might have been something I said that made Mom strike me in the face but I always attributed it to my having peed myself. I am not mad at her. She had a hard time raising me and once told me she tried the hardest with me. This must be because I was so much different and had signs of anxiety and depression at a young age.

It might be attributed to the fact that Mom was feeling rife with stress during her pregnancy with me. She might have worried that she would end up raising me alone. Diamond came around from time to time and would put headphones on Mom's belly playing *Pink Floyd* music while pregnant with me. I guarantee my personality traits are attributed to that fact. Their music is quite creative and gloomy at times, and it resonates well with me.

I would have spells as a child where I would randomly put myself into a fetal position and just ignore everyone. Mom would sometimes get me to snap out of it for a short period, but I would often revert to a slumped state of mind. Mom and I would convene for conversations and I would reveal my fear of death and hell. I would tell her that I want to go to heaven. Christianity is certainly a confusing concept for a child. I can't help but wonder if it was deep thoughts like that which resulted in what my mother describes as full-on freak outs during long car rides. This might be a normal reaction to lengthy trips as a youngster but Mom seems to think it was caused by something more for me, a greater anxiety. She was really concerned because I guess her first two kids didn't react the same way. I don't recall these fits but I do remember always being in my head.

Ear infections are horrible and I would reap them frequently. When I was about six or seven years old, I had an infection in both ears. Bilateral ear infections can be rather serious and require rather strong drugs for alleviation. I remember excruciating pain in my ears and taking the drugs that were prescribed. Mom was tucking me into the top level of my bunk bed when things started to get weird. Mom appeared to be shrinking or falling and I started screaming: "Mom, you're falling!" The medication must have been making me hallucinate. It was either that or a mixture of the drugs and the sickness that made me experience la-la land temporarily.

I am not a fan of drugs or medication of any sort. My dad was always the same way and wasn't fond of the idea of getting me on to antidepressants. Nevertheless, my actions eventually concerned my mother enough to have me see a doctor. I was diagnosed with Social Anxiety Disorder, so I was *SAD*. I was prescribed Paxil when I was approximately 11 years old. This drug is no longer considered suitable for children.

South Mulberry Street was not the safest place to grow up. We lived about a block away from a corner that notoriously had a high rate of violence. Kids would steal my bike, and loot my brother's skateboard right out of our back yard. Fights broke out often between me and neighborhood boys. One time a gang of probably about eight kids were chasing me and just wanted to fight for no reason. I darted through the field behind the elementary school. There was a hole in the fence that I intended to head through and cut straight to my house. Due to fear and scrambling I was unable to find the hole that I used so many times before. I became trapped and surrounded. They wanted me to fight one kid, when I refused, they decided to all take turns punching me. I just stood there and took it. They eventually got bored and departed. The leader of that pack was a kid named Joseph whom I had the most trouble with time and time again. I basically consider him my arch nemesis.

Joseph was a few years my major and picked on me frequently. One day he was following me home from school and eventually decided to cold-cock me in my ear from behind and then take off running. I calmly walked into my house, dropped off my backpack, and told my mom that I was going to beat up this kid Joseph. Mom came along in support. When my eleven-year-old ass found his thirteen-year-old ass I went right at him, standing up for myself. This was right in front of my best friend's house, So Robert Codder got a front row seat. I landed some swell punches on Joseph's face but he was older and bigger than me so Mom eventually had to pull him off of me. Though I didn't necessarily win the fight, I did win the day. I proved I wasn't going to take his crap anymore and he never bothered me again.

Another bully got word that I had a protective mother and I got into a scuffle with him at the playground. He said if I got my mom after him that he wouldn't just beat me up; he threatened to kill me. I went home and told my parents. Dad rushed to the playground angry. The kid didn't mention me telling my dad, in fact he probably didn't even realize that some kids have fathers. Dad shoved the bully onto the ground and had some words with him. I am lucky that I had two protective parents.

I fought with not only bullies but also numerous friends. You might say I struggled with anger management growing up. I wouldn't say I still feel any resentment today. I am curious as to how some of my childhood bullies wound up.

My ire wasn't exclusive to the playground as I had issues at home as well. Mom and I would argue a substantial amount. I remember Mom talking about me on the phone with friends of hers. Whether or not she said positive or negative things didn't matter. She revealed so many personal circumstances and this annoyed me considerably. I would request that she didn't do it but I would still overhear it happening. Mom was very open and practiced honesty to the utmost. I am grateful that her preaching helped shape me to be an honest adult but her sharing of my secrets made me irate as a child. At one point I was showcasing my anger and mimicked the action of a swinging fist towards my mother's face. I intended to miss purposefully as a warning but miscalculated and struck her in the nose. I also tore down the stairwell handrail multiple times out of wrath. I don't know if I would have behaved like that around my father, as I was more afraid of him even though he never struck me. Mom was always the one who spanked me. One time I was messing around swinging a bat in the living room and I accidently broke the chandelier. I hid when Dad got home and heard the news, but he did nothing.

Drama in the house built up the more my mother watched soap operas and the more my dad drank. Jackie was always a stay-at-home mom while Diamond worked carpentry and enjoyed a few beers every Friday night, occasionally peeing in the kitchen sink. Mom seems to wear her emotions on her sleeves, whereas Dad prefers to hide his emotions in his shoes. How they made it work for over ten years I don't know because they are complete opposites, and they fought a lot.

When I was a snotty know-it-all teenager, I got into an argument with my father on a day he'd been drinking. He was not a compliant individual when under the influence of alcohol, he would become extra critical, pretentious, and arrogant. I don't remember what was said but I ended up getting an elbow in my throat. My reaction was an immediate and forcible shove resulting in my dad falling down the stairs and spraining his ankle. It was not a proud moment for either of us. We never spoke about it; we had a silent understanding of humility and regret.

One of the most frightening moments of my childhood involved my sister Amili when we were somewhere around four to six years old. She had an asthma attack of some sort and I remember seeing her in the hospital. There she was completely still, lacking color, and had tubes in her nose. It was the freakiest thing I could have seen as a young kid. I worried that my only friend and only sister would die. We were pretty inseparable as children and always played together. She didn't die. Years later I became worried again when I received news that Amili had been hit by a truck in an attempt to cross the street on her way to school. It was mentioned over the intercom at the High School. She survived that too but was knocked out unconscious for a while. I love my sister and was always protective of her, even if we too had some disagreements during our teenage years.

Not all times were bad during my childhood. In fact, if you ask me what age I would prefer to be forever I would say nine or ten. I experienced much happiness and fun times during this part of my life. The family had gotten bigger as my dad was now supporting himself, his wife, me, Amili, Zach, and the newest addition: my cousin Jeffy. Mom's oldest sister Georgia had come into difficult times and was considering submitting to have Jeffy live with a foster family. Being a good family-oriented person, Mom insisted he come live with us instead. We also adopted a puppy. Dad picked up the black fur ball from a neighbor and carried it home in the palm of his hand. When Dad walked in the door and held out the four-week-old lab-chow mix he asked "Do you guys want this?" It was a unanimous yes with immediate smiles. We named the dog "Onyx" and he would become a tremendous blessing to us.

I don't know how Dad was able to afford to feed all of us but there was always food on the table and shoes on our feet. I did however have duct tape holding together a pair of Nike's that I didn't wish to part ways with. We were eligible for free lunches at the school which was sort of an embarrassing thing when other kids at the school started to understand why. We got by okay; I am not complaining.

Jeffy was a few years older than me but we ended up both attending the elementary school within walking distance down the street; he was in fifth grade when I was in third. Jeffy was a fun loving and goofy kid for certain. We admired him greatly. He was big into sports and I had just gotten into sports myself; I commenced becoming active. It took me nine years but I finally initiated interest in sports and I am sure it made my dad ecstatic. He almost went pro as a baseball player and tried to get me into it early on. I would swing the bat left-handed even though I was right-handed. Diamond was the opposite and swung right-handed even though he was left-handed. I entered little league baseball and started playing football, hockey, and basketball all in the same year. I liked football the best and this was something that Jeffy and I bonded over. My absolute fondest childhood memory is of Jeffy and I going down to the playground and playing football together. We would play with a bunch of eleven-year-old boys when I was nine. Jeffy was always the first pick when we picked teams, and I many times was the second pick. We were the stars on the field. Jeffy was too quick and had rabbit like reflexes; he juked everybody out like my football idol Barry Sanders. My playing style was more about toughness and pure speed; nobody could ever catch me. The cut lips, the bruises, and the grass stains on our jeans were all like the greatest trophies. Yeah, we played full blast tackle football without pads back in the day.

No kidding, I was the fastest kid in the school when I was a fourth grader, and that includes all fifth graders. I remember being in gym class and the teacher was timing us all on a shuttle run. When she clocked me doing a 9.9 second run, she must have second guessed her stop-watch and made me do the run again. The second time I recorded a 10.1 because I was winded, but that 9.9 must have really impressed her and was the best time recorded that day. I pretend I have the all-time record at Bester Elementary School for that drill.

Football runs in my genes. My granddad Fern played football in college as a fullback, Diamond was a Quarterback and so was my uncle Curt. During Curt's senior year at Keystone High School in Pennsylvania he played against famous quarterback Jim Kelly and lost by one measly point. I got signed up to play football at the Washington County Junior Football League. We were late for the sign up so I had to wait for someone to quit. We were summoned by the Bears and I went to my first practice. Upon arrival the coach threw me my jersey: Number 20. This was Barry Sanders's number and I was lucky to sport it. He was my idol because he was an amazing running back but was also very quiet and didn't celebrate his touchdowns; he was a true class act. I still wear this jersey number today in my adult league. I now associate it to "Exodus 20" which contains the ten commandments. I live my life per these commandments due to some life experiences that I will explain in the next couple chapters.

- Chapter 3 -
The Attempt

By the time I was twelve the issues at home had escalated to new heights. My depression and social anxiety had been getting the best of me. Dad may have ignored the signs, and Mom may have overreacted to them. The fighting between them had grown and the fighting between myself and Mom had grown. During this time Zack and Jeffy both had moved out, Grandma Adams had passed away, and Amili started growing up to the point where we may not have been best friends anymore. Jeffy moved back in with his mom so I must have been missing him big time. Zach had been getting into a heap of trouble, mainly because of his graffiti habits and basically was kicked out while he was still a teenager. And although I didn't see him around much in the first place, perhaps that bugged me too. Home life wasn't as fun as it was a couple years prior.

The medication I was taking only seemed to make me gain some weight. I feel like the weight gain affected my speed on the football field. I started feeling resentment towards my mom for making me take the medication. I can't explain why I felt the way I did, but I started having feelings that I wanted to hurt myself. It didn't feel like it had anything to do with any of my surroundings at all; it honestly felt like I had no reason at all to feel the way I did. It was explained to me by the psychiatrist that I had a chemical imbalance in my brain and that the medication should act as a mediator. I don't know if I took the medication as prescribed because I do remember my father telling me to hide the pills.

I attempted to hurt myself by jumping down the stairs. Why I put padding on my elbows and knees though didn't make sense. I guess I didn't actually want to feel pain. I wanted the pain to slip away. I'd go into crying fits for no reason. One particular night with nothing memorable to prompt it, I was having a hard time. I was crying, arguing with Mom, and felt like I wanted to end it all. Suicide had been on my mind for a while. At the climax of the argument with Mom, I ran down the stairs and into the kitchen, with her chasing me. I reached into the drawer and pulled out a knife. I tried to pull it into my chest but Mom had her hands on mine and was stronger than me. She always was rather strong physically. I don't know for sure what would have happened that night had Mom not been there for prevention. Maybe it was a bit of a cry for attention, I don't know. I continued weeping as Mom drove me to the hospital lost for ideas on how to help or fix me. We went in and I sat on a chair crying like a baby at twelve years old. Some man was looking at me and I recall muttering the cliché "what are you looking at?" The police had convened at this time and informed us that the situation requires a mental hospital stay for me. We started pleading that I was ok and we just wanted to go home but there was no use. I was put in an ambulance and taken to the Brook Lane Health Services institute.

A change of scenery might have been necessary. Perhaps it helped put things into perspective to an extent. Mom grabbed a bag of items for me with clothes and all. I had a small framed photograph of Onyx packed but they made me take it out of the frame. The frame had squared sharp edges and it wasn't allowed. I was also permitted my Walkman and headphones with a few tapes. I had gotten into *Pink Floyd* music pretty heavily and surprisingly my roommate, also twelve years old, also enjoyed their tunes. We decided to play the album "The Wall" and placed the headphones in between us at maximum volume so we both could hear. We went to sleep in that position and when we woke up, I noticed my device was missing. I was pretty upset when I beseeched a counselor as to its whereabouts. They took it and put it away in a container. I don't understand why they did it, and I don't know why they are allowed to touch my personal belongings and I think I expressed that with a strong tone. When we got into our daily circle to discuss goals and such, I didn't have any ideas. They suggested I had a little bit of an attitude and to work on that. This again angered me but I hid my emotions. I actually moderately enjoyed most of my time in the mental hospital. We did a plethora of crafts: painted bird houses and melted beads together to form images. I was good at art and always earned amazement from my peers due to the outcome of my projects, so I enjoyed that. We also participated in some physical activities which is another area I excelled in. We played volleyball indoors with a big beach ball. There were a lot of interesting kids there too, one of which escaped and ended up running around on the roof. I only stayed at the place for a few days and they released me.

Back in the real world I wondered if my school knew where I was because I missed a few days, but I was excused with a doctor's note. At home, Amili and I had a bunch of stuffed animals that we no longer played with so we decided to bag them up in a big trash bag and donate them to Brook Lane. I had one particular stuffed animal picked out that I wanted to give to the crazy roof running kid but upon arrival they told us he had been transferred to a different institute or something. That bummed me out.

We had hope that our situation would improve at home. Dad started selling homes for a company called Forest Homes. With his commissions we all dreamed about getting out of the dumpy downtown half duplex and building a home with an actual yard, one of the homes from the Forest Homes booklet. He sold a home to one of my childhood friend's family: The Berrys. They built their house in West Virginia which is cheaper than Maryland, but we aspired to move to Pennsylvania, the state my father is from. We all liked Greencastle and often drove past a lot my dad aspired to purchase and dreamt about what could be.

Dad was working on a big development deal with Forest Homes. The deal involved 350 lots to build homes on. The new development would draw in an ample amount of commissions. The pitch was agreed upon but the company claimed bankruptcy, terminating my dad's employment. They quickly got back in business and took my father's deal. It was a scam to eliminate the middleman and the company pocketed the would-be commissions. They screwed my family out of an estimated total of $1.7 million over four years. They screwed my family from a chance at a better life. They screwed my family from our dreams. I think this put a huge toll on my dad's state of mind. To have your hopes build up just to be dropped on your head has got to be the worst thing a human can deal with. Dad looked into filing a lawsuit but in the long run he concluded it wasn't worth it. Dad kept his emotions to himself, and I think he was unable to express his feelings or even confide in his wife. Thus, I don't think Mom understood the weight that this had on Dad. Dad may have resorted to booze to try to battle the frustration and lack of support that he needed. I wouldn't justify all of his reactions though, as sometimes he would take it out on his family, mainly Mom. Dad's nickname for Mom was "Mum the Bum, the Big Fat Bum." He would repeatedly call her this and laugh. He would continue to do it after Mom said to stop. He had no realization that others did not find it as funny as he did and would continue to laugh.

My parents would ultimately split up. I was old enough to be granted the opportunity to choose who to reside with. After Dad was kicked out of his own house for a short while, I lived with him in an apartment he started renting. Amili was not old enough to choose and stayed with Mom, although that's probably what she would have chosen anyway. My choice was based on the fact that living with Mom was frustrating to me and I thought dad's discipline would be better at molding me into a tough adult man. He would soon prove how tough he really was with his battle with cancer. I will speak on that later. Diamond lost a lot of weight over the whole divorce ordeal. I think having me around gave him a reason to be ok. We moved back into the house when Mom and Amili found some low-income housing in the south end. Mom barely ever worked in her life but started a job as a grocery store clerk. Mom was able to carry on even after her own uncertainties. She is strong physically and mentally. She was even able to quit smoking pretty much cold turkey around this time. She created a happier and healthier life for herself. I am proud of her because she too had struggled with social anxieties much of her life. All of our lives were changing around this era but little did I know there would soon be an event that would transform my mental state forever.

- Chapter 4 -
Fern

Fern Stanley Adams was a decorated war veteran and more importantly he was my grandfather. He fought in The Korean War and in the Second World War. I believe he received two purple hearts for his service and we all respected him immensely. We didn't get to see him a whole lot because he lived pretty far away in New Jersey. He paid a visit to us one particular time that would end up engraving itself into my brain. He had not been open about the occurrences he experienced in his Army days, but for some reason on this particular day he had come prepared to tell all. Some of the stories were humorous but some were down right bone chilling.

Fern was a Sergeant and basically the leader of his pack. At war, during one occasion, he and his crew were packed away in what I interpreted as a small underground bunker of some sort. They intended to sleep for the night but a peculiar noise kept alarming them. There was much fear that the enemy may have been shuffling along right above them and perhaps even discovered their whereabouts. They needed to know for sure so someone had to peek out and see what was going on. Everyone was worried that stepping out would reveal them and imminent death could occur. Being the leader, Fern had to be the one to poke his head out to verify what the noise was. So, he did. When he stuck his head out the opening, he noticed that the noise was just the wind blowing the grasses around above them. They were completely safe, and they shared a laugh.

Another story is remarkable. Sergeant Fern and his men were transporting by foot somewhere in the Middle East during World War II. In the middle of nowhere they get greeted by a dog. The shepherd must have been really far from home. He was really friendly and didn't bark so the crew decided to basically adopt the dog. For weeks he would just hang out with the crew and add some much-needed joy to their situation. One day the dog randomly started barking which was strange because the dog was normally mild tempered. Initially they figured it was just being a dog so they thought nothing of it and continued on their path. They were about to cross over a pretty steep hill when suddenly the dog got louder and even jolted up to Fern and started tugging on his ankle. The crew all stopped and looked at each other. Fern told them to hold on as if maybe the dog knew something that they didn't. They all got down and Fern crawled up the hill to look over to the other side. What he saw he couldn't believe. The enemy was all lined up and ready for battle. They were going to walk straight into an ambush. The dog had saved their lives. At night's end they woke up to notice that the dog had disappeared.

The last of Fern's stories that I will share is the one that impacts me the most.

"Walking With God"

As a first sergeant with a heavy weapons company, my duties were to scout ahead of my men, search out enemy positions and call back the information for coordinated direct fire. I did this safely and successfully many times. However, one instance burned itself deeply into my memory.

My radioman and I had slipped about 300 yards ahead of our troops, drew fire and thus located enemy positions. We quickly took cover behind a rocky ledge where I instructed the corporal to call back for gun-cover setups. Within moments, he reported the radio had failed. We were trapped – no way out, no way to communicate.

Instinctively, I told the corporal he would have to go back and get a good radio, but immediately I realized it was an impossible instruction. As he stared at me with tear-filled eyes, a clear, firm voice spoke to me: "Do not send that man to his death. You go. Nothing can hurt you."

Now I was the one in fear, searching my mind on how to do what seemed unreal and unachievable, yet impelled not to refuse the command, Again, the voice intoned, "Do not be afraid. Nothing can hurt you."

Crazily, all terror subsided. I took the radio, slung it over my shoulder and began to walk. Bullets whistled on all sides of me, some visibly spitting up dirt over both boots.

Bible verses were running through my mind and I still was unafraid. As I got closer to my men, I heard many yelling, "Get down. Get down."

When I finally arrived and took cover behind a hill, the men were convinced I had lost my mind and walked aimlessly towards them. I assured them that I was under great care and must take a good radio forward or we would soon be surrounded and overrun.

Grabbing a radio, I walked the same trail back under a hail of bullets. We did not lose a man that day.

This event still haunts me. Yet today, some 49 years later, I know it had to be a miracle from God. How could there possibly be any other answer?

-Wray, Stanley Fern, "Walking With God,"
The American Legion (Magazine), Vol. 149, No. 3, Sep. 2000, p. 46.

Yeah, he even got it published. What he failed to mention in his writing, but that I got to hear first-hand, was that he could actually feel the wind from bullets passing by on his ears.

I learned that God has real communication with people. My grandfather heard God's voice and achieved an impossible task by the hand of the Lord. I always considered myself a Christian because I came from a household of Christian people, but hearing this story enticed me to become a real believer. The way I see it, had God not been there that day to help my grandfather then he would not have made it home alive. Fern would not have fathered my dad Diamond, and then I would have never come to be. I attribute the day Fern told these stories to being the day I was saved, the day I became a believer, and the day that would alter the path of my life for the better.

Granddad Adams kept those stories to himself for many years. When he finally shared them, it was the first time I or anyone else in my family heard them. Perhaps Grandma Adams heard them at some point. The pair were separated for as long as I can remember but were never officially divorced. I had some good memories as a kid with Grandma. She was friendly, fun-loving, and hilarious. We used to all go to an amusement park in central Pennsylvania called "Bland's Park." We would meet up with grandma and some other family. I enjoyed staying in the hotel with grandma. Unfortunately, she died of cancer in the mid-nineties. It was probably due to smoking. I remember her having a real raspy voice which may have also been a result of smoking.

Grandma's spirit lived on in our hearts but I theorize that she lived on by a greater scale. We adopted our dog around the same time that Grandma died. I like to say that Onyx was actually Grandma's spirit bringing us an extended joy that we all needed. Fern's story proved that dogs do have some special power. Perhaps it's a spiritual thing.

As a teenager, I had another phenomenal spiritual experience that wouldn't seem real to another person. Sometime after the impact of my grandfather's stories, and sometime after I accepted Jesus as my savior, I was lying in bed. We all have those moments when you're half asleep and your whole body jerks a little as if an electrical impulse shot through you. This particular day was a bit different though. Take that jolting feeling and multiply it by 100. My body was literally lifted up off of my bed a few inches, and then plopped back down. It was a rush like nothing else. Something seemingly impossible happened and I didn't understand it. It felt like a wave of energy was expelled from my body. Before that time something had a hold of me and I felt possessed with sadness, confusion, and fear. I believe my faith fought off and exported a bad spirit that night, a demon perhaps had left my body. Ever since Granddad's stories, I have kept my faith. Through every step of my life I remember him. I know that he decided to bequeath those stories when he did on purpose. I needed to hear them. Ever since that day I have never had another suicidal thought. Whenever I start to have doubts I just think of Fern and his proof of God's existence, it helps me to carry on. God saved him for a reason, and he is saving me for a purpose too.

Daddy Diamond developed cancer. It seems to run on both sides of my gene pool. Dad claims he didn't start smoking until he met Jackie. Mom quit but Dad's addiction never ended and cancer showed up in his throat. This all came about not long after their divorce. Perhaps stress is a factor in deadly diseases. My uncle on my mom's side actually passed away shortly after his separation with his wife. Mental states can really affect you physically. My father's cancer required surgery. He had already lost a lot of weight seemingly from stress; he was at his weakest point. My dad was always there for me in support and help. He didn't have much but he always thought of me. My dad couldn't die. I needed him. Even though I was a young adult, I was still very immature mentally and emotionally, and Dad was the only human I could count on. So, I had to pray. I wasn't actually very worried because my dad was always a tough and resilient person, some traits I like to believe were passed on to me.

Surgery required removal of a portion of Dad's throat and a chunk of his tongue. The surgeon would slice an incision on his neck from ear to ear. Dad joked that they're "cutting his head off." Some family and I went in to see him after the surgery, and he was in rather high spirits. He couldn't talk but we would write notes to each other. I told him that he was my hero. This sentiment may have helped rejuvenate his push towards health. After surgery he went through a lot of radiation treatment but did not do chemotherapy. If you ever saw the movie *Brian's Song* you might understand why. It seems that chemotherapy may have actually been the thing that killed Brian Piccolo, not the cancer. The movie is based on a chapter of a football player's autobiography. *I am Third* by Gale Sayers is one of the only books I have ever read and I highly recommend it. The concept of the title is to put God first, loved ones second, and yourself third. The phrase has become my personal mantra; I try to apply the sentiment in my daily life as best I can. Gale, Fern, and myself were all God-fearing football players so the book resonates well with me.

Though my dad is struggling with some after effects from the radiation he did survive cancer. The same cannot be said of my grandfather, Fern. He died from lung cancer February 20th, 2007 at the age of 82. Granddad was proud of me. I was his only grandson even though he had six kids of his own, and Diamond was the only one to produce offspring. I am the last male with our family name so the pressure is on me to reproduce. Granddad came to watch me play football and I considered following his footsteps and attending the same college he did: Juniata. He even wrote a letter of recommendation for me. I did not end up going there because I had to figure out some things, and in a way, I wish I could have done more to make him proud while he was alive. Before his passing I did take the opportunity to write him a letter. I explained to him how much he meant to me, and how much his stories shaped who I am. This I am very proud of. I hope it made him feel like his life was worth it, and that his legacy will carry on. I hope God revealed his purpose and that he died solemnly and peacefully. I love you Fern.

- Chapter 5 -
Falling Leaves

In this chapter I will delineate how all the leaves fell into place. I will describe how everything came together for me with impeccable timing according to God's will. With God's hand I wrote a poem in the midst of my adult struggles and finding my career path.

> I must progress my creative mind to an atmosphere more tangible. I mustn't be lazy or let negative minds wither away at my soul. I won't let society define me or alter the path of my goals. I will eliminate the useless, gather wisdom and seat myself higher, for greatness is dire. And unnecessary are wild thoughts brought on by obsession, this depression won't last.

> The inevitable spirit of my blood will continue to pump. Long after these obstacles surpass, new life begins in the heart. The fabrics of my soul are tightly bound and moral can't break apart. I will decrease intensity, count my blessings and live in true bliss, for I'm stronger than this. And determination will carry on, drowning no deeper, I'm the keeper of my own life.

Having goals isn't just important to me but it is a necessity. I always strived to achieve eminence. I did well in school and remember being disappointed with my first "B" letter grade because I prided myself on being a straight "A" student. This was in second grade, but it actually seemed like a long time before that first "B" surfaced on my report card. It's laughable today looking back. I might haven't gotten a "C" in third grade, but I was typically an all "A's" and "B's" student from then on.

I had a few friends in school growing up but became known as the kid that never spoke. Although I did speak occasionally, I was very shy and never raised my hand to answer a question even considering that I typically knew what the answer was. I didn't enjoy reading and especially disliked reading aloud in class. I remember my classmates scoffing at one point when I had to read aloud and I don't know why. Perhaps I had misread something and the kids thought I was dumb? That's just a little insight to my thinking patterns.

In Middle school I may have talked even less. It seems to me that there is much diversity in middle school, and so many things start to change. Some kids start to go through puberty, weights change, heights change. Some kids start "dating," and some kids are years away from that. Some kids clearly are dressed by their parents, and others get a sense of personal fashion. It was a transitional period for me just like any other kid.

I got in my first in-school fight in middle school. I got in plenty of fights at the playground before but this was my inaugural one during school hours. It was during gym class; some other boys and I were playing basketball. This one kid who was much larger than me on the opposing team kept accusing me of fouling and started shoving me around at his leisure. I tried to let it go but I became very frustrated. The last shove came with a tipping force, and I couldn't take any more so I retaliated, swinging frantically through the air, with some fists landing. This caught everyone by surprise because I was always the mellow and quiet kid. He ended up grabbing me and I didn't want it to become a wrestling match because I was smaller than him so I used our momentum and slung us around, throwing him to the ground. On the ground I wound up in a head lock and started to poke him in the eyes. This was when the teacher finally made it on scene to break it up. As we headed back into the building the teacher inquired of me about what happened, and I responded with "what?" He asked me again, and again I said "what?" I think I was too disoriented to communicate but the teacher said something like "don't you just 'what' me," and sent us off to In School Suspension (ISS). I was only in the suspension room for about 15 minutes when I was directed to go back to class for a test. I think they knew that I was the good kid and the other belonged in ISS because he was a continual trouble maker. The aura around me gained a little popularity after that incident.

I almost got in trouble for writing the word "pecker" on my folder. I drew and wrote nonsense on all my belongings and I accidently left a folder in English class once. Mrs. Rentrub was awful. I already hated English class but she made it even worse. She always kept us on edge, reminded me of a white-haired witch, and wasn't very nice. It was my science teacher that notified me about the folder. There was apparently banter about it in the teacher lounge and he said he would take care of it. He was cool, and probably my favorite teacher ever. I didn't get in trouble because of him, and it's weird that I almost got in trouble for something so trivial.

I had a girlfriend in 8th grade, I will talk about Melanie in a later chapter. But right now, stay in school kids.

In high school I took all of the courses that would gain me the "Certificate of Merit," and also took a bunch of "Advanced Placement" courses. So, I was presumably in with the nerdy crowd. I also played sports so I was kind of in with the "jocks." I was very artistic so I was even in with the "out there" crowd. I joined the "Fellowship of Christian Athletes" so I was in with them too. I didn't belong to one particular group. I was later told that I was popular even if I didn't know it. I still was barely talking to anyone except my close buddies. I met my friend Robert Codder in elementary school and by the time we were in high school we had basically become best friends. We watched our first pornography together, and drank our first beer together. He was big on video games, movies, and sports. We often played sports together. On one occasion we were playing basketball and I jumped up to save the ball from bouncing over the fence, only to land on the fence myself. The pain in my side was agonizing, but I shook it off and kept playing. When I looked at the painful area later, I discovered why it hurt so bad, there was a giant bloody gash. I have a nice scar there now.

Robert was great at baseball in Little League, he had so much contact that it created power. I think he hit 17 home runs the year I had 17 total hits. I wish he would have decided to play high school ball with me. He got a job at the video store and has been a workaholic ever since. We were both smart so ended up in a lot of the same advanced courses together through High School.

High School was where I met my friends Matthew Whittaker and Daniel Abrams, each of which I'm still close to. Matthew looked like Peter Griffin from *Family Guy*. Matthew was nerdy and intelligent with an absorbing memory. He spoke with a strong tongue and was not sparse with minutia to the point where I didn't always understand him. He was into metal music and wondered why I liked *Pink Floyd* so much. I taped the album "Animals" off of my dad's vinyl record, brought my Walkman into school, and let Matthew sample the song "Pigs." I think this is where I got him hooked so I divvied more discography with him. I bonded similarly with Daniel. He was also attached to music and even beat away at the drums in his leisure. He had an interesting taste in music and lent me a mixtape of songs by the band *Melvins*, I ended up really digging them. Daniel's appearance was that of your stereotypical stoner with longer hair and all black apparel although he had one of the most colorful personalities, always goofing off in the art class where I initially met him.

Matthew, Daniel, and I formed a trio and ended up getting together to formulate some videography ideas I had. I had gotten my hands on a video camera that my brother Zack lent me. We would film various humorous and strange skits in a series that we would ultimately call "A Casually Colossal Collage of Crap." It was basically a mixture between *Saturday Night Live* and *Jackass*, with some random spaced out oddities added. Yes, we did have some scenarios that focused on legitimate "crap." One skit is from the perspective of a man in a port-a-potty having a bowel movement as an impatient stranger starts banging on the door in an effort to hurry him. We would mix in poop jokes like "this is taking a lot out of me." The majority of the skits did not involve feces at all though.

One of my favorite ideas for a skit, was a quick shot. I thought it would be funny if someone was sitting on a bench and tried to trip a passerby but fails and just ends up falling off of the bench himself. Many of my ideas came from brainstorming sessions in art class. We were to write random stories or anything that comes to mind for a few minutes at the beginning of each session to get our creative juices flowing. One day I ended up writing a bunch of nonsense about potatoes and that ended up being a skit we called "West Virginians Talking About Potatoes." Lines included banter such as "man, all brown round things ain't potatoes," followed by the drawled response, "potatoes ain't *wound*, they oval, you square."

The others had superb contributions as well, sometimes the improvisations were just as brilliant as the scripted scenes. Matthew did a shot we dubbed "Nut Flavored Chips." We're not talking about the type of nuts you consume. Daniel was good at humiliating himself by walking into poles and falling down steps. We experimented with adding music for ambiance and even tried some special effects. We simply paused the camera and had me ascend up on the roof to make it appear like I magically jumped up on it. The movies would become classics to our small circle of friends and we produced several parts: Part 1, Part 3, Part 4 and Part 5. You might ask yourself; you might say to yourself, "whatever happened to the part 2" Was there a Casually Colossal College of Crap Part 2?

Matthew was in the same grade as me, but I missed him senior year due to his departure. He didn't drop out (nor die) but had the opportunity to graduate early so he did just that. I am not surprised because he is quite impatient. We had a few heated moments during our movie making times because we both had a bit of a short fuse but the spark never reached dynamite. I am pleased we enjoyed fun times together and remained friends. After his graduation, Matthew, myself, Robert, and a couple of our other friends set off for a camping trip. None of us were really experienced with the experience but the leader of our pack was our *dawg* Dexter Hoss. We had made no reservations and just followed him to wherever like puppies. When we found a spot, we set up the tent and the coolers and were just about settled when a ranger came in to investigate. He said there shouldn't be a problem but needed to make sure one of us was at least eighteen years of age. We were all seventeen but Dexter just handed him his ID anyway. The ranger glanced at it, said "ok," and left. We thought we got away with one but a few minutes later he came back claiming he is not good at math and we had to vacate the premises. At our next stop, again we got situated and settled. This place had electricity for our boombox. Another ranger made us leave because there was to be some kind of an event the next morning. At our final destination we ended up needing to hike from our cars to the tent pitch area. This accommodation was predominately meant for hiking backpackers that slept in hammock-like tents of some sort, but at last we weren't discharged. After the chaos it concluded to be a fun outing but the hilarity was in the logistics and that's what I remember best. It's my last memory before commencing 12th grade.

Playing football my senior year was thrilling but suffering a knee injury wasn't. It started off great as we had an exceptionally talented team. I was a key player on both sides of the ball as I started at running back and strong safety. My photograph appeared in the paper under the headline, "players to watch." My long-time classmate Savaal Quickly ended up practically taking over the running back position because he was just too darn fast. We were nine games in and I still hadn't gotten my first touchdown. Our quarterback was egocentric and anytime we were in scoring position and the play call was to give me the ball, he would just bootleg around the end instead. He consistently ended up scoring because he was a legit super-star and I felt I couldn't complain. During the Middletown game I injured my ankle and expelled myself. Shortly afterwards the coach attempted to put me in when we were near the goal line, but I couldn't return. Not only was my ankle hurting but my knee started hurting as well. I ended up missing the traditional North Hagerstown versus South Hagerstown game and the playoffs. We were the first team in South Hagerstown High School's history to make the playoffs. We were legendary. I feel like we would have had a chance to beat Beall in the second round of playoffs had I been able to play because I was pretty good at protecting the edge on defense and it seemed they ran a lot of sweeps. I strained and/or partially tore my MCL and didn't require surgery but I wore the obligatory giant brace for several months. The brace extended from my ankle all the way to my upper thigh. This made me miss my indoor track season that I did every winter up until this point.

Senior year I decided not to play baseball. My knee had mostly healed by spring but I was worried I might re-injure it playing baseball due to all the twisting involved in the sport. I wanted to make sure I was healthy enough after the year in order to play college football. Wouldn't you know it, the one year I didn't play baseball, the high school won the state championship.

I ran outdoor track senior year instead of playing baseball. I thought it would better help me prepare for college football. I was a sprinter and was on the relay team for the 400 meter and the 800 meter. I was running "second leg," which is where the slowest guy usually runs. I had lost a step due to my knee injury, otherwise I was going to run the anchor leg. I was the only senior on the relay team as we had two juniors and a sophomore, but we were really fast and competed in the state meet. We got 8th place for the 4x200 meter relay (800m). When we ran the 4x1 (400m) the Sophomore Jack got a decent start for us, then when I got the baton, I felt dominant and seemed to pull away so our chances of winning the event felt good, but then I had to handoff to my buddy Martin. We never had much issue with the handoff but for some reason that day we had a mishap. I don't know if Martin was extending his arm too high or I became a ramshackle due to exhausting efforts but I remember the baton bouncing off Martin's hand and flying off the track, so we were disqualified. This was my last high school sporting event and I was upset. I took my cleats off and launched them over a hill.

I got an award for my scholarly efforts. It was the Washington County Career Connections Award of Excellence in Drafting Technology. The Technical Drawing instructor submitted me for my architectural classwork. I spent long hours sitting in front of that computer next to this guy Tim who thought he deserved the award. This is the same guy who said he would have gotten the sportsmanship trophy in little league (also awarded to yours truly) had he not punched our teammate. Although I ran away from home and fled to Tim's apartment back when I was struggling with my suicidal thoughts, and he was a friend of mine, there's one incident that really infuriated me.

Tim and my sister started messing around and it was weird to me. She is two years younger and I already didn't like the idea of them dating. I had gotten word that Tim was going around bragging to everyone that he had sex with Amili. Tim, Robert, and our friend Bill usually met at my house in the mornings to ride to school together. Robert had the cool car: a red 1995 Ford Mustang. He always blasted the latest rock music with the treble turned all the way up. Yes, I said treble not bass. *Anyhoo*, I had informed the guys that I intended to punch Tim the next morning after I found out about his conduct and loose-lips. When he sat down, I came over and asked if I could see his class ring that he just got to see if it would fit me. I put it on my hand then asked him "you fucking my sister?" When he started to rise and explain himself, I clocked him with his own ring. He previously had crossed eyes but I struck him so forcibly that I knocked them straight as he fell back down into the chair. I am kidding. He had just gotten surgery to correct his vision and I was sure not to hit him in the eye. My point here is that I am protective of my family. I must have had some premonition because I later found out that Tim was physically abusive to my sister, and that is not cool.

They were restructuring the SAT testing and I was part of the last class of students who utilized the old form of the SATs. I think I got a 620 on the Math portion which was good and a 440 on the English part which was average. My final score of 1060 was ok but not as good as I could have or should have done. At any rate I did achieve good grades, my GPA was about 3.8, and I was on the National Honor Society.

At the end of senior year, we got our yearbooks and I was awarded "most artistic" with a picture of me and the female winner together. The yearbook also had a picture of me doing an art project with a note underneath reading "One day Adam will be famous." I am still trying to live up to that expectation. I had an oil pastel (my favorite medium) drawing that hung in the library window for a long period of time. It was a self-portrait on one half and the other half was an example of what I thought I would look like when I became an elderly gentleman. I could have also gotten the vote for "most shy" had that been a category. I rarely talked to anyone other than my close friends. I think people might have thought I was mean and didn't want to talk because I never even smiled. People were surprised when I exemplified having any kind of personality at all. I didn't even attend senior prom. The info by my senior portrait reads that I intend to go to college and become an automotive designer. I was thinking either that, graphics, or architecture.

I considered many colleges on my quest for future education including Shephard, Shenandoah, Juniata (where Fern went), Penn State Mont Alto, and Frostburg State University. I considered the curriculum, the distance, the football program, and the cost. I determined Frostburg to be my best option and they were giving me a full scholarship as long as I stayed on the football team. It was division 3 so athletic scholarships weren't allowed but I got an academic scholarship. Dad also allotted me 450 dollars to help. Yup, that is all.

A few days before arriving at Frostburg State University for a short football camp a week before school started, I partied. I partied with a strange new friend named vodka. I had not tried vodka before and it affected me strangely as I still felt hungover for days leading into my Frostburg arrival. When I got onto the football field the coaches asked me what position I play and I responded: "running back and strong safety." Without hesitation they threw me a T-shirt that read "defense" on the back. Perhaps they thought I couldn't be a running back because I am white, or perhaps they just had too many running backs and didn't feel like giving a freshman the chance. We were tested on running the 40-meter dash and I was timed at 4.8 seconds. This was a disappointment to me because I expected to run something closer to 4.6 secs. I had a temporary dorm room to myself for football camp, and sleeping there alone and so far away from home affected me negatively. I overheard many players and coaches talking about partying after games as a way of bonding.

That wasn't really my scene and nothing felt right to me. I only lasted a few days before I made the move back home; I had to re-evaluate myself and my life plans. I was too young and not yet prepared for such a drastic change in my life. Dad came to pick me up and when we were leaving the coach actually said that it was a shame because I looked like I was going to give the upperclassmen a "run for their money." To this day I still wonder if quitting was the biggest mistake of my life. I almost wish my dad would have forced me to stay for a month or a year or something to see if I could get used to it. But I left and never returned.

I considered going to Hagerstown Business College and paid them a visit. They performed what was like an entrance interview and it was awkward for me. Even with my parents there by my side I still experienced a bit of a panic attack. My social anxiety was getting the best of me. I almost teared up but the interviewer could tell I was struggling and stopped the interview and we decided to move on to a tour of the school.

It was clear I needed to go back to therapy. Mom connected me with a particular therapist and psychiatrist. The psychiatrist had turrets syndrome and would randomly stomp his feet on the ground while twitching his face. This was the first time I witnessed anything like that. He prescribed me the drug Lexapro. The therapist was a nice calm gentleman and we just sat in his little room and had very boring conversations. I don't know if I got anything out of it and I eventually just stopped showing up. In these times of struggle and doubt what I would do is remember my granddad. This would always remind me that God is prevalent. I would pray and carry on ok.

I got my first real job at an arts and crafts retail store called A.C. Moore. I recall a moment when the manager said something about the way I "mope" around. I was a good worker but I just wasn't a "people person." I eventually informed the manager of my social anxiety and therapy and I think he backed off of me a little once he learned that about me.

The majority of my colleagues were young girls. I eventually would become pretty good friends with all of them too, even if it took a long time since I rarely talked. I burped one time and asked this girl if she could detect what the pitch of it was. She was a music buff and apparently possessed perfect pitch. I had a big crush on Shawna Madison but I was dating Jessy at the time. When Shawna inquired if I had a girlfriend a reluctant "yes" was uttered. Shawna was unique, she wore overalls, and would pick up dirty tissues from the bathroom with her bare hands. Of course, she assured me she'd wash her hands immediately afterwards. She had dark hair and a goofy yet cute smile as she snorted with laughter. She looked like a short brunette version of Taylor Swift. I think she ended up getting fired, perhaps because she couldn't hold her composure after a fight with her boyfriend, I don't know.

I became pretty friendly with Cierra, the little blonde that worked there, and I think the other girls thought I liked her on a level of romantic attraction, but I did not feel that. She is now a meteorologist and you can see her grace the weather maps on television. I became good friends with Stephanie Steele who was a big time Christian and Charlotte Flutie who was dating a guy named Ray. She always had to differentiate which Ray she was talking about using certain hand gestures at work. I think the up and down movements of her hands represented the straps of our smocks and thus meant she was talking about me. I believe the other gesture was more of a sexual thrusting motion to represent her boyfriend. Or maybe I made that up in my head. A girl named Stacey Starr joined the team later and I instantly had the hots for her. She had "Prom Queen" written all over her (literally in a tattoo on her lower back, just kidding) and was dating the basketball star at her high school. Aside from probably Stacy I later learned that most of the girls at A.C. Moore had crushes on me. At one point the whole team went bowling and I came to find out it was sort of a way to see who could try to win me over or something to that effect. I remained friends with Stacy, Charlotte, and Stephanie. Charlotte and Stephanie even came and visited me later when I was in Pittsburgh. I ended up making out with Charlotte that night. It was a little awkward but we remained friends. The two of them came to a Halloween party I threw a couple years ago and it was a blast. I eventually took Stacy out on a date one time, sort of, I will describe that in a later, sexier, chapter.

Around the same time I began working at A.C.Moore, I started attending Hagerstown Community College. It was a resourceful way to attain some basic education credits at a fair price before transferring to a four-year college. We had a student art show and I took home first place for a realistic colored pencil drawing that I composed. If you guessed the subject was a car, you would be correct. If you guessed it was a 1951 Mercury, you'd be wrong because it was a Lincoln. I joined the track team at H.C.C. too. I had a crush on a little dark-haired long-distance runner, but barely talked to anyone. It always takes me a long time to warm up to people. I eventually did go to a house party one of the track members threw. I got tipsy and started sharing quips and it was the first time anyone heard me speak. I asked the lone female at the party if she felt weird because of the fact. When she answered "no," I replied with "me neither." We shared a laugh and it was a memorable moment for a simple individual like myself. I crashed there that night and when I woke up, I realized I was the only person there. That was a strange feeling. My shining moment at an actual racing event was when I was up against another white dude. He was the only other participant in that particular race and I knew I would become victorious because there is never a Caucasian that can defeat me in racing. I was correct, and I won the event. This same assumption came to fruition when my new college roommates wanted to race, after I finally decided where to go.

The Art Institute of Pittsburgh had an Industrial Design program. After some research and discovering such a field, I knew it was what I wanted to pursue. The Art Institute of Washington had it too and was closer but I decided to go to Pittsburgh because I don't like Washington and actually wanted to get out and away a little bit to force myself to grow up. Industrial design involves the aesthetic appeal of products as well as their functionality and engineering. My love for making things, my creative ability, and my skill in technical drawing and math led me to believe that this was the perfect area of study for me. They did not have athletics but I was convinced it was the right move for me.

Roommates were designated before arriving at school and my future roommate Richard Fogart summoned me by phone one day. We exchanged a chat about what we expected, what we were bringing, and that nature. I told him I'd bring a toaster oven and that was all I needed. He later told me that his first impression of me on the phone was that I was sort of a bum or a simpleton. When I first got acquainted with him in person, he mentioned that he goes by Dick. I did not want to say Dick all the time so I decided to just call him Rich. He became known as Rich to the rest of the Pittsburgh people because of me, and goes by that name alone to this day. Rich was an 18-year-old lanky white kid studying Graphic Design. He was a straight-edge hard-core Christian with a big-time goofy side to him reminiscent of Jim Carey. We immediately became best buds. Our other roommate was a 21-year-old African-American straight out of the Air Force named Demetrius Charles. He was studying Gaming Design and was big into high-tech gadgets. He was articulate and full of wisdom, already had a business making and selling apparel, and was just one heck of a dude. We admired him greatly and frequently sought his advice. He was writing a book called *The Cheat Doctor*, Subtitled *How to Cheat and Get Away with It* (or something to that effect). He claimed it was more of a warning than anything. Demetrius wasn't actually any good at Game Design though and ended up going to school later for business. I remember Rich and I once asked Demetrius what "fo shizzle my nizzle" meant. He said it means "for sure." Rich was like "ok but what about the 'my nizzle' part?" Demetrius said "It means 'my nigga,' now don't you go around saying that, Rich," with a stern yet giggly tone.

YouTube was a contemporary thing when I first started big time college in 2005. A college buddy was converting my VHS tape of *A Casually Colossal Collage of Crap* to DVD and thus into digital format for me. Meanwhile I recently bought a webcam and recorded myself at an angle that looked like the viewer was in a point-of-view boxing match with me. I used my own fists to simulate the viewer's. I thought the video was reasonably humorous along with the "CCCC" videos so I created a YouTube account in order to post up some of the content. One of my initial videos was called "Monkey Fight," and it was just a scene of me battling a stuffed monkey with a bunch of camera cuts. This video quickly garnered a bunch of views. YouTube eventually advanced their algorithms for view availability resulting in less views for the video. Initially it was solely based on the title of the video versus what people search for; "fight" and "monkey" were both typed in rather frequently. The video didn't reap as much praise or view time as higher quality videos would typically get so it's understandable. This hasn't deterred me from creating or posting more videos of course. I currently have about a quarter million views on my channel for all videos combined. Numerous videos of mine are time-lapses of me doing art projects. Some of my most popular videos are of me making Halloween costumes of particular famous characters such as Scorpion from *Mortal Kombat*, Duff Man from *The Simpsons*, and The Shredder from *Ninja Turtles.*

Later that first year in college, I was introduced to a couple that owned a Deli and a boxing gym in downtown Pittsburgh. These people would become a wonderful blessing to me. I worked for them in the Deli and helped out with the boxing stuff too. Jimmy was a retired police officer who ran an amateur boxing league. I helped out with the events and had to build the ring on numerous occasions. One of the beams was about 500 pounds and I recall one time it was just me and one other dude setting up the ring. It wasn't the variety of rings that was meant to be rebuilt frequently but nevertheless we did. It was stored at Heinz Field, and we even threw an event in the stadium one time. I was actually on Heinz Field because of it; I stepped on the grass! I had to walk across the field to get to the other side where we set up the Ring on the platform behind the end zone at the south side of the stadium by the river. Another time we had an event at a country themed nightclub during the day. Me and the crew set up the ring, watched the event, then took the ring down. Afterwards we just kind of hung around as the doors were opening for the "21 and over only" night club scene. I was 20 at the time but no one knew. They card at the door so the bartenders inside assumed I was 21. Naturally I started buying beers. Everything was going fine until I made the mistake of going to a different section and asking a different bartender. She demanded to see my ID and I refused and walked away. A manager and bouncer found me and I had to show them my ID. When the guy said "You're not 21, you have to leave," I was like "yup" and just trotted out of there hastily. It was a 45-minute walk home to the north side where the school's sponsored housing was from station square where the night clubs were. So, there you go, I actually got kicked out of a place once.

Jimmy's wife Gloria mainly ran the deli or café or restaurant or whatever you want to call it. It was simply called "3rd Ave Café." The gym was called "3rd Ave Gym." I worked at the café pretty regularly and got paid under-the-table six dollars an hour. We mostly made sandwiches and coffee but even did occasional catering. We catered to an office high up on the Steel Tower one time. That is a really big building. I remember us pushing a cart several blocks through downtown Pittsburgh (occasionally dropping baskets of bread onto the streets). I remember an office lady muttering "I thought we were getting chicken marsala." We had made chicken with marinara sauce, instead. Jimmy and Gloria were hilarious and wacky and I owe them so much because they catered me with free food throughout my entire college life. Additionally, I got to work out in their gym for free. I tried not to take advantage of their kindness and I was grateful for the privileges. One time another guy was working for us and he was attempting to get "on-the-books" and with better pay. He beseeched the owners with the question, "how am I going to be able to get a car?" I looked at him and said, "sounds like you need a real job." Rich even started working there too. I have a lot of fond memories at the corner of 3rd Avenue and Ross Street.

I got a membership at the YMCA right down the street from the school. If it was because of the swimming pool or because of the girl who worked at the front desk I won't admit. This girl was literally the cutest girl I have ever seen in my life. She may have been an islander or mixed with Japanese or Hispanic or Hawaiian or Greek or something I don't know but she was gorgeous. I don't believe in love at first sight but that feeling I had was the next closest thing, so I had to try. When I got her phone number, I legitimately could not believe it. Nothing ever came of it but that was my shining moment when it came to talking to girls. I forget what her name is now though. The rest of my YMCA experience was rather strange. The Y is notorious for gay dudes and I got hit on by a gay dude there. Then one day I came back to my locker and noticed my things were missing and the super gay dude came to the rescue. He might as well have been wearing a cape. He found my pants but my money and cell phone were stolen. I had to be nice to the guy for helping me and one evening he was practically begging me to come try a meal he prepared at his house. I took the opportunity at free food but tried to make it clear that I was heterosexual. So, I went home with a gay dude, ate some spaghetti, then had him take me home when the awkwardness became too much for me. I tried to avoid him after that but he made up some kind of phony award, framed it, and brought it into my workplace, it was weird.

One of the fondest or weirdly humorous memories I have of college was a time that Rich and I played practical jokes on our new roommate. Demetrius moved out so we were informed that we were getting a new roommate named Dave. The plan was to create and maintain particular wacky characters for ourselves to masquerade as around Dave for the first week or so. I think Rich adopted a British accent but wasn't supposed to be from Britain. Meanwhile I modified my voice to a native American that had smoked too much or something to that effect. My most brilliant idea was to make it so that the first time Dave was to see me I would be wearing nothing but underwear in an attempt to make it appear that I just went around all day like that. In reality I called Rich when I was coming home (I actually had one of my first cell phones at this time) and asked if Dave was there. When Rich informed me that he was then I would go to the apartment building's laundry room and change out of my clothes. I proceeded to walk from the laundry room to our dormitory/apartment. As I walked in Dave was sitting on the couch, I said hello as I walked straight to my bedroom. We had a whole conglomeration of other antics we would perform. One of them was to write out house rules for him to follow, but we did it in Spanish. Every time Dave was out, we decided to move the refrigerator to a different place in the apartment and just act like nothing happened. On one occasion Rich and I jammed out on our guitars purposely terribly yet purported belief of much quality and skill. One day we pretended we were watching our favorite TV show, but the TV was off. We literally sat there for a half hour with occasional laughter as if something funny happened in the show. On another occasion I ran around flapping my wings like I was a wacked-out Daffy Duck. Even with all of our efforts we never even got any kind of reaction out of the guy. We made it about four or five days in and I finally gave up and just said "Hey Dave, I'm done playing jokes on you, do you want to go meet the girls." I then took him to a small party where some of my female friends were including Ashly Dankworth who was a hoot in her own right. I never could understand how she can lean so far back on her chair or barstool and never fall off.

I have some sour memories of Pittsburgh. I had a new apartment in Mt. Washington that was creaky and old but cheaper than school sponsored housing. I was there two weeks before I ever met my new roommate who attended one of the other colleges. One time the furnace broke and I froze for a few days; the landlord was rarely available. But the worst thing about living there was the neighborhood. One morning I headed out to go to work but didn't see my car out front. I instinctively wondered if I parked off the side road for some reason the previous night before it dawned on me that my car had been hijacked. So, I walked into work and called the police to file the report. They found my 1988 Buick Park Avenue a few weeks later. I had to pay a 50-dollar fee to retrieve it from the junkyard. It had the back-door window busted out, and the steering column plastic cover ripped off. GM cars of that era were easy to steal because once you got that plastic off the steering column there is a metal thing that you just push and it starts the car right up. The thieves stole the stereo out of the car and nothing more. That particular head unit wasn't even a very expensive one, and seems like a lot of trouble to go through just to cause me frustration. I drove the car back home to Hagerstown (a three-hour drive). There was a big yellow marking on the side reading "Stolen," a busted window, and I could start it with my finger so I am sure it would have been interesting for a bystander to see. In addition, it started to rain and the wipers weren't working.

Another sour day involved me walking to work early on a frigid morning. I saw steam coming out of a manhole cover located on a crosswalk. I stepped over it hoping it might give me some warmth and boy did it ever. I jumped up as I felt a sting and quickly went into the café. I took a look at my leg and noticed a blister about six inches long by 1 inch wide and it was unreal. I ended up going to the hospital and getting Pittsburgh to pay for it. I contacted PACT (Pittsburgh Allegheny County Thermal) and spoke with their insurance representative. It was a process that took so long that my medical bill went to the credit bureau before I saw the money. I even had to complain about not getting enough money initially but was surprised when they eventually granted me the requested amount. They paid enough to cover my medical bill plus a thousand dollars.

College unquestionably helped me blossom mentally and socially. It was something I desperately required for personal growth. I think more growth sprung for me in those three years than in any other period. There is one instance however that proved I still had that social anxiety in my soul. I was required to take a speech class, and I fretted terribly over it. The only way I was able to get up in front of the class and read my prepared script was to come to class intoxicated. So, I performed all of my speeches half drunk. Before doing the final speech, I calculated out the grades and realized that I already had enough points to pass the class with a D (yes, a D grade was considered a passing grade at that school). I skipped the final speech, I never even prepared one. I later saw the professor; he was so cordial and even said he would still allow me to perform the speech just one-on-one, and I could get a much better grade. I declined the opportunity and accepted the poor grade. This was the only time

I can recall where I did the bare minimum in anything in my life. That must be a signifier of just how much I hated it.

I was on the product development track and would have to present my projects to the class often. I think my passion for my art helped guide me through the fear and anxiety in those instances. I was really interested in car design and joined the transportation design club. The school was working on developing a transportation design track and I would have considered doing that but it came around too late for me. I do not regret studying product development. The variety was amply satisfying and I had substantial fun while learning. I excelled with hands-on projects and ended up making a scaled model of a car that I designed. This model ended up being displayed in the school showcase for a significant amount of time. I succeeded in my main courses of study. I had a professor who headed the car club and taught most of the related courses. He was a stickler for details and what people might call a "hard nose." Many students disliked him but he actually was my favorite. He saw my efforts and I got "A's" in each of his classes.

The last six months at The Art Institute of Pittsburgh was the busiest time of my life. I was working nearly full time and was a full-time student. I woke up most days at 4:30 AM to go work at the Café/Deli. Then I would normally have an afternoon class or two. After class I always stayed at the school to work on my projects in the workshop. I often wouldn't arrive home until 10:00 PM. So yeah it was hectic, and somehow, I maintained a girlfriend at that time too. For my thesis project I opted to design and build a guitar with a built-in amplification system. I also wanted to make it headless and positioned the strings backwards putting the tuning pegs in the body of the guitar. This ideally would prevent accidental detuning of the guitar. My target market was young beginners who might not be able to afford an amplifier in addition to the guitar, hence the built-in speaker. I tore apart an old guitar for the hardware and took a piece of MDO to the CNC and created magic. I played a working prototype for my presentation and got an "A" grade for the course. Looking at it now there is so much I should do differently to make it better.

Instead of walking on a stage to be handed a fake diploma I opted to treat a portfolio review as my graduation ceremony. It was a big event with all the graduates displaying their projects. I feel like I presented myself well and had a good showing of my various skills including technical drawing, processes, 2D graphics, and 3D modeling. It was a proud moment for me. My mother and my brother Ralph and his family came for support. After college I decided to return to Hagerstown as I learned the big city life wasn't for me.

I didn't end up remaining very close to too many people from my college years except Rich. We did have a fall out though. He was involved with a woman who didn't favor me. I was supposed to be Rich's best man at their wedding. His fiancé bent something I said out of proportion and ended up convincing Rich to remove me as best man and delete me from his life entirely. Five or so years passed and they had a son together but she continued to manipulate him until he finally woke up. One day not too long ago I got a message from him saying "you were right." He informed me that he's getting a divorce. I never intended to hinder their relationship and all I ever said was "you know many of your sister's friends used to have a crush on you?" That is the sentence that broke up a great friendship. I am genuinely happy that we can be friends again and do not hold it against him.

While searching for a career out of college I was also searching for a new way to get into football. I love it too much; it gives me more pleasure than anything. I regularly affirm that football, particularly running someone over, is the most exhilarating feeling in the world and it even beats out the feeling of sexual release. Football is number one and sex is number two. With that in mind it was necessary that I find a league to play in. I discovered there were Semi-Pro teams all around and found out that Chambersburg had a team. Chambersburg is only about a half hour drive from Hagerstown. The football team was called the Cardinals and I contacted them about joining. There wasn't much of a try-out as that level of football isn't extremely popular. I bought myself a uniform and was officially on the roster starting in 2008. The uniforms were black and we played in the summer, so sometimes we were sweating like dogs. Dogs don't sweat, that doesn't make sense. I didn't have any college playing background so they didn't think I had much skill but I did get to play on special teams and got quite a few tackles doing so. We won the BNEFF championship in 2010. I missed the championship game though because I had a scheduling conflict. I had just started my new job at the prison and wasn't able to get the day off when the team moved the date of the game at the last minute. Looking back, I should have just called off sick but I was worried they would terminate my employment. I didn't play in 2011 and that is the year they went into a national tournament and won it all! My timing is impeccable. I returned to play in 2012 but management had started to deteriorate and the team folded the following year. The team had gotten too big and too political but I did play on various other teams having some success and heaps of fun.

Possibly the best times I had playing football as an adult was with a team called Tri-State Storm. The owner/head coach was a huge Italian guy from New Jersey that went by Cap. Cap has become one of my better friends. He was great at building confidence in his players and creating a family-like atmosphere. He was no slouch, worked us hard, had a lot of passion for football, and extensive knowledge as well. We worked out frequently under his leadership during the off seasons and at one point he clocked me running the 40-yard dash in 4.44 seconds. It's a number that may have been human error but I still use it to brag about how fast I was. Cap let me design the logo for the Storm and the flyers for our events. I did program covers for the Cardinals for some real-world graphic design experience before they folded.

"Diamond Rocks"

Diamond Rocks, what am I thinking?
I don't know just what I'm seeing
It is like a pointless point of view
Flash on back to a place in time

Where these things weren't on my mind
And I knew what I was supposed to do
Sputtering stars on the ceiling
Is this really a field of dreaming?
Diamond Rocks have never crossed my brain
Loss of appetite, should I sleep at night?
I am so confused, have I lost the fight?
Everything you say is all the same
Diamond Rocks, am I in Richmond?
Virginia stars, they aren't glistening
Déjà vu in a foreign place
I have got to speed at my own pace

That was the resulting creativity I had from playing a particular football game. Could you guess what it was about? I suffered a concussion that made my head spin. I was playing kickoff return for the Cardinals and squared up to block a man sprinting right at me. We met head-to-head in a stalemate manner but I was instantly dizzy, although I didn't black out. When I got back to the sideline, I kept asking myself, "are we in Richmond?" and "are we playing against the Hornets?" I did not tell anyone about it until I confessed to my buddy on the car drive home. This is where I started feeling nauseous and my buddy warned that I better not go to bed or I could slip into a coma. Now, reread my song/poem with concussion in mind and it may make a little more sense though I prefer the mystery.

My career after college got off to a first-rate start. I had applied to an architecture firm in Frederick and got hired as an architectural assistant in 2009. It was really good money for someone with no experience, and the people in the firm were all really amiable and copacetic. I was reasonably adequate with my Auto-Cad skills and my tasks were not extensionally difficult. I would just do what they called "red-lines" which meant editing something from existing drawings. I came to find out that this was the company that did the renovations to my high school while I was still enrolled. I told them there was a traffic congestion problem in building C as there were kids shoulder to shoulder in the funnel style intersection of the hallways between class periods. Hopefully the school learned to employ the rooms in building A as regular classrooms instead of the specialty use that they had for them at the time. This would help balance traffic flow. I was gifted the original blueprints for the South Hagerstown High School renovation project as a piece of memorabilia. I would have amazing feelings of euphoria on my drives home from work. I was at a point where I felt accomplished as if my hard work had paid off. I had a meeting with the President of the firm at one point and he gave me much praise. He found me to have great work ethic and intelligence so he actually offered to pay for schooling so I could get the specific studies for our line of work. It was something that should have been a no-brainer for me but I hesitated and took my time to think about it. Some time passed and we were bidding on getting the opportunity to be the architects of the new library in Hagerstown. We were not awarded the job so the company would have to downsize and I was the first to go. The vice president was cordial enough to leave a positive remark on my LinkedIn account upon my departure.

I had just bought a V8 Firebird and was still making payments when my employment got terminated. I had to take action and filed for unemployment post-haste. Being mostly conservative I don't necessarily agree with free government handouts but it was available so I figured why not. After 6 months I finally decided to give up the benefits and took a job at a Subway making far less money than I did while on unemployment. Being in my mid-20s, working at a Subway, already losing my hair, and living with my dad makes me regard that era as one of the lowest points of my life. I had to look for new opportunities.

A guy I played football with mentioned working as a guard in either the county jail or at one of the three local state prisons. I assessed myself and determined I had the right toughness and mentality to be ok with such a job so I went ahead and applied. The sheriff's department had a vigorous screening and testing process. We were tested on running a mile and a half and how many pushups we could do. I aced those tests. I did 49 pushups in a row by the way which was far more than needed. Then they took me in for a lie detector test which I can confirm is absolute nonsense. There is a reason why they are not considered viable in the court of law. They hooked me up to the machine and asked me a bunch of dumb questions. I had an itch on my face and was waiting for an opportune moment to scratch it because I knew they were looking for that kind of thing. They asked me if I ever stole anything worth 50 dollars or more, and I responded with "No." I waited several seconds then finally scratched my nose. When I did so I noticed the officer looked up at me in a peculiar way and proceeded to jot something down. He later came back to the thievery question, asked it a few more times. At this point I am having nerves because it is clear to me that they think I am lying. The detector reads your nerves. I may have passed the question the initial time but since they noticed me scratching my face, they decided to ask it again. I never stole anything in my life aside from a pack of *Ninja Turtle* trading cards when I was about eight years old. I didn't receive another call back from them. If a lie detector test isn't 100% accurate then it is 0% accurate because how can you know? You can't, it's stupid.

After six months at Subway I got a summon from the Maryland Department of Public Safety and Correctional Services. I had applied to them before I started the job at Subway but the screening process took that long. They brought me in and I started at the training academy. We were the last group of hires before they changed the pension program. We would be able to become invested after five years of employment whereas the next group of hires would have to wait ten years. I believe this is another example of God's perfect timing. I was hoping to only work there a couple years though and thought the pension re-adjustment wouldn't affect me.

The academy was only a couple months long but it was kind of neat to bond with the group of people in the class. There was one guy that no one wanted to bond with though. He was obnoxious in a way, and he was proud of getting a former colleague fired from their job. We don't know the full story of his former workplace, but his camaraderie was suspect and we feared he would cause problems inside the prison. It didn't help that he was a homosexual, something that shouldn't matter, but added discomfort. During defensive tactics everyone had to pair up and me being slothful socially meant that I ended up partnering with you-know-who. Aside from him making everything awkward it was interesting to learn some skills for personal protection. I now know the best means to defend against a headlock, seven different ways I can elbow you, and what the weakest part of your hand is for when I attempt to remove a weapon from it. It was not obligatory but we were encouraged to get our eyes sprayed with mace during one of the sessions. This was an attempt to let you know just how real it is. The gay dude and I were the only two who opted out. I deem I'm a creature who doesn't depend on learning by doing. I have sensitive eyes and knew that it would be extremely uncomfortable. When I witnessed everyone else follow through with it, I started to feel dreadful, like I had an unfair advantage, or like I wasn't a part of the team. They turned red and flushed their eyes out with water and couldn't hardly see for approximately 15 minutes. It looked horrendous. After the session I asked the instructor to perform it on me but he said it was too late. At the next class I brought a whole bunch of donuts for everyone to basically apologize for not getting sprayed. I think they forgave me. I graduated from the academy and officially became a Correctional Officer, which is the fancy term for prison guard.

The only form of protection we had inside the barbed wire fences was mace. Firearms aren't permitted in the facility, we had them at the perimeter outside the gates. That might be a surprise to many people but there are many other things inside the prison that will raise an eyebrow. First off it is not nearly as frightening as one might expect. It is almost reminiscent of a college campus, with numerous inmates walking in the yard from building to building for various reasons. Inside the prison you have buildings for housing, a medical area, a chapel, plenty of exercise areas, a store, schooling, and the administration building. Inmates get free housing, free health care including free ibuprofen, 3 free warm meals per day, free electricity, and free clothing. Inmates are permitted televisions and video games in their cells. Inmates can still work a job inside the prison to earn money. Inmates can still attain an education. Inmates can even write up an officer for doing something incorrectly. The general feeling inside the prison was that the inmates got more rights than the officers. I honestly don't see how the current prison system deters people from doing bad things. The return rate is 75% so the statistics support me.

The prison was not a fun place though, mostly because almost everyone inside was a jerk, inmates and officers included. I have a few stories about some crazy crap that happened inside Maryland Correctional Training Center. I typically worked in the yard area equipped with a regular small bottle of mace and a giant one too that we called a "fogger." I never ended up using either of them. My duties were to just scope out the yard and make sure the inmates were going where they belong and not attempting to escape or start fights or anything. Many inmates are associated with gangs and on one particular day a giant fight broke out between seven members of "DMI," and one "BGF." DMI stands for Dead Man Inc and consists of mostly Caucasian men. BGF stands for Black Gorilla Family and is made up of only black persons. There is a system in the prison system for determining membership but I digress. A "10-10" call was announced on the radio which meant a fight broke out and all available officers were required to respond by running to the site and putting a stop to the mayhem. When I and a bunch of other officers arrived, we all tackled someone and tried to cuff them. I was about to cuff up one inmate who was complying when one of our female officers approached and sprayed the guy in the face while he was already on the ground. I thought that was uncalled for but did not say anything. Meanwhile someone had sprayed fogger all over the place and it was like a giant cloud of mace in the air and made it hard to breath. We put the inmates in holding areas in the medical building for analysis. I watched one inmate who must have gotten a heavy dose of mace because he had a lengthy strand of snot hanging and dangling down from his nose almost reaching the ground. We would give the inmates paper towels to clean up their faces which was humorous to us because we knew the paper towels would just intensify the burning sensation. The stuff is real and I myself had a burning sensation under my fingernails after that day for several more days. It might have been because I put gloves on after the fogger went off in the yard and may have trapped some chemical inside.

On another date I was working in the segregation unit which consists of inmates that aren't permitted in the general population for protective or disciplinary reasons and just stay locked down in their cells at all times. Everything comes to the inmate in that unit including the medication distribution. One of the inmates threatened to rape our nurse on that day. He was already on lock-down and writing him up would probably only lengthen his lock-down time. We all felt that wasn't enough discipline.

-This section was deleted intentionally-

In that same unit on a different night we were transferring inmates to the showers. Each cell had two inmates and one of the inmates was denied a shower on that night for whatever reason. I was working the switch board as another officer was handling the inmates. The one inmate who was denied a shower tried to come out with his cellmate to take a shower. When the officer tried to keep him in his cell a scuffle broke out. This inmate had a neck brace on but we knew it was just for show. I had to quickly shut down the switch board and run down onto the tier to help my fellow officer. We had to tackle the inmate a few times and make sure the other inmate stayed out of it.

There were many messy days that an outsider might find inappropriate. The people that write up the in-prison rules have never even stepped foot inside the prison. I don't think they understand, nor do I think anyone outside the prison walls understand, even if they may have watched some popular documentary. It's a really difficult job.

My claim to fame at the prison may have been a time I tried to be goofy over the radio. For some reason the prison acknowledges Ramadan, so we had to do a special chow hall for the participating inmates after dark. I was working the yard one particular night and had to call a couple of the housing units to send those inmates to the chow hall. On the radio I said "house six, send your *ramadamadingdongs*." Later on, I said "house seven, send your *ramadamadingdongs*." I got many laughs from my co-workers. The Sergeant in charge of the yard got chewed out by the Lieutenant. The sergeant confronted me as he should have but it was clear to me that he also found it funny, so I didn't reap any serious reprimands. The next day in the muster room (a gathering area for overview and announcements before each work day) the Major had a few things to share about it. He didn't talk directly to me but he warned us that the inmates could overhear what I said and it could cause a riot. He was correct, I was an idiot but luckily nothing like that happened. The thing is, many of the so-called Muslim inmates are not in it for the religious reasoning. I would have respected their faith had it been genuine. Many of them are in it for the perks and the protection. Really within the prison system Islam is just another form of gang membership. We would occasionally have problems with the Muslims versus the Crips or whatever. The Muslim gang was even one of the more violent of gangs; it is sad but true. It's hard to differentiate in my head the way Muslim inmates were compared to the way a Muslim may be on the outside. It's hard to keep that negative view off of the religion itself, but it's something I am working on.

I had a scare on one occasion working at the prison that found me in the hospital. We were conducting "cell searches." This is when we go into cells and look for contraband. When I was searching through one particular inmate's things, I found a jacket and reached into the pocket only to get pricked by a needle. The needle was from a homemade tattoo making machine and the inmate got in trouble for possessing contraband. Meanwhile I went to the hospital to get tested or treated for the possibility of HIV or other diseases. The doctor looked at it and determined I wasn't pricked deep enough through my skin for any of that to concern me but they still did a blood test. They tested the inmate too, and both of our results came out negative to my relief.

Some of the inmates seemed really honorable and decent when exchanging banter. We had an inmate who was a tier worker in one of the housing units. He was one of the hardest working and most respectful inmates I ever witnessed. He shared with us that the reason he was in prison was because of a drug deal that went sour, but then said he had twenty some years left on his sentence. It didn't make sense to have such a big sentence over drugs so we asked him why. He nonchalantly replied "Oh, I had a murder too." He proceeded to describe how this guy was mouthing off to him and kept on doing it even while he was pointing a gun at him. He told us "since he wouldn't shut up, I had no other option but to pull the trigger." It's clear to me and most civil human beings that *not* pulling the trigger would be the more beneficial option, but the inmate didn't see it that way.

I was making pretty good and steady pay working at the prison and so I ended up purchasing my first home at the age of 27. I was looking at this house for months. The asking price dropped significantly starting at around $140,000. I ended up purchasing it for $89,000. Amongst the houses I looked at this one was the readiest to move in. Everything was in good shape and didn't require repair. It is a brick rancher with three bedrooms and one bath. There is a full unfinished walk-out basement with plumbing for an additional bath. I eventually added another toilet down there and kept it wall-free and out in the open for my own amusement. There is also a detached garage with its own electricity. The only thing the house was missing was a refrigerator, a washer, and a dryer. The kitchen had black appliances so I bought a new black refrigerator to match. I bought a used washer and dryer and got my home set up perfectly. Other than having to pay city taxes, this house is perfect for me. I immediately started painting the blank white wall canvases different colors and proceeded to build my gym and workshop in the basement. This is the first time I ever lived somewhere that had a front yard. I immediately felt rich and accomplished when I bought the house. It was a milestone in my life that I yearned for and prayed about. God was good. Perhaps God gave me the prison job in order to give me my home. I had a few roommates join my living quarters but now my dad has moved in after he sold his home. I said he could stay with me until he finds a new place and I am glad he got out of the old house I grew up in because it's not the best area and it's getting worse.

At work we had gotten a new female to work in the food service section at the prison. I came to discover that it was my old crush from A.C. Moore: Shawna Madison. When I initially saw her inside the institution, we barely recognized each other because it had probably been ten years since we saw each other. She looked at me and said "do I know you?" I responded by inquiring if her name was Shawna. She gasped because it isn't recommended to use first names in the prison for privacy reasons. I informed her who I was and we got to reconnect. She was still looking stupendous and all the other officers and inmates as well were *goo-goo-ga-ga* for her. I had the benefit of knowing her beforehand so I had the upper hand as some of the others were probably jealous.

Shawna and I talked and even hung out outside of work. She came to my house after work one time on her motorcycle. Here I showed her the high school picture of her that she had given to me so many years ago and that I had kept. My dad randomly showed up and basically cock-blocked me. Shawna played in a softball league and I came to see her play one time. There I talked to her mother and she remarked about Shawna not being "a saint." I thought that was peculiar, then afterwards her dad was goofing off and told me to hold her hand because she is single. She had a daughter and I don't know the story about the father, but some suspect she was still in a relationship with him. At work some of the officers told me stories about hooking up with her. I assumed they were making stuff up. She ended up getting fired from the job apparently due to bringing in contraband. I haven't heard from her since her departure from the job. The truth about my crush will always mystify me.

I worked on the evening shift for a year then decided to switch over to the night shift. Less headache causing events happened on the night shift and I could do life necessities during the day. Night shift is where I met a friend who has played a large part in my development as a human. Frederick Wolfe was a smaller nerdy Officer on the night shift with pale skin and vitamin D deficiency. He appeared to have no business inside the barbed wire fences but I believe he aspired to be someone who changes people's lives for the better. He worked at the prison as an officer but was studying theology and was one of the most intelligent people I have ever come across. He and I became considerably good friends and would talk about Christianity and classic rock often. We bonded over music like I do with so many people. He loved the band *Queen*. The thing I grabbed the most from him was his realistic and straight forward approach to Bible scripture. It intrigued me and I found myself seeking his insight frequently. He was the first person to tell me that there is a blow-job in the Bible. It is truly in the book of Solomon (chapter 2, Verse 3). He taught me how to understand scripture in a different way than I was used to. He described things in a way that sounded smarter, stripped down, and less molded by time and tradition. He taught me that Jesus sometimes had a sense of humor such as when he said that a rich man has less chance of getting into heaven as a camel can pass through the eye of a needle. Some people might take it literally, some people say the "eye of a needle" was another term for some other thing that was small but not impossible for a camel to pass through. I believe Wolfe is right, Jesus was being humorous, and it may have been common trope of the time. Wolfe has also made me ponder over how some people follow certain parts of the Bible but not all. Why do they do that? Did God not want us to read and comprehend all of it? How can any of the Bible be right if all of it isn't? It makes sense to me that the Holy Bible would be presented to us in the manner that God wants. I am grateful for having met Frederick Wolfe because he got me reacquainted and reinterested in my own religion.

Officer Wolfe was a member of the Church at Martinsburg and I joined him a few times. I favor it because it was all about the people and all about the facts in the Bible. It felt like a good place to learn and become a better Christian and less like a formality or a tradition like many churches felt before. Maybe that's why I don't typically go, nor enjoy going to church. There is another church close to my home called Tri-State Fellowship that is similar so I try to attend it when I can.

I didn't enjoy working at the prison; the inmates were horrible. Officers often teased me about my white teeth (as if I bleached them) and also about my shirt. I had hemmed up the polo shirts we were given for summertime because the sleeves seemed too long to me and bugged my elbow. One of the more annoying officers came up to me and said "let me see your sleeves, I heard you hemmed them up to make your arms look bigger." He even grabbed me to get a closer look, with his hands. It pissed me off but I didn't do anything about it. I started to grow miserable at the prison like I was wasting my life away. Stress levels are notoriously high for Correctional Officers and divorce rates are high too. Suicide rates for Correctional Officers are amongst the highest of any other profession. This was a time in my life that I had to regularly remind myself of Fern, and that God is real.

I was lonely working in a yard shack through the middle of each night for years. I found a Bible in the drawer there though. It was an ESV (English Standard Version) which Wolfe had described to me as a word-for-word translation, probably the most accurate translation, and one of the easiest to read. As I opened it up, I would concur with that argument. I was accustomed to the King James version that has a plethora of old time English words and phrases. The ESV seems to use more modern words but also utilizes a back to the roots approach. It is my favorite translation and I got a lot of use out of that Bible while I often had hours of nothing to do at my post. I became more accustomed to the ten commandments. One of them is to keep the sabbath holy, and it was becoming more bothersome to me that I had to work weekends and break that commandment every week. I hoped I would get to respect the sabbath sooner than later.

Around this time, I had decided to go back to school. I already had most of the credits needed to earn an associate in graphic design so I went to Hagerstown Community College to take the remaining courses. I also intended to run track again. I just ended up pulling my hamstring twice. I also felt a little bit weird being a good bit older than everyone else on the team. I had fun nonetheless. I excelled in the courses and felt like the instructors had a lot of respect for me. I graduated with an Associate of Applied Science in 2012. I did it backwards because I received my Bachelor of Science in 2008 at The Art Institute of Pittsburgh.

After some time, I finally pushed myself to rummage for a new job. My five-year anniversary at the prison was coming up shortly and I didn't wish to be there any longer than necessary. I decided to go ahead and get my five years in which meant I would become invested in the pension program but was going to quit as soon as possible. My mental state was heading downward in that dreadful job. I applied to a sign company in Rockville, Maryland. Accepting the employment offer meant taking a gargantuan pay cut and having an hour commute each day. The benefit would be I would get my foot in the door of a job related to my field of study, I could work regular hours, and I would finally escape prison. I got support from my girlfriend Blessica who lived in Rockville, and that was a big push. I called MCTC the day after I got my five years in and told them I was quitting. I gave them no notice, after all why would I risk any more negativity? This was the best decision of my life because I wanted to leave the negativity behind me.

I would have preferred to get hired by SMI Sign Systems in Frederick, Maryland. It is so much closer to me and I applied to them at the same time but they never called me back after an initial interview. Two months into my new job I finally did receive a call from SMI. They were surprised that I quit the job at the prison to start a career in the sign industry, and so they wanted to bring me on board. They offered me more money than the Fastsigns in Rockville could give me but I still declined because I had just started and wanted to stick it through a bit longer. I am a loyal and dedicated individual and thought it was a righteous endeavor. Then SMI offered me even more money so I finally accepted. I started on the floor at SMI as part of the production staff. After a couple months one of the designers resigned and they needed me to fill in for him. I proved that I could handle the job with ease and quickly became a full-time designer for the team. When I got my own cubicle with a name plate sign that said "Ray Adams – Designer," it was one of the proudest moments of my life. I checked off another goal. I have bonded with the Art director here at SMI and we have great respect for each other. He helped progress me to where I am today and I am so thankful. I have gotten many raises already and am now making as much as I did at the prison. My job though, it is so much more exhilarating than yelling at disobedient people. I get to draw on my computer all day long. It is a dream come true for me even if sign design is the most basic of design jobs. I feel fulfilled like this is what I was meant to do. I told one of my co-workers that and they were surprised. Living a life of stress at the prison has put the things we take for granted into perspective. I could never feel as much stress as I did. This new job seems completely stress free to me even if others might disagree.

I have so many blessings. One thing I am mega grateful for is my family. Seeing extended family has come sparsely. I always wish I could see them more. My dad's side of the family is pretty spread out but we all occasionally meet up near his hometown near Amish country in Central Pennsylvania. The Alexanders are all pretty close to where I live though and we don't gather as much anymore ever since Nana and Pappy died. Last summer (2016) I took it upon myself to throw a family reunion for the Alexanders even though I am an Adams. On a large piece of cardboard, I drew out the family tree. I put big squares for each member and instructed everyone to draw a self-portrait. Directly under Nana and Pappy are their children from oldest to youngest: Georgia, Randy, Jaqueline, Frank, and Carol. Randy is my mom's twin brother and a successful dental laboratory technician. Uncle Frank has passed away and is sorely missed. Then my two Aunts are quite silly. The tree continues on and I have a bunch of cousins and they have a plethora of kids so it was sensational to gather them all together for some family fun and festivities. The reunion was a success. Amili's daughters

Willow and Ivy got to play with their cousins with squirt guns and I had fun joining in and soaking. I played basketball with my brother Zach and my cousins Jeffy and Preston. This was the premier instance I can think of that we were all together to partake in such an activity and it felt amazing. I felt pride in knowing that I was able to gather people together. My cousin Preston approached me with a question: "what made you decide to do this?" I responded, "I just wanted to see some family." I might have to do it biennially.

I have a new job, and a new life, and I am loving every minute of it. I know now that everything in my life has led me to where I am right now, where I am supposed to be, a state of realistic contention, and hope for the future. I now have the opportunity to thank God for the many blessings he has bestowed upon me.

- Chapter 6 -
Crop Circles

In this chapter I will try to explain some strange occurrences that I have experienced and try to make sense of it all. I will try to address some societal issues. I will express some theories and some opinions, and I will probably open more questions than close cases. I may make your head spin as I showcase the crop circles in my brain.

Why I don't talk:
First off, I'm not 100% sure I know what my opinions are.
Second, I'm not sure I'm saying what I didn't know.
Third, I'm not sure I'm using the correct vocabulary to say what I didn't fully mean about what I didn't know.
Fourth, I'm not sure my body language is portraying the same thing as my lips are saying the incorrect vocabulary to what I meant to say about what I didn't know.
Fifth, I'm not sure you can correctly interpret what and how I'm saying something.
Sixth, I'm not sure if when you respond, you can match your body language to the incorrect vocabulary of what you didn't mean to say about what you didn't know, and whether I have the capacity to interpret the meaning of a conversation which seems to only have 1% accuracy. Understand?

Does anyone else repeat conversations in their heads? After every chat I have with another human being I repeat it multiple times in my head and analyze it. I always conclude that I should have said something more, or something better. I am always self-conscious about how I interact with people. It bugs me, like a bug.

I theorize that spoken language could fade into being nearly obsolete someday. Screens are taking over. Texting has become the favorite over phone calls. In many workplaces email has become the number one form of communication. It seems ridiculous to think the future could be rid of spoken language, but some things we've read about in our past seem ridiculous too.

One day we'll have the ability to transmit smells through our phones. There will be sensors that read the scent, send the code, and little capsules with different smell values will recreate the smell on the other end. It'll be almost like mixing colors in CMYK values except with smell. Mark my words.

Is there a doppelganger effect on occurrences? I have noticed things happen in pairs and it is peculiar. The weirdest one I can remember was an incident in gym class in high school. We were playing kick ball for some reason, I guess we had nothing important to do. When I got up to kick, I kicked the ball with excessive force and it flew to the back corner of the gym and swoosh, it went right through the basketball net. The next time I was up to kick the very same thing happened and we were all stunned by the consecutive swooshes (the balls literally didn't even hit the rim, they were both "nothing but net"). Later I dated a "Jessika," immediately followed by a "Blessica," but did not date a "Shmessica" afterwards for it would have added a third to my two similar sounding girlfriend names. When I was hired at my current job, a Russian man trained me on the production floor, then when I got promoted to designer another Russian man trained me. They are the only two Russian people I have ever met. Whenever I put a shoe on, I always seem to put a second shoe on immediately afterwards, weird. I am literally constantly noticing strange occurrences happening in doubles. It can be very minute things like finding a penny then finding another one but I am becoming skeptical of the phenomena.

We have found out the earth is round and circles the sun. Does history do the same thing? Does time go in circles? What if timelines aren't lines? What if they are in the shape of a spring, and we are always close to something that already happened before?

Clovers freak me out, particularly of the four-leaf variety. Superstition suggests that they are good luck but I beg to differ. I have come to suspect they are actually of bad fortune or something evil is associated with them. I can explain. When I was young, my aunt gave me a four-leaf clover sealed in plastic. Around this time my grandmother passed away. When I happened upon one as a young adult my grandfather passed away a week later. Then it happened yet again with my other grandfather. On Sunday June 15th 2014 I went down to Western Heights Middle School and did an agility workout with cones. When I bent over to stretch, I discovered a four-leaf clover. The next day a woman and two kids were found dead in a car at the middle school parking lot approximately 100 yards from where the four-leaf clover was unearthed. I always close my eyes when I bend down to stretch now.

Flowers have similarly weird phenomena behind them. Every time I have purchased flowers for a girl, they broke up with me right afterwards. It happened with Samantha in high school then again with Katherine in college. I went on a date with Stacey whom I used to work with at A.C. Moore, and after giving her a rose, was not awarded a second date. I got a girl named Michelle flowers then got stood up. It is a curse, the flower curse. So, I refuse to get girls flowers anymore.

You know the common cartoon joke about a dark cloud of rain following a character around? Well I experienced the antithesis. I have noticed for several years that the rain would stop whenever I had to go somewhere. It would literally stop just for a few seconds when I walked out to get into my car. It got to the point where I believed God was purposely giving me this random luxury so I decided to pray to him. I told him that I would rather he gave the luxury to someone else. Not long afterwards I got rained on at work, and it made me very happy.

My neighbor Kerrie directly across the street from me had two kids. Their names were the same as me and my sister. The one kid's middle name was the same as my last name. Kerrie's eldest son, the one I share names with, actually committed suicide a few years back. We talked about certain important dates in our lives and they match up in a phenomenal way. The date coincidences present some weird juju.

I have always been interested in psychology, insanity, psychedelic art, and anything about the mind. My favorite movies include *Eternal Sunshine of the Spotless Mind*, *A Beautiful Mind*, *Butterfly Effect*, and *Defendor*. Let me pose a question: If an insane person accepts what does not make sense, but a sane person cannot accept it and it drives them crazy, who really is the crazy one in this scenario? Perhaps this justifies the phrase "ignorance is bliss."

I believe that someone's presence is greater than their presents. I believe an individual being present is the best gift. Presence > presents.

I do not value trust! But I do value trustworthiness. After all it would be foolish to trust a non-trustworthy individual wouldn't it? If you value yourself for being trustworthy then you won't have to worry about someone trusting you. I don't need someone to trust me, because I know I will do the right thing. I won't have to worry about trusting you if you are trustworthy.

Do a good deed without expecting recognition, it's a personal victory. But then is it selfish to feel good about yourself for practicing benevolence, and helping others? If you do something for the cause and not for the reward then you have a truly good heart.

You could say a gay man is essentially attracted to straight men, and a gay woman would be attracted to straight women. Neither of those situations would work out. My solution is to have gay men date gay women. A gay man is basically a woman trapped in a man's body, and a gay woman is basically a man trapped inside a woman's body. Since opposites attract, the woman minded person would be attracted to the man minded person, and vice versa. So now the pair of a gay man and a gay woman match up mentally and physically; they can even do the *hoo-ha* stuff in the bedroom. Perfect!

Realistically it's none of my business what orientation a person is or who they decide to love. I do believe marriage is meant to be a spiritual thing. Therefore, I would take the government out of it entirely and just let it up to local churches.

Feminism is sexism. It ends in an "ism" doesn't it? Equal rights are not fair rights. It's a simple fact that women and men are not equal, we have differences between us and that should be respected in order for true fairness to be prevalent. Equal Employment Opportunity doesn't seem fair to me. A company may be forced to hire a minority whether or not they are better qualified for the job. When you empower one category of person you take away from another person. There is only so much energy in the world, so that energy will need to come at the expense of someone else.

Hating a political party is prejudiced. This should be another "ism." Perhaps we will create a word: "*politism*." How is this hate between political parties not considered taboo the way hate between other groups of people is? It seems that it is acceptable by the general public to hate the opposing party. I don't think that is honorable and aim to put an expiration on the two-party system. The only way I know how to accomplish that at the moment is to support a third party. That is one reason why I typically vote Libertarian.

Supporting or loving someone or group of persons because they are the same color as you when you have no other reason to is a racist action in my opinion.

There is a lot of rhetoric about racism these days. Racism is wrong. Racism is hateful, but I think we've gotten to the point culturally that we consider other non-hate-based things to be racist too. Someone might make an imperfect comment such as, "You are one of the good ones," and get labeled a racist even if they are not a hater.

I think certain terms or phrases have been created in an attempt to battle oppression, but I argue who is really oppressed in America? Our culture has long been trying to give minorities every bit as much a chance to succeed as the majority, if not more. As an example, I don't think there are special college grants for people like me (white skinned) but there are specific ones for other demographics (multiple scholarships for black people only). One term that has popped up is "white privilege," and it suggests it's easier for Caucasian people to succeed. Being white, I do feel privileged in the fact that I don't have to carry around as many negative stereotypes. I feel bad for the virtuous black people out there that have to face that judgment consistently. I have seen black privilege in sports though. I found in my experience that people routinely assume the black kid was a better athlete than me. People would often be surprised when the "white boy" did something good in sports. I was never particularly fond of being called "white boy" nor when they called me "Forest Gump." Maybe in my eyes I thought I was a better athlete but in reality, maybe I wasn't. Judgment should be based on facts, but it's hard to see facts and not be biased depending on your skin color.

Police brutality is another popular argument but when I looked up the statistics it seemed that white people get killed just as much as black people. We only see one side of the story in the media. This is one reason I despise television.

You'd think I would witness systematic racism first hand in the prison but that is not the case. The predominantly white officers disliked whites just as much if not more than the black inmates. The statistics are overwhelming as the prison I worked at was about 75% black and the national population is about 13% black. Statistically 1 out of every 2 black Americans will go to jail at some point in their life. Can systematic racism be at fault at such a large scale and right under our noses for so long? Everyone I associate with agrees that racism is reprehensible... So how would it be possible? I don't think it is, but maybe I have too much conviction in the judicial system and humanity. Honestly from my experience it makes sense because about 1 out of every 2 black persons I've met were completely hostile individuals. Maybe the system made them that way. The truth is that white people fear black people. White people fret visiting areas where black people dominate the population. This is due to a history of violence and gang activity. And now many black people fear police because they may generalize black people to fit that stereotype. White people in general also fear being labeled a racist, and I think this prevents many arguments from surfacing. It's sad that both sides have these fears. Is it ok for me to be proud that I am white? I feel like the system has gotten me to ponder questions like that, and I think that's sad too.

All this being said, I wish for racism to cease, judgment to be reserved, frustration to be eliminated on both sides, and love to conquer, but this is a fairytale dream. I am not smart enough to suggest how we go about addressing these issues. Does this make my points moot?

I am a Caucasian, heterosexual, conservative, Christian, male, and I feel hated by every other group. I feel like my demographic gets blamed for everything. I myself preach love and don't do things to hurt anyone so it's a struggle personally to feel like the general population dislikes the type of individual I am. I strongly believe in individualism and don't like the fact that we have these groupings. I don't want to be a Caucasian, heterosexual, conservative, Christian, male; I just want to be Ray Adams. I honestly don't believe I have the feeling of "needing to belong" that many people may possess.

It's been said that if someone doesn't take action for a cause, that makes them just as bad as the opposition. I feel like this statement is manipulation and attempts to guilt trip people. I don't think it's very nice. Please don't drag me into your problems. People that help with other people's problems have empathy and deserve praise but people that mind their own business do not deserve blame. Of course, this depends on the severity of the situation and if the right thing to do is obvious. *The Bible* says "So whoever knows the right thing to do and fails to do it, for him it is sin" (James 4:17 ESV). In the end people get mad at you because they expect you to see "right from wrong" the same way they do.

Are you offended? Being offended equals having a problem with something someone said. Having a problem with something someone said equals intolerance towards that person's opinion. So, this proves that intolerance equals being offended. Let me rephrase this. If someone is offended then they are intolerant! I'm in a conundrum because I am offended when others are offended; I'm intolerant of your intolerance towards my head-scratching statement. Should I not tolerate the intolerant? It's hypocrisy.

Human DNA commonly has many strands that are stagnant or inactive. I think this suggests that human traits can vary vastly, and we could be much more different than we appear today. I think this is a hint at microevolution. There is proof that people have changed through the years. Abraham Lincoln was considered freakishly tall at 6'-4", and the average male back then was only 5'-8". So, we are taller on average today (but really only by an inch or two). I think this is because certain parts of our DNA show up more than other parts as an evolutionary thing. I think the final extent of who we are does not change, thus I do not believe in macroevolution. I do not think we came from monkeys. I do not think DNA can morph from one thing to another. You say that we have found bones that belonged to "monkey-men," or the missing links to our evolutionary history. I think most skeleton findings are only partially complete and a lot of what you see in a museum is fabricated. I suggest that maybe the monkey-men skulls we found are a result of the varying degrees of human DNA, or perhaps of another species of monkey-like creatures. Maybe our DNA at one point had an active portion that made it possible for humans to breed with monkeys. I think about the sterile Liger that is possible today. A tiger can breed with a lion and create a strange one-off creature. Perhaps we were able to do that with ourselves in the past. Or perhaps we had scientists in the past that played around with genetics and created monkey-men. Anything is possible. I don't understand how we all collectively consider one absurd thing to be true over another.

Some sciences weird me out. Playing with genetics, DNA, and stem-cell research all seem wrong to me. It is like we want to play God. Being religious, I believe some things should be left alone. When we clone a sheep, it turns out all messed up because it is just unnatural, and I despise the unnatural. I generally don't like medicine, I don't like altering our bodies, and I certainly believe that abortion is wrong. I also don't think in-vitro fertilization is right. Some folk believe that both of those things can be a blessing for people to fix something that otherwise can't be fixed. But for us to choose to abort our own offspring disturbs me. I get physical pain in my chest when I think about it. I believe I have a connection with God and I believe he puts that pain in my chest to let me understand that it is wrong. It is popular to say "It's my body," and "Woman's right to choose." These are phrases that the socially liberal society invented and try to pass as fact. Here is the fact: it is another human being inside of you, so it is not your body. If you are a Christian then even your body isn't your body; your body is borrowed from God and should be respected. Why would we think that women have the right to choose to kill an unborn baby? The baby is physically 50% the father's as it has 23 chromosomes from each parent so why wouldn't the father have a say? If Women get to decide whether or not they want to keep a baby then Men should get to decide whether or not they want to pay child support. That is a joke by Dave Chappelle, but it is genius. If I had the ability to get pregnant, I would feel *honored* to have the *opportunity* to *sacrifice* my body and my life for the child. I think that is love, and I am bewildered why other people don't feel the same way. Maybe it is because of society. One individual gets an idea, whether it is bad or good, and it spreads like a diseased wildfire. Jesus would say "Forgive them, for they do not know." I try to remind myself of the phrase "What Would Jesus Do" often when stuck on certain difficult subjects.

The death penalty is another tough concept. I don't have the answer, but it seems to me that people who are for abortion should also be for the death penalty since they want to eliminate nuisances. This doesn't align with popular political standpoints. It seems like many people just follow what is common for a certain party and don't have a mind of their own.

My theories are based on common sense (sure we could argue what common sense is for days) and clues that I have gathered but I am certainly no scientist. One theory I have doesn't match well with my other theories or mimic my religious beliefs, nonetheless it makes sense to me. Brace yourself for the following. Aliens are just evolved humans from the future, and the U.F.O.s are their time machines. If you look at the theory of evolution, we evolved from the monkeys. Monkeys lose their hair, grow bigger heads, and smaller mouths as they evolve into humans. Continue on this pattern of change and you may wind up with something that looks much like the omnipresent image of an alien. Monkeys are strong, humans not as much, and aliens are depicted to look quite frail. If future humans gained the ability to time travel, do you think they would want to go back in time to investigate and do experiments? I would answer probably a big yes. Also, time travel might explain the mysterious patterns of U.F.O. appearances.

The moon's orbit is changing. The moon is getting further away from the earth. Laser measurements support the theory. This could lead us to think that days on Earth used to be shorter. If this is happening with the moon then who is to say it isn't happening with Earth in relation to the sun? Maybe the earth is getting further away from the sun and years didn't take as long to complete in the past. I theorize that this explains why biblical characters lived so long. Methuselah was 969 years old and Noah was 950. If a year was shorter in their era then maybe their life span would only feel like approximately 100 of today's years. Time is relative. We base our timing on the planets. If the planets aren't fixed then our timing is inaccurate.

Time really is relative. One year seems really short when you are a 50-year-old because it is a small fraction of your life. When you are an 8-year-old, that same amount of time is a much larger portion of your life: 1/8. This will make one year seem much longer because it's relative to your entire life. Therefore, time itself is different for an older person than it is for a younger person.

Noah had an extremely difficult task during the great flood. He was to gather two of each animal on to the Ark. Can you imagine ancient humans getting two tyrannosauruses onto a boat? I theorize that many dinosaurs became extinct because Noah was unable to protect them from the floods. We now have proof that carbon dating has inaccuracies. I suspect we may eventually debunk uranium-thorium dating as well, which apparently can date something up to half a million years old. Will we ever be able to date something as old as the dinosaurs? How do we assume that dinosaurs lived millions of years ago? I think that assumption is crazy.

You can't teach a duck calculus. What I'm trying to convey is that there are things that a duck's mind will never understand, such as calculus, and so much more. What if I inferred that there are subjects that the human mind will never be able to comprehend? What if we became the duck in this scenario? In addition to spirituality, religion, and God himself, I bet there are many other things that we simply cannot be taught. You can't teach a duck calculus!

Here is my viewpoint on luck. Someone might say "I don't believe in luck." That to me doesn't make sense. Luck is just how we define the results of occurrences due to chance. I have a fun theory on why certain things are considered bad luck and the examples follow. Breaking a mirror is bad luck because you might cut yourself cleaning up the glass. Walking under a ladder is bad luck because a bucket of paint might fall on your head. A black cat crossing your path is bad luck because it's difficult to sight and you might run it over making an unsuspecting neighbor quite upset. I think I have been very unlucky when it comes to women. Clever segue?

- Chapter 7 -
Relationships

"Damn girl!" could be the light-hearted approach to describing my feelings towards my general relationships. I have many girls to thank because I have used heartbreak as fuel for many of my art pieces in the form of poetry or songs. Maybe I have seized wisdom from my relationships or maybe I have grown to accept God's will. Having this social anxiety and unquestionably erratic personality hasn't exactly helped. It is harder for me to meet people and harder for me to talk to or relate to people. From my perspective I can be pretty good when it is one on one, me and her on a date, charming in my own way. Yet I don't have another personality to compare my experiences with. How would my relationships be different had I been a social butterfly? It's too bad I'm a social centipede.

One thing I am grateful for is the era I live in. We have texting which benefits people like myself who simply don't like talking and get nervous thinking about how we're judged by others because of what comes out of our mouths. Then there is also online dating, which to me has been a colossal help. I could pretty much never see myself walking up to a good-looking somebody at a bar and strike up a conversation let alone coax a girl into coming home with me. That is not my scene anyway, and I have never had a one-night stand. Of course, I fantasize from time to time about a promiscuous lifestyle but inside that is not who I am at all. In this chapter I explore each of my relationships and I include the good, the bad, the ugly, and the pretty.

Jasmine was pretty, she was my first kiss, and it was 1996. I didn't have to reach far because she was my sister's friend. Two years apart is a lot when you are 11. Yeah, Jasmine was 9 years old. It didn't feel like a huge age difference and 2 years is certainly not much as an adult. Back then it was sort of taboo; I even remember someone hollering at me on the street mentioning how gross it is to date someone so much younger. It's not like we were "dating" although for a brief moment I had my first girlfriend. This is of course if you don't count the "girlfriend" I had in first grade; back then I thought a girlfriend was a friend that is a girl, so a female friend and I called each other "boyfriend" and "girlfriend."

Jasmine looked similar to the likes of Jasmine from *Aladdin*; she was tiny with long dark hair and big dark eyes. We snuck outside behind an old abandoned car and got down on our knees to share a first kiss. We closed our eyes and leaned in, but then I bumped my head on the side view mirror of the car. We shared a laugh and tried again, but with fruition. It was soft and nice and I liked it. As far as the relationship, it didn't last long and I don't remember how it all ended, but we did not remain close.

A few years passed and I was in middle school. In 1999 I was in eighth grade. I remember having a crush on so many cute girls, it was probably 50% of them. I came to learn that someone actually had a crush on me and her name was Melanie Jetson. She was starting to blossom from a chubby kid into a beautiful young lady but she still had chubby rosy cheeks and braces. She had curly blonde hair and blue eyes; she was quite cute. We started passing notes to each other day after day. This was a time before cell phones. We would call each other's house, speak to a parent, and ask for permission to talk to each other. Most of the time it was just her blabbing and me sitting there listening. We continued to pass notes and I started to compile quite a mass. We would sit together at lunch and hold hands in the hallway, but that was about the extent of our relationship. We never hung out outside of school and I conjecture she wasn't technically permitted to date yet considering we were only 13 or 14. I warned her one morning that I was going to kiss her at the end of the school day at the bus departure area but I remember her turning her head, I only got to kiss her cheek. She dumped me via a note that I ended up drawing a skull and cross bone on, she didn't want to continue dating me through summer and into high school. I can attribute that as my first heartbreak. We were telling each other that we loved each other but it was weird, and clearly only teeny love. In high school she blossomed, braces gone, and had become one of the popular girls. I kept a bag full of the notes she sent me, each folded in her special way. There was probably 100 of them, and I held onto them for several years. I would talk about her from time to time, and my buddy Matthew would tell me I am obsessed. I didn't want to admit it, but I do have a bit of an obsessive personality.

Shortly after "the bad" and horrifying occurrence of 9-11, I was approached by Becky Zimmer. She was quite possibly the prettiest girl in the entire school but she was "the bad." We were both fifteen years old but I was a sophomore and she was a freshman. She had been held back a year once and her past accompanied trouble. She had a sexually abusive uncle and I think that caused a downward psyche in herself. She was stunningly gorgeous with fair skin and looked like a mixture between Liv Tyler and Megan Fox with her long dark hair, green eyes, and juicy lips. I couldn't believe she liked me, the quiet good kid, and I couldn't believe that my lips would touch hers, and they were so soft. To this day I believe they may have been the softest lips ever. I got the opportunity to visit her at home. She was living with her aunt and uncle of good virtue (not the uncle from before) and good fortune as well; they had a nice house. We watched a movie with candles lit and snuck out for walks and kisses. The sex appeal and feelings were something new to me as was the addition of tongues to kissing. To add to the experience, she also had a tongue ring. She was far advanced for her age and not a virgin like myself. At one point whilst taking a shower she spun the *Nirvana* Album: "Nevermind." I've listened to some of their music before but got to hear the album in its entirety and it amazed me. It was the perfect soundtrack for the time.

As time passed, I came to realize just how bad Becky really was. At fifteen years old she smoked, drank, and had done other drugs in the past. She skipped school and made fake hall passes to try to get me out of class. One time she was hanging outside a liquor store asking people walking in if they could buy alcohol for her. I know this because on this particular occasion it was my father she had asked. Rumors would spread that she made out with one of my teammates in the stands after a football game and that she even had sex in the dugout with one of the bad boys. The latter I don't believe to be true. One night she had nowhere to go, something was amiss at home, so she ended up staying at my house. She had been drinking and I could taste the alcohol in her mouth when I snuck into the room to get a kiss only for my dad to holler and make me go back to my room. She was friendly with the music teacher and I met her in his classroom one day after school as if he was counseling her or something. Looking back on this I wonder what was really going on because that teacher ended up getting fired for an inappropriate relationship with another dark-haired student, or so is the rumor.

Becky would remain a mystery to me long after our short-lived relationship that had ended over a telephone call of which she mentioned not believing in God. She came in and out of my life a few more times and I believe she went through phases of sobriety. Later on, she told me that she had found God and I was happy to hear that. She actually is a really nice individual but I think she was never able to shake the traumatic childhood and ended up getting involved with the wrong people. She spent some time behind bars and in halfway houses. While she was living at a halfway house, I was having a bit of a rendezvous with her. I had randomly seen her at the library and it was a joyous meeting. We hung out a handful of times but I ended up getting freaked out as if I could lose my job because I was working at the prison at the time. I never got to make love to her and part of me regrets that, but I am glad that she and I are still cool, even if she owes me money.

My junior year in High School I started dating a long-time friend. Samantha Blakeny and I have been schoolmates ever since elementary school. She had red hair and a proudly bold personality to match the strings of fire on her head. She didn't always make sense but she was different, interesting, and had developed an oh-so desirable hourglass figure. We were in the club called Fellowship of Christian Athletes together and that is where we initiated romance. After a few months of dating, something gave me the idea to buy flowers for her. She worked at the mall so I was going to bring her in one flower every hour: a romantic gesture. I even made a tee-shirt that said "I love Samantha Blakeny" on it. When I arrived at her little novelty store, she wasn't there. I attempted again and she still wasn't there. She was avoiding me and didn't make me aware that she had off that day. I ended up dropping the flowers off at her house and later getting a telephone call from her where she explained that she no longer wanted to date me. I don't remember crying, but I probably did, being that I am a crybaby. That was another heartbreak for me.

After my football injury senior year, I ended up running track instead of playing baseball. Had it not been for the misfortune of that knee tear I may have never met my next girlfriend.

Jessica Strongly was a young member of the track team, she intended to throw discus and run a few short-distance running events. I had been admiring her backside for a while because it was so perfectly round. One day in practice I possessed the courage to go up to her. We were warming up just running around the track when from behind I came and said "hey would you like to get to know me better?" When she said yes, I handed her a piece of paper with my phone number pre-written on it, and then I took off running. This was the first time I had the confidence to approach a girl like that, I don't really know what came over me. Even though Jessy may have been faking injury to refrain from running and even though I found out she was only fourteen years old to my seventeen, we ended up hitting it off pretty good. Yeah, some people may have been muttering some gossip about the age difference but she made me feel comfortable and her parents didn't seem to mind. Her mother actually adored me and I was welcome over to their house at any time. Not relevant to my life or this story but it's funny to note that Mrs. Strongly was about six feet tall and Mr. Strongly probably wasn't even five feet tall. Jessy got the shorter trait but her sister Becky got the taller trait. Becky was also on the track team and threw the Shot put because she was big and strong. Both of the girls were also proud cheerleaders.

So, there I was the senior football player dating the freshman cheerleader. I graduated high school and no longer had to deal with the snotty remarks from teenagers. Jessy and I were inseparable and sensed we were in love. This must have been why her mother decided to put her on "the pill." We hadn't had relations yet but it was basically an invite for us to do so. Naturally we took advantage of it. We were both virgins so we got to share the experience with each other. We were staying the night in her living room with the sofa bed pulled out. She got on top of me and tried to push it in but it hurt her and she started bleeding everywhere. It was actually quite gross. We eventually became rabbits and nearly got caught a few times.

We did everything concertedly including attending our first concert together: Aerosmith. We both loved the classic rock stars and Jessy even did a review for the school paper about their new album at the time: *Honkin' on Bobo.* Our song was "I don't Want to Miss a Thing," and they almost didn't play it live but did it as the first encore, so that was pretty special even though I liked the second encore better: "Train Kept a Rollin'."

Jessy acquired the attic of the family house all to herself and they were installing decorative mirrors all along one of the walls. I feel like her parents surely treated Jessy and I pretty special whereas the older sister Becky may have gotten raw ends. My buddy Matthew would come over with me occasionally and he was immediately attracted to Becky. They ended up dating and have a whole story of their own.

At the end of the summer it was time for me to depart for college and Jessy's mom provided some gifts including bed sheets and an alarm clock. They engraved an assurance that they would be there for me if I needed anything. They made it easy for me to quit college and after a few days I did just that, but I don't attribute it to my reasoning. I hadn't grown up enough just yet.

We took a golfing trip one day at a small par three place in Hagerstown. Little did we know it would become unforgettable. We saw some guys we knew from high school and joined their game. After about 9 holes there was a dude behind us that clearly was getting impatient with our retarded speed so I figured we could let him go ahead of us after the hole. Before we had a chance to offer it to him, he started shouting at us and called me an "asshole." I did nothing to earn that but still didn't let it affect me. Jessy couldn't resist shouting back at the man standing at the beginning of the hole with his 10 or so year-old son. She told him to shut up but the man responded, "You shut up you fucking slut!" Jessy's eyes and mine unanimously met as we knew without speaking that we had to do something. I dropped my club and we quickly walked across the green. Along the way the only thing I said was "no one calls my girlfriend a 'fucking slut'!" As I got closer the man started to speak, "the best thing for you to do is just turn..." but before he could finish his sentence my fist lunged through the air and landed on his face. I snapped, fists kept flying, and the kid started crying. Jessy even kicked the man. I ended up having him on the ground smack-talking him. I said things like "Did anyone ever tell you that one day you would say something to the wrong person, today is your lucky day," and "you just got beat up by a guy in a pink shirt and a girl." While on the ground he bit my right bicep. I still have a scar there today. I enjoy seeing the reaction now when I show people my "human bite." After the fight, I proclaimed I was a minor to scare the guy even though I was actually 18. Needless to say, we got kicked out of the place. I have always been protective of the people I care about. I am not exactly proud of the events that took place that day, but my father recently informed me that he was secretly proud. That is the last fist fight I was ever in. I am prouder of that fact. I forgot about WWJD that day.

Jessy and I shared many blissful memories that added up to almost two years, and it has been my longest relationship yet. Near the end we were arguing too much and I was trying to grow up but the age difference might have caught up to us. I recall an unhealthy exchange where I ended up punching a wall and breaking my hand for the first time. I was young, stupid, and frustrated. The last fight had us screaming at each other in the car over some insignificant crap and saying some hurtful things that are regretful but I knew I had to end it. I am sure I broke her heart, and I never wanted to do that, but I attempted to keep a friendship going with her. Later on, she ended up getting married and having a kid so all turned out well for her in the long run. I am happy for her.

Matthew was dating Becky for a little while, but it ended in heartbreak for Matthew. He is an intense and emotional guy. For years he struggled and thought about Becky on the constant. I'm happy to announce that they have gotten back together. It was sort of a movie style story in itself. It's rare that the boy gets the girl back. The memory of me around the Strongly family must have been negative for a while because it seemingly strained my relationship with Matthew. There was a time that we weren't talking substantially but remained friends in the long run. I did end up attending Matthew and Becky's wedding. They now have two children and have been together for about a decade. So, if my dating Jessy meant nothing more than being the pathway to love for my friend then I am glad.

Approximately two years passed after Jessy and I broke up before I even commenced dating again. I found myself fooling around with my sister's friend Sarah Chaplin. She was an introvert like me, very mellow, very thin, and had a jubilant Anne Hathaway smile. When I was away at college, she was actually living at my dad's house with Amili for a little while. I think Sarah actually wanted to date me but I knew we had too many differences and it wouldn't avail. We did end up hooking up one time on the floor at my dad's house. Afterwards I said, "we probably shouldn't have done that." But her response was, "it's okay, I just wanted sex," as she puffed her cigarette. She eased the situation although looking back I am not certain of her actual feelings. She is always nice and friendly and we remained friends like it never even happened.

Immediately upon my arrival at the Art Institute of Pittsburgh I started conversing with some girls, which was actually surprising to me. Day one I talked to a girl in the elevator at the school sponsored housing. I mentioned we didn't possess a shower curtain and she had one we could have. Later that day I strolled over to her door and talked to her about it but it was dirty or something and the situation felt awkward and I never got the shower curtain. I still felt accomplished at the fact that I actually talked to a pretty girl so I penciled it down as a success even if I never spoke to that particular girl again.

I think Stephanie Nikeflori needed sugar one day. She must have had a class with my roommate because she knocked on our door and my roomy answered. I remember chilling on the couch in a muscle shirt, and I caught her eye. She must have found me attractive. She wasn't bad looking herself, she had an athletic yet small frame, smooth dirty blond hair, and a huge smile. She reminds me of *Natasha Bedingfield* and the song "Pocket Full of Sunshine" for some reason. Steph and I ended up hanging out a bunch. Cuddled on the couch, her head on my lap, we were watching TV one night. Unexpectedly she popped up from my lap and kissed me quickly then plopped back down. It took me by surprise so I asked "did you just kiss me?" I felt like we matched pretty good, she was of catholic background, was studying interior design, was into sports, and was even into cars big time like myself. She introduced me to the folks who owned the café/deli and boxing gym downtown. So, Stephanie basically found me the job that saved my college days with the gift of free food. I stayed in her room one night and she was laying right on top of me. Being shy and nervous prevented me from making a move. I ended up sweating a lot in her bed that night and I think it grossed her out, meanwhile I was embarrassed. Our relationship faded, I essentially wasn't outgoing enough and couldn't prove my worth. My efforts were otiose. Later she ended up dating a guy for a long time but now she is actually dating a girl! Should the square shoulders have given away her orientation?

Some girls lived right above us at the school sponsored housing and I threw chunks of bread onto their balcony for their attention. Ashly found it humorous but her roommate wasn't amused. Ashly was a slapstick, I inquired what her last name was and her response was "Homestore." I didn't get it initially but her real last name is Dankworth, which is just as funny. She was an Ohio native country girl, four years older than me, and much more experienced with partying. We weren't allowed to bring alcohol into the building so we would sneak it in by slinging a rope over the balcony edge. We dressed up for a Halloween party where I went as "Le Drunkn' Luigi" and her costume involved a whole story about a construction worker who becomes a bar fly. Needless to say, we had loads of fun. I remember returning from a date and we were in the elevator with some dude and I blurted out "we just went on a date." I wanted to make her my girlfriend but I did it the awkward way by making a gift for her and basically proposing a relationship to her. The gift was a mix of ZZ-Top music, she really loved them. Her response was "no" but asked if she could keep the CD. We remained friends and even became roommates for my last six months in college. No, we never slept together even though the opportunity was probably there. Actually, when we were living together, we were both so busy with school and work that I probably only saw her a handful of times those whole six months. One time though, her friend Eve stayed the night with me in my bed, that was an interesting night. Try being in bed at peace when suddenly a half drunk yet pretty faced woman you barely know just randomly climbs right in bed with you. She needed a place to sleep.

Photography student Katherine Oral was my next relationship in 2007. I was 21 and she was 17 when we met. I waited for her to turn 18 before getting involved this time, but I admit I like younger girls. Rich actually had a crush on her too which led to an awkward stare down at one point but I won over the girl. She was quite cute, thin, and pale skinned, with dark pixie hair, and big eyes. She was a former cheerleader, into creative stuff like me, and had a religious background so I thought she was a good match for me. She had that stereotypical naughty catholic school girl edge to her too which was a turn on. She claimed to be a virgin and we ended up sleeping together with an orange condom her roommate provided for us. I violated the experience afterwards because I brought up that she didn't seem like a virgin. It didn't hurt her and she didn't bleed so I was puzzled and thought maybe she had lied to me. Later I did research and learned that women indeed can break their hymen through physical activity. In some cases, it can just stretch instead of break. At any rate I apologized and we moved on.

Katherine and I were in my place at the school sponsored housing cuddling one day. Rich and I had just gotten a new roommate, Sam. Sam was a creepy nerdy kid and had a crush on both my girlfriend and Rich's sister. Katherine and I were on the couch, and Sam was supposedly asleep right behind the curtain in his bedroom which was converted from a dining room. Katherine and I were getting frisky and saying dirty things to each other but she was worried that Sam could hear us. Later I found out that Sam indeed could hear us and in fact was leaning right up against the couch listening to everything we were saying. He told Rich all about it.

Katherine and I did the "I love you" thing and I even brought her down to my mom's cabin for a visit. Introducing her to my mom was a pretty big deal to me so we had gotten pretty serious. On one particular night Katherine said she wanted to stop having sex out of fear of getting pregnant and I guess religious reasons too. I went along with it and she was impressed that I would stay in a relationship without sex so she gave me a sweet kiss with an even sweeter "I love you" attached.

We had fun times, living the college life. I threw a party at my new place and remember an easy dream-like instance where Katherine was perched on my lap during the wind down of the party. It felt kind of special to me but not everything was peachy. At another party I belittled her last name "Oral" by making a sex joke. She told me she would expect other people to do that but not me. I had even told myself I never would, so it was definitely the booze talking; a sober me is better. It was not nice of me and left me with shame and regret. At one point, I remember getting news that she had made out with some other dude. I confronted the guy and said, "do you think I am an asshole?" Maybe I was more upset that he might have said negative stuff about me, even if I really was an asshole. I was prepared to fight but he whimpered. I forgave Katherine for the mishap because she was honest with me about it. One day I was leaving school, walking with some friends, and chatting with Katherine on the phone. She said "I love you," but I didn't have the guts to say it back that time. I don't know if it was because I was surrounded by people at the time or what but we engaged in a fun conversation about it later. I told her I do love her and I don't know why I didn't say it. We let it go.

Valentine's day with Katherine was pretty memorable. She came over to my new place and I tried to set up a romantic scene with candles, wine, and flowers as I made her dinner. I concocted a heart shaped pizza. Yeah, I wasn't quite the master chef yet. She bought me a stuffed bear, the kind you push on the belly and it says "I love you." The bear sounded desperate and put extra emphasis on each one of those three words. It really sounded weird.

Spring break for us was shortly after Valentine's Day. I had already taken Katherine down to my mom's cabin earlier in the year but it was my turn to meet Katherine's family. Her Hometown is Syracuse, New York, and it would be about a six-hour drive from Pittsburgh. We decided to go up together to alleviate her father from driving all that distance, since she didn't have a car of her own. On the way up it became dark and there was a lane shift ahead of us. The car beside me didn't realize he/she was supposed to shift and Katherine didn't realize that either. I guess they both interpreted it as a lane merge. The car nearly collided with mine but I was able to brake and prevent a wreck. Katherine started yelling at me proclaiming that it was very irresponsible of me. Meanwhile I yelled back asserting "it was a lane shift," I held up two fingers, "two cars shifting, it's not my fault, the other car didn't shift." The remaining few hours of our drive was silent.

Upon our arrival Katherine didn't give me a proper introduction and remained taciturn. Her mom was the only one there and she was courteous. I went out with Katherine and her friends for ice cream and her friend was driving her Jeep pretty erratically. Of course, they were all giggling, Katherine included. I guess it was ok for her girlfriends to drive carelessly, but I had to be a perfect driver. Days went by and still I was getting zero interaction from my supposed girlfriend, she even pushed my hand away when I was trying to pet her one night. I slept in the top bunk of her little brother's bed. The little guy wasn't there for whatever reason. Finally, in the morning Katherine gave me some attention. She climbed up in the bunk with me and we were kissing and rubbing. We had decided to refrain from sex but it started to get frustrating. It's one thing if you never have sex, but to have a sexually active relationship and then stop is more difficult, I think. We were dry humping, and I really wanted to climax but she told me to go into the bathroom and finish. I didn't want to do that, so I just dealt with being teased.

The final straw was the final night when she was in her room and I came in and just wanted to cuddle but she was still ignoring me. I told her I love her and asked her if she loved me. She said "I don't know." Fed up, I decided to grab my things and storm out. She grabbed her mom and they tried to convince me to stay at least until morning but I couldn't take the disrespect any more. I told Katherine to tell her mom what she told me. As I headed to my car, I heard her shout "I love you!" I replied, "yeah right, now that I am leaving." So, I drove six hours through New York and Pennsylvania in the middle of the night to my home in Maryland. I felt like she just used me for a ride to her parents' house. The whole thing was a calamity.

After a few days of cooling off we got back to school and I still wanted to work it out, but it didn't work out. She and her friends came over to confiscate her belongings and I didn't have them bagged up because I really didn't want her to exit my life. She told me that I seemed like I wanted to get married straight out of college and she didn't want that. I took this failed relationship thoroughly hard. It lasted only a few months but I was still crying on my mom's shoulder some 9 months later. They say it takes half the length that the relationship was in order to move on emotionally, but for me it's much, much longer. Katherine and I have never spoken since the split to my dismay although I tried to hit her up a couple years later and got a negative response.

A pair of girls came into the Deli that I worked in one day. I was attracted to the shorter brunette and the taller buxom blonde had her eyes set on my co-worker Phil. Somehow, I ended up dating the blonde by the name of Dianna. She was a Pittsburgh native and shared the same last name as one of the Pittsburgh Penguin hockey players. She was attending a University at the time. Pittsburgh is definitely a college town as there are bunches of colleges in the area. We went to a Penguins game together and it was the most exciting live sporting event I have ever experienced. It was my first time at a hockey game. The seats are so close to the rink and you feel like you are right in the action. As a gift I got Dianna a Penguin jersey of the player with her name. Her and I also got to go to a Steelers game together. I was visiting some buddies in Baltimore and received a call from my uncle inviting me to a Steelers playoff game. Initially I said that I couldn't make it, but quickly changed my mind and called him back. He had two extra tickets so I called up Dianna and told her to cancel whatever plans she had because I had a surprise. I drove five hours back up to Pittsburgh and we made it on time to see the football game. They wound up losing to the Jaguars but it was a memorable experience.

Dianna was Christian, rather intelligent, and enjoyed my humor so we made it work for a while. She may have been too liberal for me and I may have not been open to love anymore as a result of Katherine so it was never going to work out. Dianna is the only girl I ever cussed out. I remember getting into an argument with her on the phone over who-knows-what, but I concluded the debate with a, "fuck you" and a hang-up. I also remember her coming over to my place to grab her things. She was disappointed that I had her stuff together neatly in a bag and that I didn't try to argue to keep her around. It would embitter me anytime she would sarcastically say "see ya around." I don't like people entering my life and then exiting completely from it. I like to keep in contact and I am glad Dianna and I are still borderline friends, or at least civil.

I am left with faint memories of Dianna and I. Some, I can chuckle at, like how I used to cluck like a chicken as we walked around Pittsburgh to embarrass her. One time she was referring to her friend as whore and didn't realize that her phone was still on and her friend could hear her. She also didn't realize that "whore" in reality meant "prostitute" so we were teasing her about that. Dianna really was a good individual though; she was loyal to me. The physical part of the relationship was good. She had what seemed like a special talent with her mouth. She knew how to *savor the moment*. My funniest sex story involves her. We were having sex and I was sweating bullets. A droplet of sweat fell down on her and landed right between her eyes. That is not the kicker though. I was wearing a condom but at one point I looked down and discovered it was missing. We thought it must have slipped off somehow so we looked around for it with no victory. It wasn't until nearly a week later that she discovered its whereabouts. The condom was stuck inside of her vagina the whole time. It is funny because I even mentioned that to her the day of.

I don't know how I managed to be in a relationship those last six months of college in 2008 with Dianna. Not only did she and I hang out frequently but I also worked full time and had a full schedule of schooling including my thesis project. It was the busiest time of my life. When we split up my roommate wondered if it was because I was graduating and moving back home but I don't think that was really a factor. It just wasn't meant to be. That phrase means nothing, the truth is I wasn't passionate enough about her or the relationship. I will always hold respect for her and all women I've dated even when I wasn't great at actually respecting them.

I met my next love interest in a hot tub. After playing in a semi-pro football game, me and some of the guys hung out in the backyard of this dude's house who was a friend of ours, but he wasn't even there. It was a fancy setup with a pool, a hot tub and an outdoor bar reminiscent of a tiki lounge. The guys and I were just hanging out at the bar when we noticed some girls coming out of the hot tub sporting only underwear and asked if any of us wanted to join. I was checking out the one girl, she had a pretty cute butt. We were all drinking and I decided to strip down into my *"whitey-tighties"* with the two girls and one other dude. I settled next to the girl I was checking out and she told me her name was Michelle. She ended up sitting on my lap and there might have been some touching or kissing but I don't exactly remember. I do remember getting out and jumping into the pool in my underwear and claiming to the guys that I only wear that type of old-man underwear to football games. By the end of the night I was too drunk to drive so Michelle gave me a ride home to my dad's house of which I was staying for a period of time after I graduated from college. The guys noticed I left my car behind and left with Michelle and of course later inquired if I "got some." I responded with "I don't kiss and tell." They saw through my bluff and knew that meant "no."

Michelle Randall and I kept on communicating proceeding our extreme first encounter. I asked around about her and discovered that she had a kid and a bit of a wild side. My co-worker Dorian from Fed-Ex (I briefly worked as a package handler), was really good friends with her when they attended high school together at Boonsboro. He said she was really cool but then started sleeping with everyone. He followed that up with a "JK." When Michelle and I went out I recall some of her party animal friends teasing her and saying that she is a "butt girl" as in she enjoys anal sex. Gross. I called her one time and one of her guy friends answered and just screwed with me and didn't let me talk to her. That was pretty disrespectful but she apologized promptly.

With a banging figure, a cute face, and dark crimped hair, Michelle came along with me to the beach with some friends. She asked me to rub suntan lotion on her. Gladly, I did, and I kept rubbing long after necessary as I just wanted to touch her. Back at her abode one particular night she had put her boy to bed. She assumed the attic of her parents' house for her and her son. We cuddled and caressed but she just lied still. I sense she may have craved more aggression from me, but forcing myself on someone is definitely not a feeling I enjoy, so we never had sex. I asked when her parents would come home and if I should stay or leave. She said I should probably leave, so I did.

There was a special event happening that the architecture firm I was working for was attending and I was to go. Michelle would be my date. I would introduce her to my work friend Annabella Bell and the others. I bought flowers and headed over to pick up Michelle. I knocked on the door. I knocked again. I called her. I called again. I was stood up. I informed Annabella that I wouldn't be making it because I was stood up and felt lowly. She insisted I come and said that she was going "stag" too. I wasn't able to muster the social and emotional energy to make it though.

My job was immensely satisfying at the time and working with Annabella added to it. She was an amazingly smart and down-to-earth human being whom I respected a lot. She was the intern at the firm and was really fervent about the work. We chatted over our computers all the time while at our desks and became good friends. She played softball in college and had a strong build and a bubble butt. I even recall teasing her about her bubble-butt that I secretly thought was amazing. I wasn't attracted to her initially but the more I got to know her the more I admired her. She had perfect *"AutoCAD-ed"* white teeth as I would call them. Annabella must have liked me too because she complimented me often and said she thinks she is a pretty good judge of character. Then she invited me to join her and her aunt at a family timeshare at Massanutten Resort for some snowboarding and other activities.

I was very excited to be going on that trip and with good reason. Annabella was probably the most amazing human being I had ever met, and this was one of the coolest adventures I had ever been on. It was the first time I ever snowboarded and as soon as we got off the first lift I was already falling and taking Annabella down with me. She laughed it off; a trooper. I love snow, but snowboarding is hard, not that I didn't enjoy it. I gave Annabella my gloves as an act of chivalry but then my hands were shivering. Her aunt paid for the activities and they are rather expensive. I think the snow tubing was $60. I remember trying to give them money for it but they dismissed it. We listened to Lynyrd Skynyrd the whole time as Annabella is pretty "country." She drove a Jeep Wrangler with a manual transmission while wearing high heels! We started flirting a good bit, and I remember her secretly texting me while the three of us were at a dinner table together. Annabella's dirty blonde and curvy hair was shimmering and her curvy features glowing. She was looking really classy at this resort restaurant and her perfect smile was a delight along with her spunky yet cute attitude. Her happy go lucky charm mixed with honesty and smarts convinced me of my feelings for her.

Later at night we found ourselves in the jet tub drinking wine. We were just relaxing because we were friends and I wasn't sure of her feelings. I got to see her in swimwear because I was naughty enough to suggest getting in the jet tub and was surprised that she agreed. We got out and set up my pull-out sofa bed for the night. The big surprise was before Annabella went to her room for the night. She gave me a quick kiss on the forehead. It was the most amazing weekend and later at work I mentioned how much fun I had but also asked her to guess what my favorite part was. She didn't assume that it was the forehead kiss.

I really wanted to date Annabella and even asked our co-worker Mitch for advice since he knew her longer than I did. The problem was that she was leaving to go to Rhode Island to study for her master's degree. I also had gotten laid off at the architecture firm. So, with Annabella gone and me jobless I would enter a low point in my life. I dated a couple girls during this time but kept Annabella on my mind. When she completed her Schooling and came back, she agreed to go on a date with me. I was overly excited and tried too hard, took her to a fancy place, tried to act smart, and probably came off as ostentatious. She is a simple style girl so I freaked her out I guess, but things were different. I revealed my true feelings for her but those feelings faded away on her end. She was one girl I really feel like I could have loved, but she is one who slipped away. I recall expressing my feelings about her with my friends Robert and Amanda. Amanda said "just keep trying." I kept trying but it just pushed her away further.

Working at Subway inside a gas station I was desperate for attention. I had a little bit of attraction to this girl who worked in the Pilot Travel Center. She looked like Wednesday Addams. But it was a blonde by the name of Tammy that gave me more attention so I just rolled with it. She isn't the type of girl I typically go for and probably my most regretful situation and I will tell you why. In addition to being blonde, which I typically prefer not, she also was your stereotypical snotty-for-no-reason Hagerstown native. She was not very studious and had the baggage of parental responsibilities. She invited me over one day to her house that she shared with her "baby-daddy." She claimed that they were broken up, but living together for the time being. She got naked that first night under the covers expecting sex. She had multiple stretch marks, I didn't get aroused and I felt odd. The opportunity for sex was too difficult to combat so at the next invite I completed the task and had sex with a woman in her baby-daddy's house. She ended up moving out and staying with her parents temporarily. A few short weeks went by and she decided to go back with her kid's dad and quickly became engaged to him. I feel like I was used just to make him jealous; I feel like a wicked game was played. That guy was bizarre and even called me to ask if we had sex. I was honest with him but he didn't even believe me as if I was just trying to antagonize him. I don't understand those games. Boy was I glad when that mess concluded.

My buddy Dorian invited me to a few parties in 2010 and I sort of became part of the clique. He, Jay, and Ryan acted a lot like the guys from the show *It's Always Sunny in Philadelphia.* They talked fast with quick banter and little regard to anything. Dorian's girlfriend Bethany had a cute friend named Ashleigh Smith who would become my next crush. Ashleigh was in college to be some kind of a doctor or medical something-or-other so she was very smart. Her celebrity look alike was Julia Roberts so she was quite pretty as well. She also was big into athletics and played soccer for many years. She even dabbled in guitar playing. She really seemed like a catch. The problem here was that she actually had a big crush on Ryan who was the lead guitarist of a band they called *Missing Sarah*. I recall Ashleigh and Ryan hooking up a couple times at the end of those parties so I assumed something between Ashleigh and I wouldn't happen.

Some time passed, Ryan got a steady new girlfriend and Ashleigh was a few hours away at her college in Virginia. There was a home-coming dance party at her school and I presume the guy she was seeing canceled on her so she gave me a call. I came to the rescue, even though I had to call myself "Mark" in order to enter. We were just sitting around when everyone was dancing and Ashleigh wasn't having the fun that she deserved so somehow someway I got the nerve to take her onto the dance floor. It was a big step in me fighting my social awkwardness but I thought this girl was worth it. Not knowing what I was doing, it didn't matter because I was making her smile. We went back to her dorm room and her roommate was asleep. We hung out a little bit and she mentioned I could stay but the not-so-adventurous and good boy part of me decided to go home. As I walked to my car, I saw Ashleigh standing there in a waiting state. I dropped my things into my car but promptly walked right back up to her. A wave of confidence came over me when I saw the expecting expression on her face. I landed a big smooch on her, our first kiss. I am proud of that one.

We dated for a little while after that and I was hopeful for the relationship. I found myself running out of interesting things to say to her and still had some nervousness. We went to another one of our friend's parties but as a couple. She had some sort of a breakdown and had to leave the party early. She later tells me that she isn't fully over Ryan and so she had to withdraw from seeing me. It sucked but at the same time I understand what it's like to possess those feelings. I don't know how I would have acted had Annabella been at that party.

Robert Codder was my best friend growing up and his sister Sarah was one year older than us so naturally I felt some attraction early on. She was a feisty redhead and looked a little bit like Olivia Wilde mixed with Kristen Stewart. I remember flirting with her some as a teenager and her touching my abs as I showed them off one day in the Codder household. I used to follow her in the halls at school watching her butt wobble. I never really thought about dating her although I do recall getting a little envious when one of our friends started dating her after a campout in Codder's backyard as teenagers. Sarah ended up dating Derek Abrams for a long time. He was the older brother of one of my best friends, Daniel Abrams, who I met in high school even though he lived right down the street from me for many years prior. So, Sarah and I still crossed paths on many occasions. One night the Abrams had a party at their house and I got drunk and apparently told Sarah that I had always loved her, and did it right in front of her boyfriend. I don't even remember declaring that at all, nor do I recall why. I might have been joking. This conversation came up between Sarah and I much later when we started dating. How did we start dating? Let's talk about the beach.

Myrtle Beach nearly became a yearly tradition. It was with my good old buddy Robert and his girl Amanda. Some of Robert's work buddies who also became my buddies attended too. This includes Drake and his girl Claire, and Tyler with his girlfriend. The trips were rife with crazy actions and we had enormous fun. I remember finding a dead horseshoe crab one night after everyone had fallen asleep, bringing it up, and placing it in my friend's room for a morning surprise. I remember drunkenly yelling out of the car window random phrases to strangers such as "Hey bitch, how you like it in the rear?" which is out of character for me because I typically don't cuss. We went to a Babar the Elephant art museum that had a mysteriously racist upstairs showcase. One night out of drunken stupidity I scaled up the side of our beach house to the balcony. We played kickball or handball of some sort in the beach house once we positioned all the furniture out of the way. Many good restaurants were visited such as a Medieval Times where one of our buddies worked at. Once at a buffet and I had just filled my plate up when a fire alarm sounded and everyone had to exit the building. I brought my plate of food out with me. We hadn't paid but the food was going to go to waste anyway. That was my reasoning. I had no reason to take the plate home with me though. I have had many good times during these trips but the memory I probably hold dearest is the spawning of romance between Sarah and I.

Sarah had finally gotten over her breakup with Derek and decided to come out of *Hermitville* and into the real world. She joined the gang for a Myrtle Beach trip one summer. At the beach everyone else had their matches so Sarah and I bonded almost by default; we've known each other for 15 years prior so it was natural. One night after all the day festivities, we were all winding down and sitting around the little personal pool with candlelight and a twinkling atmosphere. I brought my guitar and some printouts for everyone to sing along. We did classics such as "Free Fallin," "Brown Eyed Girl," and other easy-to-play songs while partially intoxicated. I believe Sarah liked the creative and musical type of guys because Derek was extremely talented in that regard. Sarah wondered why Robert and I were friends because she perceives the two of us as being very different. I think it is because I have many qualities and can relate to many people. It's also hard for me to make friends with this social anxiety so I like to hold on to the ones I have. I was a little hesitant to approach Sarah romantically but Robert basically bestowed the green light and even said "I have been trying to get you two together for years."

After the musical relaxation everyone but Sarah and I went to bed. We decided to try to re-cook the chicken that everyone was afraid to admit didn't seem thoroughly cooked. It did not wind up any better but it was diverting to be alone with Sarah. Afterwards we started kissing on the couch. This was followed by more kissing with the addition of rubbing. The rubbing was followed up with more rubbing and eventually a suggestion to go up to her bedroom. In the bedroom a failed attempt at penetration occurred. It must have been a mixture of hours of teasing and what they call "whisky dick." She was totally cool and even said "I think I have whisky vagina." I eventually snuck back into my room. The next morning Robert immediately asked "what did you do with her last night?" with suspicion and judgment in his tone. I simply replied "nothing."

Sarah and I continued seeing each other after returning from utopia. We were both on the anti-social side of the spectrum and were both into music big time. She even starred in a music video that I made for a school project. The song sucked but we had fun developing the video. I took her to see her favorite band at a music festival: *Blind Melon*. We had waited through many other bands and a good bit of rain but finally they came up on stage. The original lead singer had died many years prior and the new singer might have been ok but we couldn't really hear him because his microphone wasn't working. I am glad I got to be the one to take Sarah to see them though and I even made her a *Blind Melon* tee-shirt. We had a Christmas celebration at the Codder's house and she had hand-made me a hemp necklace and bracelet. She put a lot of effort into them and it was a very thoughtful gift. She also got me a *Pink Floyd* Blanket. It is safe to say that she was the best gift-giver of anyone I ever dated. I made her a painting of a tree that also said her name in a symmetrical and hieroglyphic manner.

Sarah was not a Christian, but not closed-minded to the idea. I mentioned the book of revelations to her and how it depicts Jesus and horsemen in sort of a terrifying way. She found interest in it and asked where she could find said book. I had to inform her that it is the last book of the Bible. She borrowed a Bible from her mom who ended up thanking me for giving Sarah a little push in that direction. I pushed too much though and our differences would eventually become glaring. I recall her telling me one time that she hated everything I say and everything I stand for. That comment hurt more than I let on but I understand people can say wild things when upset or frustrated.

Our problems all compiled together to a climax with a trip to Detroit. We went to the car show and I am thankful she came along otherwise no one would have but it wound up disastrous. We got back to my old Subaru after the show and were planning on heading out to check into our hotel. Something was locked in the glove box so I gave Sarah the key to open it. She turned the key and suddenly it broke. It was the only key for the ignition to the car but I tried not to panic. We were in a dangerous city far from home and felt stranded. The parking lot worker guys tried to help but didn't seem to have a realistic answer until one guy said that there is a key making place a block or two away. He told me to follow him and to hurry because they may be closing soon. Sarah asked what she should do and I said "stay here and protect our stuff." This was not the best idea because as I was coming back from having no luck at the key place Sarah's dad, Rob, called me and asked why his daughter was crying. I should not have let us get separated and that was a mistake. Nothing happened and I wasn't far away at all but the fear I put Sarah through was a complete brain lapse on my part. We eventually got a locksmith out there who manufactured a new key for us then we went to the hotel which was another disaster. It was freaking cold and the people weren't even prepared for us. Another mistake of mine was picking that crappy hotel. We usually had mind blowing love making sessions, but that was the first instance we were together and didn't.

Our relationship was pretty much over then and there. I tried to fix it but everything I did backfired. I had never told her I loved her but I did write her a letter full of all my emotions and opinions. The response was not good. I guess I mentioned a lot of stuff that she didn't like and it inevitably convinced her to call me a "psycho." I feel like I caused her too much stress and the only thing that relieved her stress was weed. I feel like she chose weed over me. Not being as good as a plant made me feel like dirt.

I was usually too nervous to strike up conversations with women in the real world so I started doing online dating and met a girl named Linda in 2012. She claimed to be half Christian and half Jewish; as if Christianity and Judaism are races. She was funny and seemed to take relationships seriously so I was ready for that. She worked at a surgeon's office and had breast implants herself. That's not my thing but I don't judge. She got them because she had lost a bunch of weight and felt like she needed to perk them up. I informed her I am not a boob guy so much and she laughed and said "great, I paid all this money for these boobs and I wind up with a non-boob guy." She ended up communicating all the other things she wanted to do to her face and I found that weird. The fake things didn't stop there. Her moans were clearly fake and she treated sex more like a pornography than love making. She even spat on me, much to my chagrin, and it turned me off. I ended it with her because I like real and natural things; I just couldn't do it.

Ashly Manning was my second short-lived 2012 online dating adventure. She was a country girl who seemed really simple and natural. She didn't have any kids yet but wanted them so we had that in common. She ended up coming over to my house a couple times and we had fun lying in bed listening to music and trying to guess what the songs were. We never got too serious. I remember her inviting me to the club one night so I came out but she seemed preoccupied texting other guys. Needless to say, we stopped talking.

The wackiest date I ever went on was with a girl named Beth. Beth was extremely adorable looking. We met at a Starbucks, got some drinks and sat in the patio area. Here she started talking. She talked and talked without any pauses. Every time I tried to speak, she just kept going. I may have gotten three sentences in for the entire three hours that we sat there. She talked so much that I started to see foam build up in the corner of her mouth. It was wild. She was nice and cute but I didn't see her again after that.

I sent "likes" to many girls on *Match.com*. Sometimes very pretty black girls arose and I sent them "likes" as well because I don't discriminate. I didn't assume any of them would ever be interested in me but I got a message one day from a beautiful girl who happened to be indigenous to Rwanda. She simply asked me why I sent her a "like." I responded with "because I see that you value spirituality which is important to me, and you happen to be very pretty as well." So, we chatted a bit then I earned a date with Jessika Ubando. She lived in Leesburg and was studying at Northern Virginia Community College. We met up at the school and my first impression was that she was super cute. She had a gorgeous smile, and almond eyes. She had short hair and a tiny body but then bam! She had extra-wide, jaw-dropping hips. She had a pretty heavy African accent but she knew English well along with 6 other languages. I really liked that she was Christian and very much into gospel music and such. She had a good singing voice and at the end of our first date she sang these lyrics "Are you going to kiss me or not, are we going to do this or what" from the country song by *Thompson Square*. I got the hint but was too nervous to make the move so I played dumb. I did not leave her hanging on date two though. Those juicy cloud-like lips were amazing, and it was probably the best first kiss I ever had. Her nose ring ended up falling off and we couldn't find it, so we had a romantic comedy brewing.

The fastest I ever went from meeting someone to sleeping with them was with Jessika and it was on our third date. She basically invited herself over and cooked a meal for me. It was an African style meat and potato stir-fry thing or what-not. I don't know what to call it but it was tasty. Then we watched a movie. When we transitioned into the bedroom it was so exciting. I was 28 and she was 20. I was white and she was black. It felt almost like it was wrong but maybe that added to the excitement. Her skin was silky smooth and her body was perfect. She even had a sweeter taste, especially when she would squirt. That was another first for me. It was the best sex of my life. She recounted to me how amazing it was for her as well. She asked me if I was ever with a black girl before because her vagina "isn't supposed to look like that." She had vitiligo so she had discoloration but it was only in that one particularly fantastic location. Actually, you could notice it in her gums too. I felt the discoloration just made her more unique and special. She once playfully commented the classic phrase, "once you go black, you don't go back." I responded with, "once you go white, you got it right."

Jessika told me she loved me really fast into our relationship and it threw me off. It was only a few weeks in. I didn't convey it back when other girls said it, including Dianna nor Sarah, each of whom I was with for a much longer time than Jessika. I was holding on to that feeling ever since Katherine broke my heart. I said "I love you too" back to Jessika though.

I took Jessika to Virginia Beach with my brother Zach and a pair of his friends. Those two were an interracial couple as well.

Jackson was black and he was hilarious. He would lead us to the Hilton in an attempt to get us to the Hilton top party. We knew the top of the Hilton was reserved for guests of the Hilton but we followed him and tried anyway. The top of our budget hotel had a pool so we reenacted a Hilton top party on our own. I am not sure if it was supposed to be open because we were the only people up there late in the evening. Earlier in the evening we tried entering a bar but Jessika was unable to pass security with an ID she borrowed from an of-age cousin. The bouncer could tell it wasn't her from the picture, so tails between our legs we had to retreat. We were able to see an African style beach concert. It was a cool and coincidental event since Jessika was African. The following morning, she and I rented some bicycles to ride along the boardwalk bike path. The bikes didn't have hand brakes and I tried to tell Jessika to forcibly pedal backwards in order to stop. She almost ran over a child crossing the path, but only bumped the young one. The parents were confrontational but it didn't escalate. I thought both parties were wrong but kept my mouth shut.

I took Jessika to my friend's wedding. Drake and Claire had a beautiful outdoor venue in Frederick. This was my fifth wedding I attended in just a couple of years. I took a different girl to each of them. They had an open bar but I couldn't drink because I was going to have to take Jessika to a friend's house and therefore couldn't stay long. Everyone got on the dance floor but I was feeling too shy and sober to do much or even really enjoy myself. Jessika enjoyed herself as she danced with some of the other gals, and had a few drinks since they didn't card. I was a little disappointed I couldn't spend more time with her that night but she was having a sleepover thing with a girlfriend so I dropped her off and didn't complain.

Jessika was a sweetheart but she wasn't perfect. I think the main thing that annoyed me was how she would remain on her phone while dealing with cashiers. Little things like that bugged me but I could overlook them. She broke things off with me after a couple months and I don't remember her reasoning. I think it was actually because she had a crush on another Caucasian man named Joseph. I saw on Facebook that she praised him and thanked him for a fun time ice skating. This was before her and I split up. After we split up, I messaged Joseph and told him about our recent split and told him she needed a friend. I did not blame or rebuke him. It wasn't long afterwards that I noticed the two of them became a couple, of course. Another heartbreak to add to the list.

After Jessika I dated Blessica, another online match. Blessica Ann Gaviola was Filipina and Catholic. She was gorgeously cute with the prettiest face. She was short but did not have your stereotypical string bean Asian figure. She actually had a little bit of a body to her and often had people joke about the fact that it's rare for Asians to have a butt like hers. On our first date at a billiards café, the first things I noticed were her cute smile with dimples in the bottom corners, and her radiant caramel skin that she showed off with an open top. I could just lay my head on her chest like it was a pillow. This day was the start of one of my longest relationships and the one that has affected me most thus far.

Blessica, or Ann as she often went by, was studying accounting in college, living in Rockville, MD with her mother, older sister, and younger brother. Her younger brother was really tall and I told Blessica that that means her and I would end up having a big son. Our son should end up being a professional athlete and make us millions. This must be every man's dream. I also teased her and said that that's the only reason I was dating her. Her family moved to America about five years prior to our meeting but her parents split up.

Blessica spoke great English but would always say things oddly like "open the light," instead of "turn on the light" due to some words in Tagalog taking on multiple meanings. All in all, we communicated well though.

Blessica was really into an active lifestyle; she loved hiking, snowboarding, and other outdoor activities. We had that in common. Our faith was also very important to both of us, and we wanted the same things out of life. She was easy going, easy to talk to, didn't get offended, and knew how to laugh. Everything was good and I had feelings for her. We had a plethora of good times together, and took a lot of small trips. We introduced each other to our families. My family liked her and I think her family liked me. I owe Blessica a lot because she helped motivate me to quit my job at the prison and start my new job with the sign company.

Many adventures broke out for us. We went biking a few times. She preferred that flat paths but when we did a legit mountain biking trip and got muddy, that was more exciting to me. We went hiking a few times and enjoyed the scenery. Blessica was active and worked out a bunch, so we shared that. She let me into her gym and we did a class one time where I was the only male in the class. Awkward. I showed her some football drills and she kept up surprisingly well, I was impressed.

Blessica, one time, made me eat something without telling me what it was. It was some kind of specialty rice dish from the Philippines. It was really good. Then she told me it was made with pork blood. She taught me the lesson, "Don't knock something before you try it."

We went to a special concert together to see *Trans-Siberian Orchestra*. It was a theatrical event with a lot of stage props and at one point the guitarist was on a little platform that floated around in the air. They are a spectacular band and do the Christmas themed concerts all the time. Blessica enjoyed it even though it's not the type of music she normally listens to. Pop was in her normal playlist but she was open to all types of music. In fact, I also got her to listen to *Pink Floyd* and she liked them too.

I spent Christmas with her and her family. I got her a snowboard and snowboard boots. I like gifts to be a surprise but they were all accustomed to telling each other what they wanted beforehand and getting that exact thing. Blessica didn't exactly like the boots I got her; the size was a little small and the style wasn't exactly on par. I also wrapped a giant box that had a smaller box inside of it, and a smaller one inside of that, and it kept going. She wasn't thrilled to find a small piece of chocolate in the middle. Although things didn't always thrill her, she was never one to become mad and was usually very sweet and forgiving. I did however upset her when we took a trip to Pittsburgh. I didn't know why she was mad but she gave me the silent treatment for a couple hours. It must have been something I said but to this day I still don't know why she was mad. We ended up making up and making love in the shower dripping water all over the place.

I tried to love Blessica, I wanted to love her, but I just never could. She frustrated me immensely. I could ask her a question but she would be glued to her phone and couldn't even answer me as if she prioritized her phone. She would stick her finger up in a way to tell me to wait. I just wanted to know where the screwdriver was. We went to a Redskins game together which is an exciting thing to be able to do with a significant other but it was spoiled by a fight as we were trying to park. She would flip out when I didn't pull into a particular spot that she thought I should have. Then the tailgating people irritated me, and maybe I drove angrily making Blessica think I could have hit someone. Certainly, I am not that irresponsible but at this point she was screaming at me. That moment was the first time I had an urge to punch a woman. I would never do that, but having the urge was a sign that the two of us couldn't be.

We had a one-month break in the middle of a one-year relationship. I felt like the split was only a break, but she said she had gotten used to us being apart so it took some convincing to get her back. I was glad when we did because we shared so much. It's rare that a guy gets a girl back and it was the first time I ever achieved it. We shared all our secrets and were honest with each other. I was at a real happy time in my life and posted a profile picture on Facebook with her and I hugging and smiling huge. We talked about remaining friends even if it didn't work out and that was important to me. I should have loved her because she had a lot of patience with me.

The frustration eventually built back up and I broke it off a second time. I felt awful seeing her walking away crying. We tried doing the friend thing and continued to talk but I got frustrated and something compelled me to announce everything that was on my mind. I wrote her a letter with all my frustrations present. I even told her that I was never satisfied sexually with her. We didn't have sexual relations frequently and when we did it usually halted short because it was painful for her. I expressed my frustrations with her mannerisms and everything that prevented our relationship from blossoming. She responded telling me that the letter was unnecessary and just plain mean. I immediately realized she was right and wanted to apologize and build her up because in reality she deserved to be treated well. She was a wonderful individual and I did her wrong. I was unable to deliver a positive message or apology to her because she decided to block me, and delete me entirely from her life. I haven't spoken to her since. How two people who share so much can suddenly quit communicating evermore really disturbs me, but I may be in the minority for that.

- Chapter 8 -
Atmosphere ii

So here we are one year removed from my last relationship and a little over a year into a job that actually utilizes my field of study. I have pretty much reached all my life goals aside from the partner thing. I have more knowledge, am wiser, and more humbled. I have made a bunch of mistakes but I *am learned.* I have also made some correct moves establishing the best state of mind and position to better my future. I have many people to thank through the process but I thank God more than anything because his love is never failing. The closer I get to him the better my life becomes. This is what I realize when I look up into the atmosphere on this magical drive home. He is still with me, molding me. I have decided to give it all to him, and let him lead the way. I am attending church more frequently, and reading my Bible more. I may need to get an ESV version though, as this King James version doesn't suit me as well. In the meantime, I am also writing my own book of which I am thinking I will call *The Great Mountain,* because we all have a great mountain to climb much like I did.

I didn't come from much; my family was borderline poor so I couldn't be reckless in life. I wouldn't have much I could fall back on if I failed. Being smart and talented meant there was hope I could do good but I never had super high expectations from anyone given our lifestyle. I learned from my father how to pinch a penny and swing a baseball bat, but little else. I've earned most of the things that I have through hard work and self-motivation. I am proud of myself and my journey. I hope to continue greater success because I dream of buying everyone in my family their dream car. We always had semi-junky used cars. I don't need *dolla dolla bills* to measure my success though. As long as I am still there for my family, I will feel good about myself.

I invite you to accompany me on a journey in the present day to see the reality of walking for the glory of God. I have beaten depression with the proof of God's existence. Since the day Granddad revealed that he heard God's voice, I have not had another suicidal thought. God has given me everything I ever desired piece by piece. Not everything has been how I pictured it but I got through low times and confusing times with perseverance and faith. Every day I see the results of his love and my faith grows stronger; I trust he will continue to add to my story in amazing ways. I am building a mountain on my pathway to God, and every puzzle piece is coming to me through him. Perhaps the last puzzle piece is a wife?

Perhaps I am not meant to have a partner at all. I am no longer going to fret over it. I am content in being single for the first time ever, and a lumbering weight has lifted off my shoulders. I no longer feel the need to have a wife and kids. If a relationship is in God's will then it will happen. It is clear that I am to focus on my art projects, for that is my gift to the world, and it must be my "raison d'etre." God granted me with a good family, good health, intelligence, talents, and this life path that includes a good job, and a home. I am so thankful. What happens next is on him.

After taking some time to contemplate my life and my decisions I think I have narrowed down some things. First of all, my experience with Blessica put me through some spiritual turmoil. How can I let sex be a factor like that? Secondly, if I am to ever have a legit relationship, I should work out all the bugs first. I have decided to outline what would be the girl of my dreams, if only just for fun.

I am a practicing Christian and would want to find someone to grow in faith with. I don't go to church regularly but I don't oppose it. She shouldn't be an overly strict, judgmental, churchy weirdo. So, she loves Jesus, but not necessarily all the current traditions or roles. Opening up the Bible is a good idea though. As far as beliefs and views go, I am not big into politics but I lean right and am currently registered libertarian. I am accepting and non-judgmental in most cases but abortions are not ok, we must agree there. I don't think I'd be fond of someone who tags themselves as a liberal or a feminist.

I have a high level of sexuality and would want my partner to relate. That being said I am Christian and am willing to wait until marriage as I think that would be a proud accomplishment and way to give back to God.

My dream girl is smart but not smug, and humble but knows her worth. Her personality is nice, innocent, sweet, with a silly sense of humor. She is unique, caring, rational, quiet, open to new things, attentive, creative, fun, and energetic but not obnoxious.

Values that are important to me include respect, honesty, loyalty, communication, faithfulness, integrity, and forgivingness. Being trustworthy is more important than being trusting!

For a lifestyle, my dream girl and I will indulge in outdoor activities and sports. If she will throw the pigskin with me, it will be a dream come true! She would not be a big drinker or be into the bar scene. We would be able to relax but won't be glued to a television screen. I barely even have a television. Funny fact: I have bought a TV for my dad, my sister, and my mom, but never for myself. Neither hunting nor fishing would be something I would be interested in. I would never hurt an animal, or make a fish late for something (this is from a joke by Mitch Hedberg, my favorite comedian). My partner might enjoy going out to comedy shows, concerts, and/or museums. She would stay fit and healthy to a rational degree.

I am generally physically attracted to the following feminine appearances: petite with dark hair and complexion. Her ethnicity doesn't matter to me. She has a cheerful smile, and hopefully laughs often. She is in good shape, with natural looks, and is not obsessed with make-up. The way someone dresses doesn't really matter. The more you respect and the more you love someone, the more attractive they appear and the more special physical touch becomes. I like genuine girls. I dislike phony things, so please, let's cease cosmetic surgery, implants, Botox, etcetera.

Children are important people, and I want to create some. My dream girl doesn't have them yet, but wants kids someday. Loved ones come before work, I hope my partner would prioritize family. She would have moderate to high ambition to do something with life, whether through work or something else. She doesn't need to be wealthy or have much money at all, but she must have enough ambition to want and keep a steady job. That job could be anything in the world, as long as it's ethical of course.

I don't want to tolerate smoking, nor other drugs, preferably not even marijuana. Regular drinking isn't attractive or healthy, not that we can't drink, but we should do it responsibly.

Music actually has a pretty big pull for me when finding a partner, and I hope my partner and I would share some commonalities here. I can appreciate a little of everything but the following is what I prefer: Classic Rock! (*Floyd, Zeppelin, Hendrix, Aerosmith*), newer forms of rock (*Radiohead, Blues Traveler, Porcupine Tree*), blues (*Elmore James, Buddy Guy*), Jazz, Reggae (*Peter Tosh, Buju Banton*), Classical (*Beethoven, Bach*), Oldies (*Doris Day, Dean Martin*), Alternative, Instrumental Metal (*Polyphia, Scale the Summit*), Some Soul, and some R&B. I mostly dig older tunes, but some newer as well. I like *Michael Jackson, Isreal Kamakawiwo'ole, Etta James, Adele, the Coup, Alt-J*, and this list goes on. Country is ok, it's just not my go-to, and I only like some Rap. I am usually not into EDM or similar genres. I strongly dislike the following: *Li'l Wayne , Drake, Ke$ha,* and similar acts.

There are additional random things that I admire in a human. I like when they always promptly answer my questions. I like when they enjoy exploring and traveling. I am sort of allergic to cats but I love dogs so I hope to find a girl who can be accommodating. I like when people are not phone zombies. My dream girl won't mind if I burp. I am not a fan of foul language, nor saying "OMG."

Posting a listed out form of my "dream woman" seems like a good idea to weed out large quantities of people from the get-go. As I seem to know no other way to meet women, I put myself out there on *Match.com*, with the aforementioned picky list. At the same time, I also have a profile on *Plenty-of-Fish*, albeit with a much looser approach. On my profile I simply wrote "I know the majority of you that receive a message from me are instantly so excited and nervous that your hands start shaking and you drop your phone in the river, and that's the reason I don't hear back. If you are one of the lucky ones then I will be glad to talk to you." I am at a point where I am ok with the single life that God has given me and I don't need a partner, but surely deep down inside I still want one.

Mandy is the name of a girl that I am talking to on *Match* and who accepted my stringency. She is a nice Christian nurse of middle-eastern descent, and very cute. Being the only one of approximately 200 girls to respond, I try to keep the conversation going. This ratio is not an exaggeration by the way! I really think dating is much easier for women because they pretty much have the power of selection. If I had that power right now, I think I would select this girl I saw on *Plenty of Fish* named Gabrielle.

Gabrielle's profile reads in a fun yet professional way. She mentions being a practicing Christian with no compromise but not necessarily much of a church-goer. She is studying to obtain her master's degree and already has a degree in language, specifically Spanish. She doesn't watch much TV, and she plays Cello, Piano, and Ukulele. Very much into the outdoors, she loves being in or near bodies of water. Social awkwardness, and introversion are other things we have in common. Gabrielle is my type of girl, natural and real, doesn't seem to wear much make-up, and enjoys the simple things in life. She is not your typically hot chick with all the fake accessories, but looks like a natural beauty, cute in her own way. I cannot tell what ethnicity she is but she has a dark complexion, maybe Pacific Islander or something. She has moderately short pixie hair-cut, and the unique feature of a perfectly positioned mole right in the middle of her forehead. She only has a few pictures up but in every one she looks like a completely different person, and it's kind of funny to me and the sole thing I bring up in my message to her. My thinking is that it's unlikely she will respond anyway so I will just leave it in God's hands.

A week has gone by and I am looking at Gabrielle's profile again. I feel I need to put forth a little more effort, so I message her a second time. This time I bring up some things we have in common and the fact that I would enjoy a chat with her.

Having not met Mandy yet I don't feel ashamed in messaging other girls. In fact, these messages I have with Mandy are moving like molasses and aren't excessively interesting. It's been several weeks now of small talk with her and although she seems perfect and has everything I want in a woman; I am not sure it's going anywhere. So, I am going to message her and bring this up, not to try to end it, but to try to go to the next step, I actually do like her. Hopefully in person she will be fun and I will actually get to know her personality. I receive a response to the message and it's not what I had hoped. She basically says "I guess I am just too busy right now."

Movement B
GABRIELLE

- Chapter 9 -
Warming Up

The day after I stop talking to Mandy what do I get but a message from Gabrielle! She responded to my last message and this is the most excited I have ever been to receive a message from a stranger; I can't believe it! She found my synopsis of the typical female reaction to my profile to be refreshing, and that she jumped into the river to retrieve her phone in order to respond to me.

Over internet conversations I am now gabbing it up with Gabi (which is one of her preferred nick-names, the other being Gab). I learn that she is half Filipina but all American as she was born here in the States. She did some moving around but spent the majority of her childhood in Alabama. So, I assume she has that good old southern bell charm to her. We have the same beliefs and values. Each of us come from Seventh-Day Adventist families but aren't Seventh-Day Adventists ourselves. Growing in faith is an important thing we have in common. Being an enormously unique and interesting individual, I have already fallen *in like* with her. We talk every other day, the length of our messages grow and grow, and now we seem to be writing books to each other! I am eager to get to know her, I will have to ask her out on a date when I get home today, as it's been a few weeks of positive chit-chat already.

I'm leaving work March 31st, 2017. It's a bit of a gray day, it has been raining and there is still a misty feel in the air. Entering the twilight zone, I turn onto the main road. Route 15 has a pretty big single lane straight-away. Traffic seems normal and I see a maroon van off in the distance. I need to get some music going so I'm adjusting the radio to help ease the dreariness. As I look up, I realize that the maroon van is actually not moving and stuck in traffic! I slam on the brakes with an instant skid. I turn the wheel to the right to try to avoid a collision, but there's no use, I have no traction and my vehicle keeps sliding straight. There is a split moment where I just give up and accept the fact that I am going to be in my first major car accident. Poof! The airbag deploys with a puff of smoke. The force of the airbag jams my thumb up a bit, but other than that I am fine. I'm sitting here for a moment in confusion, but quickly realize I ought to turn on my flashers and get out to see if everyone is ok. The van's rear window is busted out, and the front of my car is wrecked up pretty bad but neither appear totaled. There is a big Middle-Eastern family in the van and kids of all different ages, but luckily no one seems injured. The father jumps out and says "what were you thinking?" At this point I am too nervous to think straight but I am able to gather enough sense to call 9-1-1. The mother is starting to become hysterical and I am starting to worry a bit. The police officer arrives, and I proceed to tell him what happened. He reminds me of a Canadian, and he is super friendly, but I do get a ticket for failure to reduce speed in inclement weather. I wasn't even speeding! As the family walks past us, the father again asserts the query "what were you thinking?" The cop responds with "I don't think he did it on purpose." This reassured me that there are sensible people out there. My automobile isn't even starting, so it's getting towed away. The van on the other hand is still drivable, so off they go. I still need a ride home so hopefully Tom is still at work. He answers and is right at the stop light down the road, perfect timing. He lives in Chambersburg so my home is along the way. I must thank God in a prayer tonight.

I tell Gabi the news via text because an additional thing we have in common is that we both detest talking on the phone. I also inquire if there are any coffee joints or something that we can meet up at. She brings up The Frederick Café which coincidentally is the only coffee joint I know about. It is also the perfect meeting place as it is halfway between each of our residences.

It's Sunday morning April 9th, 2017, the day I am to meet Gabi for the first time. First, I pay my friends Robert and Amanda a visit. I am just chilling here for a little bit and marveling at their huge home and ever-growing family. As I wonder how they afford their fairy-tale dream come true home, I reach into my pocket and discover a quarter. Hmm, I must not have super clean pants on, ha-ha. I check out the coin and discover an Alabama stamping on the back. I must tell Gabi! Better yet I will give it to her as a hello gift, since Alabama is the state that she grew up in. There are just so many coincidences already leading up to this point. The stars must be aligning.

- Chapter 10 -
Dates

As we approach, sun shining across our faces, the first thing I notice is Gabi's enormous and expressive smile. What could be going on inside her head? Hopefully not a rapid quick fire of semi-pro football player and ex-prison guard. I hope my shiny giant forehead doesn't alarm her. Yes, I am nervous and uncertain, but there's also an unexpected level of comfort as she reaches out her hand for a handshake. "Oh, okay a handshake," I proclaim, "I was a little worried about how we'd do that." It's delightfully awkward. I open the door for her and we walk into the café and wait in line. I pull out the quarter and say "hey look." She doesn't realize I am trying to give it to her. "It's a hello gift for you," I say. We agree that there have been many strange coincidences and our situation, serendipitous. It's our turn to order and Gabi selects a tomato bisque soup. I'll have a sandwich and a smoothie. When the barista asks what flavor smoothie I would like, I reply with, "red." Gabi is giggling at me already. Woo-hoo! I think this is going to go smoothly. She indicates that I caught her off guard with my easy playfulness. It's considerable because I am actually quite nervous in my own right.

We sit, talk, and giggle some more. We're eyeing each other up, shaking the polaroid in our minds to form a memory, all the while trying not to stare or be weird. I take notice of her charming mascara and will never forget what she is wearing: a black shirt, plain jeans, and a purple scarf. It's nothing spectacular but I want to remember this moment. Gabi does seem a little shy and kind of staggers around her choice of words, but she is obviously a very intelligent human. I find the realness of her uncertainty to be adorable. She claims she is socially awkward and an introvert, something very relatable. She notions that a strength of hers is being able to see both sides of every argument and being able to see the good in everyone and anything. It can be a blessing but also a curse, because many times she struggles with indecisiveness. She seems very easy going though, as if we already know each other. She is sweet and respectful and doesn't pull her phone out every few seconds. In fact, I haven't seen her pull it out at all. A common audible trait between us is the fact that we are both soft spoken and refrain from using curse words. I guess we are the oddballs because sailor talk seems to be commonplace socially nowadays.

Next, we take a stroll around Carroll Creek Park and find some Easter eggs hidden in plain sight. Some of these eggs have Skittles in them, which might be my favorite candy. Other eggs have little ads promoting a church, which gives us the incentive for another date. At the end of our day, with the sun falling asleep, I request a hug. I withhold the fact that I wanted to greet in such a fashion earlier today.

I'm headed to the tow yard to retrieve my belongings out of the car and to give the towers the key, of which I accidentally still hold in my possession. Secretly I am also going there to yank the stereo out of the car. It's the coolest aftermarket touch screen DVD GPS *dealie* I've ever had. I hope no one watches me doing this, I don't really know how legal this is. The insurance company is supposed to come by soon to give me a quote on repair. I've swapped out radios multiple times so this is a cinch, and I exit the premises quickly with no one scoping me. I finally receive a call from the insurance company and they determine my car is indeed a total loss, and the payout is only $2,800. This figure sucks as this was a perfectly good running SUV in great shape. I guess I will just save up and drive my Firebird around for a while. I am privileged to own two cars.

It's time for date number two and Gabi and I are going to The Church of the Redeemer to see an Easter play: "The Mercy Tree." First, we have a quick bite at The Nibbler (a Latin-American restaurant), then we head to the church to get some seats. We sit side-by-side, stealing glances and making quick comments between announcements. I wish we could have more time to talk, but what we are doing makes me feel righteous, to be on a date with a great girl at a church! We chat more afterwards as we sample the little church café on campus. It's a chilly spring evening with twinkling lights wrapped up around the trees. I tell her the story about the guardian angel in the form of a dog that my grandfather had experienced when he was at war. I inform her there are more goose-bump-raising stories about my granddad that will blow her away, but I am not ready to tell her the *big* one. There is a hubbub of church members all around but we sit and talk until we are the last of the last, neither of us wanting to leave. I already want to give her a kiss, but I am nervous and don't want anything to mess this up. Another hug is granted as we depart.

I made a collage of myself making a bunch of goofy faces. I think I will send it to Gabi, as I am sure she will appreciate it. She has already sent me a few goofy face pictures and has a silly sense of humor that I adore. It hasn't been but an hour or two since I sent the goofy image to her and I receive a response with a conglomeration of her own goofy faces in a similar manner. This girl really makes me smile like no other. She tried to mimic the faces I made! In lieu of the cursed flowers which have consistently foretold my breakups, I want to get her some chocolates. I tell her about the flower curse and she laughs it off saying, "there's no curse."

I remember a place called The Perfect Truffle in Frederick that my old workplace for the architecture firm was nigh. The gourmet chocolate place and sandwich shop has since moved to downtown and focuses solely on chocolate now. It's near the restaurant Gabi and I plan to sample for our next date. First, I think I will surprise her and take her to said chocolate factory. Yes, dessert first! The Perfect Truffle is the perfect place for the perfect girl. She is impressed with the gorgeous rows of glorious chocolate of all colors and styles, too beautiful to eat. She chooses the "Northern Lights," or a chocolate that looks like Aurora Borealis anyway.

At Brewers Alley there is a white tablecloth and anticipation between us. Gabi gets her favorite food: mac and cheese. I order lobster, and I didn't realize the whole freaking lobster, head and all, would come out on my plate. After dinner I show her my little keyboard and we grab our ukuleles. Our two-person ukulele jam-session commences on a parking deck in the middle of Frederick. We own the late night following the people to their beds. We have good acoustics as a passerby mentioned, but it is more than music, as music usually is. Our eyes meet with bashful gazes. There is so much tenderness and some curiosity too. Would I fall? Would we both?

Of course, I chicken out and didn't try to kiss Gabi again. I hope she doesn't think I don't like her. I must kiss her on our next outing, maybe I will just ask her for a kiss. Is that weird? I am a bit mad at myself, but worried I will mess this up at the same time. She seems so innocent that I don't know how she would respond if I just dove in.

The next adventure for Gabi and I is at Mt. Airy Park which is a quaint little place. I brought my boom-box, and tennis equipment. She brought her pickle ball stuff. What is that? First, we jump into a game of tennis. The stakes are high as I present a wager. If I win, she has to give me a kiss, and she can pick what happens if she wins. I see a huge smile on her face with those beautiful large teeth and she places her finger on her nose in her adorable thinking pose. We carry on with the game and it's a hard-fought battle but she wins. Did I let her win? No way! I now owe her some water time, either canoeing or some other water-based activity. She is a water baby! She recalls living in Alabama and riding on a pontoon boat all the time with her uncle. I'm not even aware of what that is but she describes it as a flat boat and sounds like a lot of fun. The next fun thing for us is pickleball, which I fathom is just giant table tennis on a real tennis court, except the crack of the ball on the paddle is utterly satisfying. As I insert a cassette tape into my boom-box I try to devise new ways to secure that kiss. I must undertake a game of truth or dare before the night retires. It feels weird to me that we've yet to seal our attraction with a kiss.

Next, we take a pathway through the woods for a walk, it's a hazy greenness kind of walk. There's distraction on the way back to our cars, finding some swings and climbing a tree. No joke we are actually up in a tree right now, I am 31 and she 26. Gabi is so free spirited and fun. Who else would ever do this kind of stuff with me? This would be a cool place to smooch, but maybe too dangerous. We're hanging up here chatting and enjoying the breeze in the leaves. When we come down to earth and lie in the grass she reveals that she wants to "wait." After the results of my last relationship I had also decided waiting until marriage for relations would be ideal so I am happy she said that! I simply tap her arm and say "well then we'll wait." I can guarantee that wasn't the response she was expecting, although she doesn't seem surprised.

We start conversing about ourselves and she brings over what looks like some school work. She has a worksheet with questions on it that will ultimately reveal your personality type. It is called the Meyers-Briggs personality test. She has already taken the test and her results were I-N-F-J. There are four sections with two types per section, so 16 possible personality types. I start to answer some of the questions and they are pretty difficult to answer, you have to take a deep look at yourself. We both agree that some of the answers could go in multiple ways depending on how you feel that day. My result ends up being I-N-T-J. So, we are both introverted (I), we both use intuition (N) for learning, and we both use judging (J) as a main form to organize our life. The only place we may differ is how we make decisions. I am a "Thinker" and she is a "Feeler." We are pretty darn similar.

Hunger attacks us so we take a quick trip for sushi then return to the park picnic table with mints. It's time for truth or dare. She keeps on saying truth, truth, truth! I finally say "you know I am going to dare you to kiss me. What? Don't you want to?" She responds "it's not that I don't want to..." I quickly say "well come on then," and I lean in. How magical it is. I want this to be a first kiss each of us will remember and I am surprised at how passionate she is with it. We keep on kissing longer than any first kiss has ever been. Then I feel a voice: "this is the last girl you will ever kiss; you will marry her one day." RING, RING, RING, we are interrupted by a phone call from Gabi's mom. As we depart, we discuss how amazing the kiss was and she says that she treats kissing like it is a conversation. Quirky girl.

God is doing an amazing thing right now. It is just unbelievable to me. I can't wait to see what else he has in store for us. I pray at night and I thank him.

Cinco de Mayo is bringing us fish and chicken tacos, a peach margarita, and an Old Dominion root beer. Gabi is wearing a classy lacy black blouse and looks absolutely stunning. I feel underdressed. After the meal, it's time to venture out to Frederick Community College in hopes that it will provide us with a piano and some heart and soul. We luck out and find a giant open room with a piano in the corner. The door is open so we waltz in. We sit and she starts playing a melodic chime. She is impressing me mightily with her musical talents and I have so much admiration for her and her mannerisms. Now I am extra nervous, butterflies rekindle, which feels weird because we had already broken the ice with a kiss on our last date. We enter the car to head to my house but prior to take off, I say, "before I forget, give me a kiss." She responds "before you forget?" and laughs, but of course is happy to oblige.

At home Gabi is introduced to good old Daddy Diamond, who is a "friendly chap," as she puts it. Dad is so ready to share my art and talents, and a piece of "cherry P-I-E," as he puts it. But now it's fort building time! We are actually building a fort together! I jokingly suggested it a few days ago but she was ecstatic to do it. No one else would ever do these kinds of things with me. We have sketches and plans and are adding some ideas. We get to work post-haste and tackle the cardboard with box cutters and red duct tape. We're not messing around. I am just looking at her in awe with her tie-dye shirt and the way she's hunkering down constructing a rather complicated dome structure. Meanwhile, I am working on a giant collapsible castle. We combine the two and bask in what turns out to be quite a fortress. I am sure my nieces will get plenty of enjoyment from it.

Neither of us are avid TV watchers, I barely own one and Gabi never had cable growing up. It's another quality that makes her and I similar. Nevertheless "Lisa The Vegetarian" is making her screen debut for Gabi, finally. It's my favorite *Simpsons* episode and I have been praising it. Gabi is so willing to share with me what I enjoy. As her reward, I smooth my way into a romantic dance in my living room, something that is atypical of me but everything feels so right with her. She says I'm sweeping her off of her feet. To cap off the day I grab my guitar and just fiddle around with Gabi listening. We share quick quips, lyrical conversations, chuckles, and guesses to songs sprinkled in between the notes and chords. Gabi says she could listen for hours, but it's late and time for her to head home. Today was May fifth, our fifth date, and we packed 5 days' worth of stuff into it. Such an amazing day it was, one of the best of my life.

I inform Gabi of my nervousness regarding my wear and she eloquently states that she finds the kind of shirt I was wearing to be the most attractive thing a man can wear. I wore a long sleeve shirt with three little buttons at the top. Gabi is weirdly attracted to that but with the sleeves pulled up a bit like I normally do. I am starting to feel like I can't go wrong.

I've taken time off work to prepare for my sister's wedding rehearsal. I invited Gabi to the rehearsal but not the wedding. I don't want to take anything away from Amili's day, plus I have taken so many different people to weddings that it just doesn't feel right anymore. Gabi and I start the day early and visit the Washington County Art Museum. There is an incredible watercolor showing. Watercolor is a medium I don't personally dabble in. I get in trouble somehow trying to sneak into an exhibit not yet open; I guess I wasn't fully convinced it was closed. Next, we take a stroll around City Park's pond and head over to Maloo's restaurant for lunch. The Scenery here is magnificent and continues the art theme. This excites me as I wasn't aware of how nice this place actually is. It is much nicer with Gabi as a guest. They situate us in a pretty romantic corner of the restaurant, although near the entrance to the restroom. I am wearing a fedora and it catches the attention of an elderly man. As he moseys towards the restroom he stops and asks for his hat back and comments on Gabi's beautiful smile. "Not many people smile like that," the man proclaims, "find me if he doesn't treat you right." I surely agree that Gabi has the greatest smile, it's not just her mouth but her eyes smile as well, and now she is blushing.

My dad insists Gabi sit up front with me in the car because she doesn't know me as well as he does. We go to pick up my almost seven-year-old niece Willow from school before we venture over to York for the rehearsal. Willow comes running down the hill from school hand-in-hand with a friend. Her dark curls bounce along and contain an energy all their own. She shares a *Fruity Pebbles* bar with us, which is just like candy. Back into the car we head out. On the way up we play "I spy" and Willow falls asleep.

At the church, the rehearsal begins. There is the natural hubbub before a wedding, organizing, tweaking, and practicing. Gabi gets to meet Amili, three-year-old Ivy, and some more of the family cast. I did not warn her of my aunt Georgia though, who is the self-proclaimed crazy one, and the oldest although she acts the youngest. Her and aunt Carol hug Gabi simultaneously in a sandwich, and it makes my heart swell with giggles. Gabi gets another comment on her beautiful smile and blushes some more. She says all the smiling is because of me. I am so happy to know that I am also bringing her happiness. One of the bridesmaids didn't make the rehearsal so Gabi stepped in. I walk down the aisle with Amili's best friend Sarah, and Gabi walks down the aisle with one of the groomsmen. Am I jealous? Is she jealous? No, even if it felt a little weird it was all good fun.

On our way back from York we played a game using the alphabet that decided something peculiar: "I'm going to Mars and I'm bringing...?" Gabi selects a torpedo, and all kinds of specialized survival items. She uses big words and impresses me and my father with her intelligence. Meanwhile I am bringing "inflatable flailing arm tube man." Needless to say, the game was full of random and silly things and at the same time got your brain working. Wow, Gabi is smart, funny, spiritual, good looking, and just about perfect. I mean, she is a perfectionist.

Back at my house I show Gabi some of my art and graphics. She takes a gander and says "wow, you are incredibly talented." She adds, "your drive to create is inspiring, and your energy is magnetic." I must admit, I love being admired. We watch the Disney classic: *Dumbo*! She has never seen it so it catches her up on her childhood while taking me back to mine. As we sit on the couch afterward, Gabi opens up to me. She expresses her spiritual turmoil regarding sex. A bad experience with a prior relationship has shut her down for three years now. It really bothered her because she felt like it was only about the physical part. But she proceeds to inform me that I am waking her up to the reality of closeness and joy. She continues to say, "there is a contentedness in letting you know me and to embrace me, to be vulnerable and open; I had purposefully stored away any desire to feel like this for so long that it's hitting me in a more powerful way." She reaffirms that she is committed to God and waiting until marriage for sexual relations. This girl is so innocent and thoroughly a good girl. I comment that I feel like I am not good enough for her. She quickly and cheerfully says, "oh yes you are," and gives me the sweetest kiss. I share with her, "I am one happy man." She lays her head on my chest and rhetorically asks, "Is this real life?"

It's Amili's wedding day and it's raining! They say that's good luck, for some reason. May 13th, 2017 is a gloomy day outside, but inside the church it's glorious: bright and cheery. My sister will become Mrs. Blaine Macdonald, and I will become a proud brother. I really am so very proud of my sister and how far she has come. I am so happy for her that she found such a special person. Blaine really is a great feller and today he is *erect*, as one of the other groomsmen put it. Obviously, that means he is very excited, but me being a lunkhead, I find it to be a peculiar word for the situation. Moving on, the cast members are all running around making sure everything is situated perfectly. Meanwhile we are all still waiting on the bride's mother: my mother. I have no evidence she will arrive on time but my heart knows she will so I assure the others. Sure-enough she is here on time. I see how emotional and exhausted she is (from the 5-hour drive) but I quickly inform her of the procedure, since she didn't make it to the rehearsal. I get to take two trips down the aisle, walking my mother then walking with Sarah as well. So here we are standing at the altar in anticipation of the white dress. The music initiates and thus comes Amili down the aisle looking as beautiful as she ever has. Emotions are high as I notice my mother with a tissue and it takes everything that I have to not start balling myself. I do tear up a bit as I realize how happy I am for the female variant of myself. Pride will not hide these tears. Vows are being presented and my dad is trying his best to keep Ivy still and mute, and it's comical to see. I hearken an "I do," then another "I do," and the couple are dubbed "Man and Wife." Trumpets please!

Blaine did play trumpet at the wedding and now he is playing a keyboard and singing to his new wife at the reception. How cool is that? He also does a father-daughter dance with his two new step daughters. The girls also dance with their pappy (my dad) a lot, and their spirits are adorable. Even though the cake has the wrong color icing, the day is story-book style. It would be cool if I could experience this human ritual first-hand someday.

Back to monotonous Monday for work. The seemingly longer than conventional day ends and I lie my head down at night's rear. I exchange the usual text with my sweetheart Gabi. She claims a comment that I made has been on her mind, and then she reiterates that I *am* good enough for her. She uses direct biblical reasoning and says to not let the devil tell me that I am not good enough. "Fear is the Devil's tool," she exclaims. How much she cares, how amazing of her to assure me of this; it's making me cry. I feel like I have been waiting so long to hear this and to finally feel accepted. It is like a real-life reflection of God's love. I love God and I was already thinking that I love Gabi, but now I know for certain. I am *IN LOVE* with this woman already, before our seventh date. This is the first time I have ever had to dry my eyes as a result of sheer joy. It is intimidating because I never felt this way before, but I am bullish about our relationship. I can't let on that I feel this way already, oh no, how embarrassing that could be. I pray to God and thank him for introducing me to such an amazing woman.

For my 32nd birthday my father awards me 32 dollars. Each year my salary goes up by the amount of one dollar. That is his tradition. May 17th, 2017 isn't bringing much more with it. I have a fun day planned for tomorrow with Gabi. It's getting close to midnight and I receive a text from her wondering if it would be weird if she didn't call me. Her and I haven't even spoken to each other over a phone call yet in our relationship. Neither of us are into it. Yet my response is "you would be the only one to." This cues our first ring-a-ding, and she calls me just in time at 11:59. We chat a little and it feels way more natural than expected for both parties.

The thoughtfulness in Gabi's beautiful brain impresses me. She gets me a 6-pack of random root beers (my favorite carbonated beverage) and a postcard that's good for another at The Pop Shop! We are at Point of Rocks to bike on the C&O Canal trail. It was raining much of the day while I was at work and I asked Gabi if she liked mud and danger. So yes, we're biking in the mud as it actually excites her. The rain has cooled the weather down and makes parts of the Potomac River foggy, hazy, and completely dreamy. We splash through puddles and chat here and there. I shake some of the branches I can reach to drench water on Gabi as she peddles behind me. She is so much more different than anyone I ever met. She loves the rain, the puddles, the biking, and the scenery. She sprightly shouts, "this is so much fun," and hearing that makes me beyond happy. Gabi expresses that the joy in these moments are more vivid and more intense when you're with someone special. We paddle along, slowing down every now and then to talk and check out the river, the train tracks, and other charms of the C&O pathway. At one stop, without warning, I pick her up from the armpits and hold her straight up in the air for a spin. I try to remain unpredictable and like to do the unexpected. She says that I keep her on her toes. We get drenched, caked, and splattered with mud, but we properly clean off in the river before our next adventure.

Hunger attacks us so we decide to go up into town to eat. We're at the mall headed to a taco joint but I see a hibachi grill and insist we divert. Everybody in here is getting special birthday attention it seems. I'm almost nervous Gabi is going to have them sing to me, but it doesn't happen, she knows me too well for that. We're considerably dirty but we don't care, the company and the food are great. The chef sprays apple sake into my mouth. I've been to many hibachi grills but this is a first. Gabi tries some as well and says it's strong, she must be a lightweight or something because I can't even tell there is alcohol in it. Neither of us want this night to end so we head into the theater for a movie: *Guardians of the Galaxy*. It has a spectacular soundtrack. My shoes are still wet and it's a little chilly but that's ok, I can shimmy away this armrest and provide a snuggle opportunity with Gabi. So, we sit and hold hands, a classic notion for a motion picture.

The next day is date number eight (yes, I am counting!). The plan is to meet at a bar called Nola, which is a rare activity for each of us. I'm having an estranged dark feeling on my way over, I think because it's a rainy, gloomy, gray evening. Am I worried she won't show up due to a car accident? Maybe I am nervous because this is the first occasion that we are to meet two days in a row, and I don't want to smother her. I see Gabi and all my fears dissipate. She is wearing a little dress, with a denim jacket: so perky looking. She explains she was worried she was running late, that she tries extra hard to be punctual for me. She hustled down the streets of downtown Frederick in her wedges and stepped in a very dark and deep puddle. She says, "I am surprised I didn't fall down into a secret aqueduct." She is so weird and nerdy, I love it! Live music is the allure at this bar. It was her idea to keep celebrating my birthday and we both enjoy the audible arts. She makes me feel so special. The band features an accordion, guitars, an upright bass, drums, and a saxophone. They remind Gabi of *Pearl Django*. I don't know what that is or if

I even heard her correctly. We are finding ourselves leaning over and yelling into each other's ears as we sit at a table in the corner by the glass wall. We're forced to do this because of the music and the cacophony of voices and conversation around us. Gabi thinks there is something intimate about carrying on conversations this way. I was feeling shy and she was acting coy especially when alluding to wanting a beverage. Ray to the rescue! I bring her an apple cider bourbon drink that she says is very strong and is making her arms feel heavy. The night goes on and we manage to take some goofy pics of ourselves. I am so glad we have the same sense of humor and some of the faces she makes will make me laugh forever.

We leave the bar and are just trotting around a very lively Frederick. We stop a few times to look around and decide where we want to go, each time stealing a few kisses. We are walking to her car but decide to stop in front of an old church. She teaches me how to salsa! It is pretty much just wiggling your hips and stepping forward and backward. Maybe we will take dancing lessons together some day. We sit at the bench and talk about everything and nothing, important and unimportant, until it's eventually time to rest our bodies for a new day.

"Will you go out on a date with me?" I ask Gabi. She responds, "I'd love to," and so date nine embarks. We meet for complimentary bang-bang-shrimp at Bonefish Grill. Gabi discovers her new favorite drink: a tropical tiki martini. She says she is glad I am with her otherwise she would have three or more of them. I'd like to see how she acts with that much intoxication; it would probably open her up a bit. In a way she is a bit of an enigma, and a little unsure of herself. We then walk around a furniture store just for no apparent reason. I see some beds and inquire of her, "What kind of bed should we get our children?" She responds, "a waterbed hammock of course." It's fun to joke but we never spoke about children before so I ask if that is something she wants. She says it's not something she really thinks about but, "someday... yeah." I told her I want to reproduce a son who will become a professional athlete, which is probably most men's fantasy. She says, "Why not an artist?"

Artists starve! Kids are on my mind today because it is actually my niece Willow's birthday. She is seven and I gave her a Lite-Brite when we celebrated on Saturday. The rest of the evening Gabi and I just meander. We end the night sitting in the car flipping through radio stations and trying to bode the song before *Shazam* can.

May 25th is game night at my house. Amili, Blaine, and the kids are here as Gabi arrives. She brings along a bunch of board games including Apples-to-Apples. She is always so prepared and brings along more than what's a necessity. We seem to be playing Apples-to-Apples pretty much exclusively as my sister really digs it. The kids bop around with Dad and Willow bops in and out of our game, making Gabi's lap a seat. Everyone is pretty excitable today, even myself. Amili points out that I look different. I must be glowing; maybe this is what happy looks like. Willow points out that Gabi and I are trying to do what her mom and Blaine did, referring to the whole marriage thing. We adults feign a lack of understanding. Ivy points out the "dot" on Gabi's forehead. With a reluctant tone Gabi mutters, "it's a mole." "It's not a mole when it's on your face," I quickly remark, "it's a beauty mark, and it makes you more beautiful." She is a little nervous to be spending time with my sister, who is pretty much the most important person to me. Everyone heads home to their beds and so Gabi and I have some alone time together. She mentions she had fun getting to know everyone's humor throughout the evening. Now Gabi is having fun watching sports with me! This is really happening! It is the Penguins playing in the seventh game of the Stanley Cup. Watching this hockey game with Gabi puts icing on the cake (pun intended). This girl is definitely shaping up to be the girl of my dreams! I give her a quick lesson on the rules and it's a good game: reached a second overtime. The Penguins make the last goal in a sudden death victory, very exciting. Gabi says she could get into hockey, that I might have her sold.

Gabi has been driving around in an old blue-silver Toyota Matrix with 200k miles on it and steel wheels. Being a car guy, I can't handle the two missing hubcaps so I decide to purchase some new ones. I install them for her and also polish the headlights. I'm glad I get to do something nice for her at the same time. She is very grateful and says I am very thoughtful and sweet. On a prior encounter we had talked about our "love languages," which refers to an infamous book. We each took a survey that listed out our love languages from priority to least important. Our results were the same: 1-quality time, 2-acts of service, 3-physical touch, 4-words of affirmation, 5-gifts. She was surprised "words of affirmation" wasn't higher on her list because she is very much into verbal communication. I was surprised that "acts of service" wasn't first on my list. We match up pretty well either way.

Date eleven is hiking day at Great Falls Park in Potomac, MD. First, I have to find Gabi because she said she parked near a Borders at the FSK Mall in Frederick. I cannot find Borders! So, I'm calling her. She meant to say Barnes and Noble, but quickly spots me with my phone to my ear. After a bite, we head down I-270 and I am the copilot with handwritten directions, which she finds humorous. I prefer driving but so does she. It's a beautiful day for an outdoor activity albeit a bit hot. There is a long line at the park entrance so we utilize a pack of cards she got from Chick-fil-A which simply present a bunch of questions. We are still getting to know each other really. We pull up and get informed that both of our main attractions, Billy Goat Trail and the Great Falls Overlook are closed. Gabi's optimistic and always positive self says, "It just gives us an excuse to come back." We won't let it spoil our fun.

There are other trails in the park and we hightail. We are just walking and talking about relationships and I mention how it is important to just be yourself. Gabi agrees wholeheartedly and "being yourself" is a mantra she lives by. I mention how I like to stay friends after breakups, but this is something she disagrees with. It's the only thing we disagree on so far. Then I bring up something that I don't like discussing but I need to know her viewpoint on: abortion. As soon as I hear her say, "I would never do it," it puts me at ease and that is all I need. I say "good, now let us never speak of it again."

We get a lot of hiking in, heading into the woods and finding new trails. We climb rocks and bouncy fallen trees. I randomly proclaim a "RACE," and sprint up a hill, Gabi keeps close behind me but is struggling with laughter. Now we are both sweating, huffing and puffing. The woods are patchy with green lights and rays of sunshine scattering on the path before us. Gabi finds a floaty white fuzz in the air and snatches it only to discover upon closer inspection that it is actually a bug. We share a laugh and proceed to talk about our families, our strengths, and our weaknesses. We climb down to the river for a break, sit, and have a snack. We rest there for a while just taking in the scenery; the sound of the churning river is calming and tranquil. Then we notice a small snake sitting on the rock beside us just chilling. This is the second time we discovered a snake on one of our adventures. Strange things happen in pairs. Sitting near each other we are at ease.

After several hours of hiking we gorge ourselves with food at the Double TT Diner. Breakfast for dinner is spectacular! It might be the post hike food daze talking but I say, "Gabi, everything is magical when I am with you," and I mean it. I sense Gabi has similar feelings. It's not sparse how often she says that I bring her "hope." She says it frequently.

In the back seat of Gabi's car, we get frisky... playing a card game. She is really into these peculiar card games and this one is called Metagame. It basically just asks what you would rather do between a few options and reveals your opinions. We are on the same wavelengths.

I've decided to expose my secret story with her tonight. I proceed to say that it's really hard for me and kind of a long story but I need to get it out. I tell her how during my childhood I suffered from depression, on and off medication. It got so bad that I basically tried to kill myself, I ran and grabbed a knife. Mom was there to stop me and had she not been there I am not certain what the outcome would have been. Maybe it was a cry for attention of some sort. Either way I was out of sorts and needed help. I contribute that eventual help to my granddad and his stories. I proceed to tell her Fern's main story that I hadn't yet. He was trapped at war but heard God's voice saying, "nothing can harm you." God then protected him, diverting bullets, some spitting up dirt on his boots and some creating wind past his ear. I explained that hearing this story in particular really is what made me realize God's realness and love. Had this not happened, my grandfather wouldn't have come back from war and my father never would have been born, and so neither would I. This was when I was saved. Since then I have not had another suicidal thought and believe I am on God's path. My storytelling skills suck and I blurted that out all pretty fast and say, "Well that didn't take me long at all actually." Gabi is taking it in with open arms. She says it was amazingly brave of me to share and feels honored and entrusted with the weight of my vulnerability. She says she won't take it lightly and that she has a story she needs to express as well. She isn't mentally prepared for that yet so I say, "whenever you are ready, I am here."

June 1st Gabi and I return to our favorite park on Mt. Airy. I rode my motorcycle today so she can see, but I don't see her around. Ah, there she is coming down over the hill, she must have been going pee-pee. I tell her I would let her ride on the back if I had more experience but having her life in my hands like that would be too much of a frightening risk right now. She aspires to ride a motorcycle on her own someday. It will be fun to add that adventure to our list. Today we will play badminton, volleyball, paddle ball, and partake in long boarding. With the sun shining and sand under our feet I bask in the admiration of this outdoorsy lifestyle we share. After volleying for a while, we sit at a picnic table next to the one where we shared our first kiss. This time we're playing Mad Gab (another card game). This game is hilarious, it makes you read some nonsense that sounds like an actual sentence or phrase. Then you have to figure out what that sentence or phrase is. I see some interesting expressions on Gabi's face as we laugh out loud. I feel like I am seeing another side of her, her inner sweet, silly, goofy, real, and natural self. This gives me a warm fuzzy, an exciting "joy" as she would put it. It makes me feel closer to her when you can just be yourself. Being yourself is something each of us preach and/or praise.

As the sun goes down, we find an essential sloping sidewalk for our longboarding idea and take several runs. She is ahead of me as we roll down again and I see her board start to wobble; she is going really fast. It's pretty funny as she takes a dive awaiting a groovy grass stain. The stain on her shoulder will hide itself in Chipotle as long as I keep my arm around her, which is something I always want to do. She often mentions longing to have my arms around her. Before departure, I demonstrate a quick motorcycle tutorial and suit up. I swoop her up in one arm, helmet in the other, and give her a big smooch. I ride off into the cool night air feeling remarkably *studly*.

It's been approximately two months and I have had 12 dates with Gabi. I know she is special. Her allure is something deeper than a physical attraction. I feel like we have kindred spirits and are meant to be. She mentions God's timing bringing us together and our season being full of joy. I had patiently waited for this kind of relationship for a long time. When I finally came to love myself and enjoy life for what it is, without even needing a female companion, God presents me with this angel I call Gabi. I have already told my sister that I'm going to marry her one day, thus believe Gabrielle is "the one." I'm so confident in our relationship because everything is different with her, it feels so natural and genuine. I never want to call her "babe" or "baby" like I did every other past girlfriend. Gabi is especially special. She is the only girl I have never gotten frustrated with or annoyed by. We never argue but have elaborate discussions. I've never had these feelings before. I don't want to frighten her and force a flee. I want to wait before I express my feelings. We have spoken about taking things slowly, and sure we are holding off on the physical thing, but my heart is ahead of schedule. To fill the void where I want to say "I love you," I just say, "I'm crazy about you." I looked up the average time it takes a couple to start saying "I love you," and it is six months in. I doubt I can delay that long but I intend to postpone divulgement until the 4-month mark.

▲

- Chapter 11 -
Her Story

Date thirteen sings to us as Gabi and I stroll around the jolly
Blues Fest event that happens once a year here in Hagerstown.
There's free admission to the outdoor theater in City Park where
various blues bands perform. Before sitting down and enjoying
music we decide to visit the art gallery, it's kind of a rickety
building but has a tasteful presence.

We lay a blanket in the grass and plop down to take in the
notes and waves of cool jives. The last band finishes up but we
continue to just lie there in the field perfectly content. We
wallow in the ambience until there is no one left but us. I
eventually take her home to prepare a meal. Stuffed manicotti is
my specialty and is a well-known pantie-dropper. Of course, I
have no intention of that happening tonight. I tell her this with a
big stupid smile on my face and she smirks. We lose track of
time and I cook the manicotti *fricking* twenty minutes too long.
The failure knows not how to defile the food, it's still good. Food
tastes better when I can lay my eyes on Gabi.

We finish up the pasta and head downstairs for some ping-
pong. I have built a *beer* pong table out of plywood and
disguised it as a *ping*-pong table. We converse and she reveals
that she is ready to tell me her story. Gabi has not been in any
kind of a relationship for three years, she recently decided to
start dating again and I am her first. She says her previous
relationship put her through spiritual turmoil. She wanted to
refrain from sexual relations. She had sexual relations with
previous partners and this guy used that as an excuse to get in
her pants. He manipulated her and basically used the "if you love
me" line. He apparently was the begging and pleading type,
claiming it was because of his strong love for her. He was even
able to convince her to take nude pictures of herself for him. She
didn't want to do it but the desire he showed was persuasive.
After a while Gabi started to realize what this guy was all about
and wanted out. She took the route of attempting to sabotage

the relationship. She exclaims she didn't know what she was doing but she was confused and ended up calling up an ex-boyfriend. She hooked up with him and thus cheated on her boyfriend believing that would be the end of it. She knew it was wrong and felt humility. Somehow though the dude was able to convince her that she was the only one at fault. He kept a stranglehold on her. He even convinced her to get tested for STDs. He beguiled her, stripping her of dignity. They stayed together a while longer but she eventually came to her senses and broke off the relationship. But that was not the end of it. This guy had saved naughty images of Gabi, and as revenge he posted them up on the internet. At this point Gabi's voice is breaking up. She continues to explain that she called authorities and a cop came to the house and she had to expose what happened and those images to her very strict Christian father. How embarrassing. The authorities are futile and there's nothing they can even do about it. The whole situation broke her spirit and for the next few years she was in therapy and just did her best to connect with God, keep the faith, learn how to forgive the dude, and learn how to forgive herself. It's not until recently that she's started to overcome the depression and come to terms with her past, but claims that it is still an ongoing process. I know not what to say but I gather in her speech patterns that she is a victim. I simply walk up to her, hold her, and say, "It's ok, you got me now." It's my best effort at comforting. I am so honored to be the one that she shares these things with. I try to assure her that whatever happened in the past doesn't matter. I do not know that old Gabi. We are in a new life form and that everything is good.

We decide to cuddle up in our little silly romantic spot: inside the fort we built. Here she reveals to me why she was reluctant to share her last name with me before. She even says she would almost prefer to have been raped. I am startled by this statement and demand: "why?" She says because that would only be a one-time thing, but now there is a possibility of tons of people gaining access to those images without her knowing. It's a constant haunting and invasion of privacy, and it is rather disturbing.

I have decided for the first time in my life to completely delete all naughty pictures of ex-girlfriends. Gabi's warmth is all I need and it is the mature thing to do. I have collected quite a few over the years, but it doesn't feel right anymore, especially after the feelings Gabi expressed with me. I feel like this is a major step for me, almost like breaking an addiction. The pictures are completely gone now, unable to be recovered.

- Chapter 12 -
More Dates

June 6th I am going Gabi's way. She shows me her house; her parents aren't there and she isn't exactly comfortable having a boy over without them here since it is their house. She plans on introducing me soon though. She shows me her room and I look around and see a bunch of sticky notes all on her walls around her laughable twin sized bed. The notes all have Bible verses on them. She keeps them there as a reminder of God's love and says it's helped her through difficult times. I also notice her jewelry collection and comment that her style is "dainty." She conveys that others have expressed the same thing. I didn't even ask but she brings up her ring size. She is a 5 on her pinky and ring finger and 7's on the rest. I am sure to pencil this down in the back of my brain.

Our next order of business is to explore her hometown. She drives me around, shows me the glories, and shares some stories that happened here and there. We have some Chinese food and then some ice cream at the coolest spot. I snuck a pun in there. Gabi unfortunately is lactose intolerant but can still enjoy the treat accompanied with a *Lactaid* pill. Next, we head to the Community College she attends. Here we locate a tiny room where we try to play "Billie Jean" on the piano. It would be fun if we could learn to play this song together, her one part, and me the other. I return home for the night and jot down Gabi's ring size in my journal. I also take note of our adventures, these times are amazing and I have to keep a record. Am I living a dream? Pinch me.

June 11th I'm bringing my dad down to the place we lived when I was three to buy a car: Applegate Apartments in Frederick. Gabi meets us here and I show her the old pool where my parents met and where most of my toddler footprints exist. I take her on a walk along a little trail behind the pool and explain how it seemed so much bigger and extravagant when I was a wee one.

Now I can connect her to a little memory of my past. Dad meets the guy selling a Toyota Corolla and discovers it's not quite as nice as he thought. The plan was that he could drive it home and then Gabi and I would be free to go off and do our own thing. He isn't buying the car so we have to drive him home and our plans hinder a bit but we'll still have fun. Gabi squeezes into the barely existent backseat of my Firebird and we drop "Daddy Diamond" off at home.

The next adventure of the day includes playing mini golf and swimming in Greenbriar Lake. It's a man-made lake/beach thing and is pretty scenic and convenient for the outdoorsy type in the area. In the front the lake has a beach area with fake sand. The whole place is surrounded by a mountain of trees and the back is designated for fishing. The place looks beautiful but then I see Gabi in a bikini! She is nervous about it but she looks gorgeous! She isn't buxom, nor does she have a perfect hourglass shape, but she has a certain natural beauty. She has beautiful skin with a slight tan, strong collar bones. Her legs are long, thin, and silky with a little bit of tone. We hop in the lake and play around like carefree children, trying to dunk each other. She tries to teach me how to float on my back but all I can think about is how she can probably see the shape of my package quite easily every time I attempt. Getting out of the water we take a walk and she ventures off on exploration mode. I am trailing her and of course I am checking out her backside. I don't even touch her butt because I specifically requested to once and she responded saying, "well, it is within the bikini area." So, I decided not to because I have so much respect for this woman and our agreement. My eyes aren't known to resist though. On our walk Gabi sees a rock about twenty feet out in the water and gets an urge to swim out to it. Everything with her is just so fun and free. She sees a fishing hook and we agree that that is probably why you're not supposed to get into the water over here; you wouldn't want a little metal rod stuck in your toe. Just then a siren goes off and signals an exit from the premises.

At her house I am honored to meet Gabi's parents today: Cobydean and Liz Tipton. I stand there, with my arms behind my back in an attempt to look as approachable and respectable as possible. I want to make a good impression but shyness forces me to say little. They are very courteous though. They head off to bed and Gabi and I do our thing.

Gabi has been craving the opportunity to do an outdoor movie for quite some time. This is something I've never done before. She grabs the projector and we head out to the side of her house to set it up. There is a charming little patio area there with a swing and a flat spot to lay a blanket down. We set up a bunch of anti-bug candles. There's an abundance of little trees, shrubbery, and specifically placed rocks in her yard. It's done up quite nicely in a manner you might expect an older lady such as Liz to prepare. Cobydean also doesn't like mowing so they decided to fill the yard with other trinkets. Gabi and I lie down and images dance directly onto her house. We are attempting to watch The Lord of the Rings but we are just too distracted with each other's presence. The lighting on her face has so much grace as candles twinkle. Our lips meet and we can't keep them apart, kissing long into the night. We are making love, even if no sex is involved. I have no idea what is happening in this movie.

June 15th, we are going to "Alive at Five" for our sixteenth date. This is a weekly Thursday event in Frederick by the creek with live music. Here I meet Gabi's friends Ashley and Tim. It is kind of a lot to meet her family and her friends seemingly all at once but I am happy she is making me a real part of her life. We all stand around taking in the breeze and sound waves for a while then decide to head to a bar/restaurant called JoJos. Here Gabi has two drinks and appears a little tipsy. It's the first time I get to see her in an alternate state and she is super cute. "Cute," is a word I don't use around her, she isn't fond of it; to her the word "cute" belittles an individual unless you use it in the most endearing way. Here I mean it in an endearing way, her smile is cute and antics are adorable. She is making these funny little hand gestures as she slurs her enunciation. She is wearing sort of an old-fashioned style dress, red with white polka dots, and she looks cute! Her beauty is ethereal to me. I admire the dress yet she second guesses it along with everything else. The couples detach to our pairs and Gabi and I take a walk to burn off some of the alcohol. A late-night chat by the church and some more kisses commence. I tell her "I want to kiss every square inch of your body... except one." She raises her chin in puzzlement and we share an awkward pause. "I'm not into buttholes," I proceed. "Thank you," she responds with instant relief in her tone. With all this making out I am sure she can feel my aroused member. She must be feigning as if it doesn't exist.

Pain in my groin area grows as my grown member spends a long amount of time without release. The red dress creates blue-balls. I really don't care because I have me the best girlfriend in the world. As soon as I get home though, I know what I need to do. This solo sexual release does not alleviate the pain. I still feel swollen and nauseous as the pain creeps up into my abdomen area. I also notice a lump on my penis, and it basically wraps around the shaft approximately where my circumcision scar is. What is this? I look up the symptoms on the internet and discover what I have is probably a busted lymph vessel. It is probably caused by too much masturbation. The cure is to refrain from masturbation. Great, now I am in a relationship with a woman who just gets more attractive every day and I can't sleep with her nor can I give myself release. I am keeping my lump a secret, and it may make our "no sex" rule easier since I don't want her to see it. I will inform her of my blue-balls though. Her response is simply, "must be painful." Perhaps guys have said that to her before as a way to try to get her naked, and perhaps she thinks it's a myth. Either way, we might be looking back and laughing at this one day.

Tattoos are something I don't think I ever want. Gabi has an ocean wave on her left foot and a mountain on the inside of her right ankle. Both of them mean something to her and what she is about. I bought a bunch of temporary tattoos to share with her on our seventeenth date. She is ecstatic when I show them to her and am glad that I can make her laugh. We slap some on our legs and head over to a progressive pizza spot since we are progressive people today. I ordered one anchovy to be placed on one slice of our pizza. The preparer had to change gloves after touching that single anchovy. He says the oil from that fish can get on other things and it's so strong that glove changing is necessary. This was a good chill day for us, but on our next encounter I hope to blow her away.

June 23rd is Gabi's birthday. We are chilling in a parking lot waiting for her parents, her sister, and her sister's husband to arrive. As we wait, I give her a card. On the inside I scribbled: "A score and 7 years ago an angel was born. Nowadays I have the privilege of calling her my girlfriend. If your birthday is half as good as every day since I met you has been for me… this will be the greatest birthday ever!" I ordered her one expensive gift that took little thought and one not so expensive gift that did take some thought. The first was a used Alexa that I got off of eBay. When I had visited my buddy Rich, I discovered he had one and anything could be asked of it, then it would answer you correctly. You could also request any song you wanted and the tune would playback immediately. I thought this would be a good tool for her and compliment her lifestyle since she always wants to build knowledge and also loves music. I show it to her and she is appreciative but I know she will appreciate the second one on a deeper level. She is really into Bollywood movies so I ordered a pack of a bunch of DVDs for her. I show them to her and she is effervescent. But "hold on," I say, "there is more, open up each of them." I wrote up a bunch of sticky notes with words of admiration and put one inside of each case. The first one reads, "*You are beautiful on the inside.*" The second one reads, "*You are beautiful on the outside.*" When she sees this one, she says, "Did you plan for this one to be right after the first?" The rest read as follows:

You are the funniest girl I know.

You are exceedingly intelligent.

You make me want to be better.

Your religious integrity is admirable.

You make me smile with the power of a thousand suns.

You are tremendously thoughtful.

Gabi is on my brain 24/7.

I am so thankful I met you.

But this isn't enough to express my real feelings. Then she surprises me with a gift, on her birthday! She knew I wanted an ESV version of the Bible and she got it for me. It is the perfect size: medium. It has the words of Jesus in red. It's perfect. I am speechless; it is the most thoughtful gift I have ever gotten, and I will get so much use out of it. It is sort of a symbol of us growing closer to each other in faith and love. I love her for it. She wrapped it in especially decorative newspaper, I've never seen anything like it before. I tell her I am crazy about her.

We enter the restaurant to eat with her family and I am so honored to be included. I feel shy as always but I am with her so I am good. I meet Gabi's sister Sonja and her husband Brendon. Sonja is my age and Brendon is a little bit older. They both possess much couth and are rather intelligent. Gabi says that Sonja and her used to fight a lot but get along extraordinarily well upon the maturation of time. Liz made cupcakes which apparently is her tradition for birthdays. She brought them into the restaurant and Gabi ate one right there. Her parents head home after a full family selfie in the parking lot and the four of us that remain take a walk around Frederick. We find a playground; it's so refreshing to hang with someone who enjoys these shenanigans. We play around like we are children for a while until the sun takes its daily nap.

For our 19th encounter I head to Gabi's house and bring her soup because she is sick. She tells me a funny story about how she plopped over on her parent's bedroom floor. Turns out she has a urinary tract infection. Maybe it is from swimming in the Greenbriar lake? She says she can only chalk it up to poor hygiene. It's an unflattering yet honest remark. We hang out in her room and test out the Alexa. So, I assume you need an Amazon subscription to get the music function to work like I had hoped. Another issue is that it seems like it shuts off randomly. This is just what I get for ordering used junk on eBay. Perhaps I should learn to make sure I only buy good and new stuff for the people who are important to me and to stop being cheap. That's about $120 down the drain.

I feel like I am in a dream land, as if I am living in heaven. I ask my dad, "did I die in the car wreck in March right before I met Gabi? Because I feel like I died and went to heaven." I love everything about my life right now and I love Gabi. Our times together are majestic, we are magnetic, a beautiful healthy magnetism that fills up my spirit. We walk and talk hand in hand, we embrace at every chance, tickling the senses. We text every day, good morning and good night and "xoxox." We share Bible scripture oftentimes and we are growing in faith just as god had planned. She is special so I don't want to call her "babe" or "baby." We give each other silly pet names all the time. I might call her "sugar plum," or "honey dove." She often calls me "Dulce," which is Spanish for "sweet." I am trying to text with her in Spanish as often as I can in order to help her practice. I simply use Google Translate. Freshening Gabi up on her Spanish will help when she goes to Spain. She plans to go in August with Sonja, Brendon, and her best friend growing up by the name of Suzanne. Suzanne is pregnant and may be pretty big by the time August rolls around. This worries Gabi a bit. In other news, Gabi and I plan on making a trip ourselves to the beach. We talk about it and I tell her I would like it if she picks out the hotel. I had that bad experience in the past picking a crap hotel. Her reaction is priceless. "A hotel together?" she mutters with an awkwardly fearful expression, "that's pretty serious." I laugh and say, "Gabi we have been dating for months now, I think it's a pretty normal thing that couples do." She is so innocent, but I got her prepared to do that. Later on, we text and decide to take a day trip, drive down early in the morning and come back later that day. I presume she doesn't want her parents thinking we are sleeping together. Over text we say our goodnights: "besitos!" (kisses).

I am working on a playlist of music to make a CD for Gabi and to embrace on our venture to Assateague Beach. Some of these tunes are numbers we've spoken about previously and some are secretly a hint at the fact that I love her. The first song on the list is one that I am really feeling right now with my emotions and my relationship with Gabi. It is called "Stay Forever," and it is by *Ween*. *Ween* is a weird band with many different sounds but this one is pretty rocking and romantic. The lyrics resound 'I want to know do you feel the same way? – cuz if you do, I want to stay forever.' Hopefully that message isn't too strong. Song number two is "Bushel and a Peck," by *Doris Day*. This is one I sent to her a long time ago because it is funny. Gabi didn't initially realize that bushels and pecks are units of measurement. We shared a cackle. "Brown Eyed Girl" is song number three. I played the *Van Morrison* tune for her on guitar a while back. "Truly, Madly, Deeply" by *Savage Garden* makes me think of Gabi because of the lyrics: 'I want to stand with you on a mountain – I want to bathe with you in the sea.' She is very much into nature and has tattoos of those exact things. "Somewhere Over the Rainbow," by *Israel "IZ" Kamakawiwo'ole,* of course made the list. It is the quintessential ukulele song. *Michael Jackson*'s "Billie Jean" is next. Number seven is "Wild Horses," by the *Rolling Stones*. Wild horses literally live on the beach that we are going to. Next is the original "I Will Always Love You," which is by *Dolly Parton.* "Caress Me Down" by *Sublime* is on the list to mix it up and because it has some Spanish lyrics in it that I want Gabi to translate. Number ten is "Come and Get Your Love" by *Redbone*, because Gabi mentioned liking it. She also likes me a good bit and once called me magical. "Magic Man," of course, had to make the list, which is a song by *Heart*. My favorite musician *David Gilmour* gets a number and it is "The Girl in the Yellow Dress." This was one of the initial songs I sent Gabi to show her my taste in music. Gabi once said "I don't like calling someone *MY* ex-boyfriend, because they aren't mine, I don't own them." That comment earns "You Don't Own Me" by *Lesley Gore* a spot on the list. *Pink Floyd*'s "Money" is next just because it's a great song. "That's Amore" by Dean Martin is next. It is love, and belongs on all mix tapes for a romance. On the day Gabi and I shared our first kiss I brought my boom box and played some *Collective Soul*. They earned two songs: "Shine" which has a bit of a religiousness to it and "Pretty Donna" which is a beautiful stringed Instrumental. I think that may be enough songs for the CD. Call me old-school or cliché but I am proof that people still make mixtapes in 2017.

A discussion about our trip is next on our agenda, so we meet at Starbucks. We each do the nerdy thing and make a checklist. We are going to bring our bicycles along so I need to bring my bike rack that we can strap on to the back of Gabi's car. I am going to prepare my pasta salad that I always make and place it in the cooler along with beverages and other snacks. I will bring my frisbee and football along. Boy would it be a dream-come-true to play football catch with my girl!

I hop in my car at 5:00 am July 1st to drive out to the Mt. Airy park-and-ride to meet Gabi for our beach trip. "Not so fast" says a cop who pulls me over on the Dual Highway before I could even get out of Hagerstown. Ticket! I eventually make it to meet Gabi and she pulls her bike out from the back of her Matrix. I say "How did you even fit that in there?" Apparently, she even puts her kayak in there for her water adventures. With the seats down and the rear window open it touches the front dash and hangs out the back. She is so independent and will do everything herself if she can. We make room for the cooler and attach the bike rack to the back for our bikes. It is much simpler this way and Gabi notions she might invest in a bike rack herself. After we head down the road, we start to hear an annoying tapping. Tap, tap, tap, what is that? We discover that the handle bar to one of the bikes is tapping on the rear window. We (or maybe just I) eventually can't take it any longer and have to pull over to adjust the situation for an easier audible sense along our adventure.

We arrive at Assateague Island National Seashore and Gabi shows me around the campsite and other goodies. She and her family used to come down here regularly. I assume that the horses are the main allure. It is pretty weird to see random horses just hanging out and drinking coffee along the seaside. I holler at one: "You should put on clothes!" Ok I am joking but the horses really do just stand there in the road sleeping and sometimes blocking traffic. It's a strange site to witness. We whip out our bikes, cruise over a scenic bridge, and site see some more. We stop at a museum and scope out some of the history and artifacts. There is a deck in the back area where I show her what distraction graphics are. It is just vinyl adhered to glass so you can see that it exists and not traipse through it. I then feel like my job is a snoozer so I just pick her up and throw her in the air acrobatically for a while. She laughs at my randomness. We then hear a calling from the beach and head down. This is good old beach time complete with snacks, swimming, and all the essentials. I always thought the girl-of-my-dreams would play football catch with me and she says she probably won't be any good at it but will give it a whirl. Not only is she willing but she is also a pretty effective teammate. I show her some pass routes and teach her some fundamentals of the game. I am having the time of my life! All the sweat convinces us to cool off in the ocean, before coming back to just lay down on the beach.

Gabi has fulfilled everything I imagined my dream girl would be. I need to tell her that I love her. I cannot hold it in any longer, and now is the perfect time to do it. I want to be suave and say it in Spanish. My heart is racing as I lay cuddled with her on the beach. I am working up the bravery as this is all I can think about. It will be the first time I ever confessed it to a girl without them saying it first. It's the first time I've ever felt this way. I don't even need her to say it back, nor do I expect it, I just want her to know. Should I clear my throat? I've been stalling for about a half hour now in anticipation, I can't back out. Here goes nothing: "Te amo." She quickly reacts with "what? in Spanish?" with a huge smile, followed by: "yo tambien te quiero." This is the greatest moment of my life, right here, right now. My heart is still pounding so I grab Gabi's hand and place it on my chest in hopes that she will feel it. I'm not sure if she can feel it but it's intense. A few minutes later she asks, "wait, did I hear you correctly?" I smile and nod. I love her smiles and how she's second guessing what happened. This is by far the best day of my life. In fact, every day I spent with her has been the greatest day of my life, Gabrielle is an angel.

I wake up on the beach, I don't know how much later, but it's time for us to go get a shower then head into Ocean City for some grub and a walk on the boardwalk to see some pretty lights. We stop for a photo opportunity in front of the Ferris Wheel and I wrap my arms around her from behind. She snaps the pic and mentions she adores the resulting photograph, that it might be her favorite of ours. We are both pooped to the core from all the activities and the heat so we decide to take turns driving back. It is a three-hour drive so we've got to keep each other cognizant. When we return to the park-and-ride and get everything situated, I hold her tight. I don't want to let go. In English this time I look her in the eyes and say "I love you." She says "aww, I love you too," with an assuring nod. Eventually cupid peels us apart and we head to our respective homes for some much-needed regenerative sleep.

Gabi had put her driver's license and her credit card in my wallet. We both forgot about it. I want to bring it to her so she doesn't have to drive without a license, but she insists we at least meet halfway. Does this count as our 22nd date? I show her my sunburn. Since I refuse to wear sunscreen it was inevitable. But I am only burnt on one side, since I fell asleep on the beach on my other side. It is pretty ridiculous looking right now and is starting to peel off in the weirdest way. It is quite leather-like in texture, and thick. I will have to wear a hat to obscure it from story seekers.

At the hospital Gabi is a lab tech, and I am meeting her there today. She has an African co-worker named Grace who is throwing an Independence Day party. Gabi asks if I want to go check it out really quick, so we do. When we arrive, we are the only non-black people there but everyone is cordial. We try a little bit of African cuisine. It's a potato stew dish of some sort and has some bite to it, pretty spicy. I am surprised but Gabi is ready to leave pretty quickly. We are both kind of anti-social. I hope Grace didn't find it rude that we came and went with such haste. Gabi is burning up in her thick dress she is wearing so she changes it and we head back into town for the July 4th celebrations at Baker Park. We meet up with Ashley and Tim again. On our way over to the field to see a country band I have to pause every now and then to steal a kiss from Gabi. I might be making her blush. After the band is done, Ashley and Tim depart but there are still fireworks to be seen. We walk back along the always perfectly leveled creek to find a good spot to sit. We find the perfect spot basically by accident because the sky sparkles suddenly started booming. The view is perfect right here so we plop down. It is a romantic situation so I give Gabi a nice big smooch, but then I hear a young child's voice squeak "eww." I assume the kid saw our "PDA" and I hope I am not embarrassing Gabi.

After the amazing fireworks we walk back to our cars and Gabi hops in mine with me because she wants to discuss something. She says she doesn't think her feelings are all fully there yet. She is not 100% percent recovered from her past. She doesn't know what is in store for the future but she thinks she will probably be transferring colleges to complete her Master's degree. She might go to Colorado out near her friend Suzanne, or possibly the Carolinas. She doesn't know if I would want to do long distance. "I don't know, maybe," is my response. She asks, "do you want to talk about this now or just wait until the time is nigh." I don't really know what to say, I am kind of taken back. I postulate she doesn't really love me. I suck in my gut and mutter, "I don't know, how about we just enjoy our summer." She kisses me and goes over to her car. I am perplexed and downtrodden and am just staring at my steering wheel. Suddenly Gabi pops out of her car and comes rushing over, so I open the door and she hops in on my lap. She whispers, "I love you" into my ear. This is so sexy and she just healed my heart right back up. "I love you too," I whisper back, "I love you too."

Despicable Me 3 has three sets of eyes glued to the theater screen. Gabi and I are chaperoning Willow to see the animated flick. She's sitting in the seat right between us. I am sure it will be memorable for the seven-year-old. July 6th is capped off with Gabi and I cuddled up on my couch for hours just gabbing away. In a still moment I hear Gabi echo, "Is this real life?"

July 9th Sugarloaf Mountain is calling our names. So, we head up to the mountain and do a little hiking. We are getting up pretty high and have a fantastic view of the land below. The world is so awe inspiring. I am surprised I found someone whom I can have this kind of connection with. Out of all the millions of people down there I wouldn't want anyone other than Gabi up here with me. We come down the mountain and find a big rock that we find cozy so we lay and nap out. Before leaving the premises, we explore the vineyard areas and a beautiful little spot where Gabi's friend got married. Outdoor weddings are admirable. I assume Gabi would prefer an outdoor setting most certainly. Coming down a paved walkway something possesses Gabi to challenge me to a real race. She thinks she is pretty fast. I explain to her that I ran track, made it to states in high school and ran track in college too. Gabi still says, "on your mark, get set, go!" I am ahead of her running pretty hard in order to stay ahead. She actually is pretty fast. I say "wow Gabi, I was almost sprinting."

Buffalo Wild Wings for dinner is good. Chicken wings are spicy but even spicier might be Gabi's wings... I mean legs. She is wearing some rather short shorts. We sit in the car afterwards and chat. She situates herself in the driver seat so she is facing me. Her smooth legs and thighs are on prominent display and I can't help but caress. I rub her legs softly and inch my hands upward. Suddenly she grabs my hands and shouts, "Stop!" Oh my, did I make her angry? I retreat back into my seat like a puppy dog and apologize. She has never gotten loud like that before. Quickly calming down she says "I'm sorry I should not have reacted that way, I love your hands and how you touch me but that was just too much." "It's ok I get it," I reply. She then asks me if she can lay in the seat with me and cuddle. I am like, "Um, yeah, can you fit?" She fits perfectly within the cavities of my body. She really knows how to pick me up. I think she knows when I need it; she reads me like a book. If only women were as easy to read. I ask her what super powers she would want to have if she could. She says to fly and to be able to communicate with all languages. I announce I would teleport and read minds.

Gabi had offered to buy me another pack of sodas way back on my birthday. A tasty place called The Pop Shop requires a visit from myself and my tasty girlfriend. I call her tasty because I want to munch on her amazing brain. She is so smart and interesting that I just want to zombie out on her. I make the munchy growl noises as I reach my hands out to her head and mumble "*braaaiins.*" She teaches me a lot about life, growth intellectually and spiritually, and is really inspiring. She has always been a straight "A" student and is still studying hard for her master's degree in occupational therapy. Today is different as I am going to teach her something. She wants me to give her a lesson about football. I actually am still playing football in an adult league. We get a couple pops and sit down at this little table by the exterior glass. I start telling her about what offense and defense is and what the objectives are. I tell her about down and distance, and about the different positions. She is holding attention pretty well. It's probably because it's a big part of my life and she wants to show interest in the things I enjoy. She really doesn't need to but I enjoy this moment. Another day where I have to pinch myself. I tell her she ought to come see me play some time. She responds with, "Yeah I should do that."

I got an invite from my old college roommate to come see him graduate with a Doctorate in business. This guy is an overachiever as now Walden University will crown him as a doctor. Dr. Demetrius Charles sounds weird. I must go to this because I haven't seen him in forever. I invite Gabi and she will be meeting me at the National Harbor right below DC, which is where the ceremony is being held. The building for the event is huge and there are tons and tons of persons galivanting around. Gabi hasn't arrived yet but I take a seat and watch the folks walk across the stage. With there being so many graduates, Gabi might be able to take her time getting off from work and still see Demetrius walk. I receive a text from Gabi, meet her in the hallway, and bring her back into the seating area. Three more graduates walk then viola there is Demetrius. Perfect timing. We are to go to a celebration dinner in a hotel for Dr. Charles after the ceremony but we have some time to kill. The air is desert-heat-like and we are both dressed in our Sunday best outfit, but we decide to take a walk and scope out National Harbor. There is some nice new architecture and a giant Ferris wheel. We are standing in line for possibly this spot's main attraction, sweating, and can't wait to sit in one of the air-conditioned carts. We finally do and it's such a relief. The ride takes us up very high and the view is spectacular. We take some pictures of the scenery and of our fancy dressed selves to store in our memory banks.

Finding the hotel, and finding the room for Demetrius's celebratory din-din proved a smidge difficult, but Gabi and I used teamwork and found it. So, we walk in and the first thing I notice is that Gabi and I are again the only non-black people in there. Perhaps this is what black people feel like when they go to most places. I look around to make sure I am in the right place then I spot Demetrius so I walk up to him. I shake his hand and start chatting then Gabi emerges beside me and I introduce her. Demetrius asks if this is the same girl, and I say, "No, Gabrielle is new." We then got invited to sit at the same table as Demetrius. I am a little startled because I am not extremely close to him and thought there would be more important persons to sit there. Here we are sitting, chatting and collecting souvenirs. The water bottles have special print-outs on them for the occasion. Gabi tells me that when I walked up to Demetrius that she didn't know what to do, and thought "should I follow him?" "I'm sorry Hunny," I reply. I really should be more attentive. Both of us are shy and she probably does feel pretty awkward. Now Mrs. Charles is speaking and introducing everybody. When she gets to us, she refers to Gabi as "Ray's *new* girlfriend, Gabrielle." I find it sort of humorous that she chose to use the word "new." After we eat, I get to talking with Demetrius and he admits that a Doctorate in business is the easiest route to Doctor status, and he finally admits that he is indeed nothing more than a professional bullshitter. I knew it all along. As Gabi and I set out to leave, Demetrius chirps to Gabi: "You better be taking care of

Ray now, he is a good man." I reply for her: "Oh she definitely does!" She really treats me with the utmost respect and I can't get over the level of comfort I feel with her. I can only hope I reciprocate it.

A mid-week rendezvous in the works, not knowing where the tires will lead us, Gabi instinctively suggests we visit Liberty Reservoir. So, in our street clothes we pull up. Immediately we are envious of the other folk with their life vests, kayaks or canoes, and basic preparation. With Gabi's sheer excitement we promenade along the esplanade of sorts. Really, it's just a path around the lake. She tells me a tale of a time her and her cousin Holly hid a small time-capsule with some notes in it. This was many years ago, maybe a decade, and now we are on a treasure hunt. We don't find said item but Gabi gets a new idea. The water and her have a sacred bond, and I am jealous. She gets the urge to jump into the water in her street clothes. I suggest maybe letting her wear my shorts. There isn't supposed to be any swimming here but she says if anyone asks, she'll just say she fell in. Without regard to possible clothing arrangement there she goes into the water. "Ha-ha," I laugh as I can't believe she did that. I adore her. I want to join in, but I don't have the bravery she does. I also prefer clean pool water but man, I wish I was freer spirited like Gabi. I inch my way closer still with consideration. Suddenly I slip a bit and almost fall in. I decide to take a seat then I ask her if she has ever skinny dipped. "No," she replies, "but one time my friend Suzanne and I swapped our tops while in the lake." Afterwards Gabi is soaking wet and so we head into a Wal-Mart to obtain dry clothes. She makes a purchase and changes in the bathroom. We hop back in her car and she puts on deodorant, men's Old Spice anti-perspirant to be exact. She is so funny, and says it works better than women's deodorant.

Another water adventure is on our agenda and I will introduce Gabi to another part of my past. We are to meet my sister's family along with my old roommate Rich at Delgrosso Park in central Pennsylvania. It used to be called Bland's park when I was a kid and it didn't yet have the water park portion. Amili and the kids are enjoying the water park as the rest of us arrive. We all go into the regular ride portion together as one big family group. It feels really good to have all the most important people to me all together in a fun scene. I have the opportunity to show the kids and Gabi around what were the happiest and most memorable moments of mine and Amili's childhood. So now this whole group is added to that memory. Rich has his own memories of this place as he grew up not too far from here. I whisper to him as we are straggling behind the others, "See that girl, she is 'the one.'" "Really?" he responds with a surprised tone. "Yup," I assure.

We all are taking turns experiencing different rides with the kids. The adults all aren't quite as thrilled about rides anymore but the kids want someone to go with them each time. The main roller coaster that I remember isn't here anymore, that's a bummer. Even more of a bummer is that they don't have the Rock 'N' Roll ride either named "Space Odyssey." It was an indoor ride that just kind of went up and down around a circle. What made it cool is that it was pitch black inside and they blared rock music and flashed light all around. There are new things to enjoy though. Gabi and I get on the new ride that just drops you from a real high height. It is actually on the scary end but Gabi shows no fear and makes me look wimpy, all in good fun of course.

The kids are having a blast but Ivy's legs are tired so I pick her up and carry her over to the snack vender. We get some ice cones and pretzels and head over to a picnic area. To our demise it starts to rain so we all head over to a roofed edge of a building. Gabi loves unorthodox weather, so I decide to grab her and pull her out into the rain. Her reaction is "what's happening?" "Let's dance," I say, and we start dancing. With a huge smile on her face we salsa, we spin and twirl. Meanwhile the others, along with many strangers, are staying dry and watching two weirdos enjoying life to the fullest. Rich got video evidence of the situation. Once the sun comes back out, we resume normal activities, how boring.

Amili, Blaine, and the kids are ready to head out but we all decide to grab some grub before departure. So now Rich, Gabi, and I remain. We have these full-park/all-day passes and haven't enjoyed the water park yet so that's what we set out to do. This is all new and amazing to me. We go into the respective locker/changing rooms to change. My eyes probably dilate when I see Gabi come out of the locker room in a bikini top and little shorts. She throws her arms up in excitement as if to say "I'm ready!" My eyes take a second look at Rich as I don't think I've ever seen him shirtless before. He is monstrously hairy. We head to the giant slide first. They have these big tubes that you grab and carry up the stairs with you. You can go in pairs or single. We switch it up and take a few runs but now Gabi and I are going tandem. Instead of carrying the tube by hand like normal people, we wrap it around the pair of us and penguin our way up the steps. In addition to the slide we also enjoy a big wave creator and a lazy river, which may be the greatest of all. Floating around on a tube just chilling alongside my soul mate and one of my dearest friends really puts me at ease. The mixture of the exhaustion from the activities and the contentedness with my life provides the most surreal earthly heaven feeling as I float along.

We change up, exit the park, and are trying to decide what to do for dinner. We decide on going to Hoss's. I notice my phone is dying and Rich worries about losing contact since we are driving separately, so I just give him Gabi's number. Gabi and I get in the car with the intention to follow Rich. Gabi mutters, "That was weird." "What?" I respond. "You just gave Rich my number," she says. I say, "Oh, I'm sorry, I didn't think it would be a big deal, it's just Rich, he is a good dude." I guess the action was much to her chagrin, although it's hard to tell because she rarely uses an alternate tone.

We flop into the restaurant, all kinds of tired, and just start philosophizing. Rich sounds so much different right now compared to what I am used to. He has a lower pitch, and less humor coming out of him, but at the same time sounds intelligent and professional. Rich and I recently got reunited so we tell Gabi the story of his ex-wife and how she prevented us from being friends for many years. Our conversation subject changes and Rich asks Gabi what she sees in her future. She describes finishing up school and her desire to start running an Occupational Therapy service in a series of hut-like buildings possibly out near the beach or a lake. I am thinking it would be like a compound of Quonset-like huts except built in a more elegant fashion than how that resonates. Each hut would concentrate on a particular line of therapies. It's a rather intuitive and clever ambition to have. Hopefully I'll be by her side helping push her along.

Back in our neck of the woods I see Gabi take an old tree that has been carved into a giant stringed instrument and create music. The cello makes an impressive tune at the hand of a multi-talented angel. She lets me try and I cannot even achieve proper tone. It takes a certain skill and a certain pressure to make it sound off correctly. She transitioned from violin to cello because apparently the violin didn't resonate well with its high pitch right near the ears. This girl plays four instruments and speaks two languages. She gets perfect grades in school, in addition to working part-time and still finding time for me, usually a couple times per week. How does she do it?

We visit the Great Frederick Fair and pet some Llamas. Are these llamas, or alpacas?

July 30 is drawing day at Gabi's house. Her cousin Holly is invited and beats me to the house. I meet her and she is a young pretty lady, wearing a floral dress. She is talkative, and has high energy. She looks similar to Gabi probably because they are both half Filipinas. Holly seems a lot more mainstream though, and definitely not the type of individual I would normally hang out with. I wouldn't dare tell Gabi that though.

Gabi gets all the supplies out and we settle onto the quaintly decorated patio area for art day. Gabi has some silly coloring books so we start there. We are sharing wine and it is such a pleasant atmosphere. Holly randomly beseeches me a question, "Where did you guys meet?" She thinks she is smart, trying to catch me or something. I respond, "at The Frederick Café." "Liar," she quickly replies, "you met online." Technically the first place we met in person was at that café so it wasn't actually a lie. I attempt to explain myself but she starts blabbing off to Gabi. Ok, I already don't exactly like Gabi's cousin Holly. The two of them are very close and although very different it's good for them to have a bond. Holly is kind of crazy though. She is a divorcee and is currently engaged to a man she just met a couple months ago. They actually met online too. I don't really get her. She claims that she's been through marriage and knows what to look for now.

We all continue coloring and I move on to free drawing. I bet Gabi and I look cute to Holly because we are giggly and keep tickling each other. I am now looking at a picture of Gabi and I on my phone that we took at National Harbor so I can draw it. The weird pelicans I colored in before impress the ladies a bit, but this portrait of a loving couple should impress more, that is if I concentrate. I really don't have much time and it turns out ok but it could be so much better. Gabi likes it and says "wow, no one has ever drawn me before." She will probably be the subject of many drawings to come being that she is the apple of my eye. I do caricatures of her all the time. I have multiple doodles all over my documents at work. Cartoon Gabi is simple to draw: square jaw, round forehead, 60's style neck length hair, Asian curvy eyes, button nose, a big smile with a long smooth bottom lip, tall narrow teeth, and her iconic beauty mark. Cartoon me includes a pointy bald head, squinty eyes under a dominant brow, big bridge nose with round blob at end, a small slit for a mouth, and monkey ears. I do a caricature of the two of us here too. Gabi looks so stereotypically Asian in this particular one, it's hilarious. In reality she is beautiful. I have comprehended her celebrity lookalike and it is a mixture between two: Aubrey Plaza, and Kina Grannis. Gabi may share some personality traits with them as well, from the awkwardness of Plaza to the sweetness of Grannis.

We all hop into Holly's car for a random roll. She notices my firebird and mentions that she used to have one. I purposefully and arrogantly remark, "was yours as nice as mine?" "No," she replies, "only one of the headlights worked properly." They are flip ups and some of these cars do have issues with one not retracting like it should. They then wink at you. I hope Holly understands that I will take care of Gabi much like the way I take care of my vehicles. Along the drive I notice Holly's huge engagement ring. She says, "for your information, this is 2 carats." She also says, "for your information Gabi wears a size 5." "Yeah, I know, it goes 5-5-7-7-7," I said. I look back at Gabi and smile, and she mutters, "I actually don't think my thumb is a 7." Either way I know 5 is the number to remember and it's good to know what a 2-carat diamond looks like. I honestly can't imagine Gabi would want something that big and gaudy.

They are looking for a sunflower field to frolic in and they find it. Hastily parked, the girls run out into the field. I am sitting here in the car feeling like a third wheel but decide to get out and look around a little. I am glad Gabi makes so much fun out of everything. I find her and take a snapshot of her with a giant sunflower. She is so dear. We make it back to the house and Holly leaves.

Liz gets home and we exchange pleasantries. I mention I met Holly and she is crazy. Liz asks, "what did she do?" I respond, "nothing in particular, she just has an interesting personality." I think there is some kind of weird dynamics with that side of the family. Apparently, Holly's brother Chris doesn't even talk to Gabi or them anymore. But that is territory I don't understand yet.

Next Gabi and I head out for a walk and she presents a pathway in the community with some trees, benches, and other interesting decorations that her father actually built. Cobydean is a big part of the community in addition to his work in the medical field. Liz also works in the medical field and maybe they expect Gabi to follow. Her parents paid her way through her Bachelor's degree and she feels a good bit of pressure from them. I tell her she is lucky they paid for her schooling as I still have big student loans to pay. She mentions she thinks her dad is happy that she has finally decided on a career path with occupational therapy. We sit and continue to chat on the bench about family and life. I ask her what annoys her the most at home. She replies, "when I am asked to do chores while I am trying to play the piano, I hate doing dishes." We have that last part in common but I find it funny that a 27-year-old gets asked to do chores. She also gets a little annoyed with her father's right-wing agenda and attitude. She loves her parents though because they are always there for her. It's night time and it's time to leave. Gabi walks me to my car and hugs me. "I love you," and "I love you too" proceeds, followed by a lingering hug. This is the longest hug ever; we simply don't want to let go of each other. This is an amazing feeling to have.

When I finally arrive at home, I pray to God and thank him for his grace and this relationship. I also ask him to help give Gabi strength when it comes to the family dynamics she spoke about and to help her along her path of career and schooling and everything else. I have nothing to ask for personally, I have everything I want, and the future is wide open and so promising.

- Chapter 13 -
My Sneak

It's Saturday August 5th and I am home alone having a few drinks. It doesn't really bother me to be alone doing the *George Thorogood*. I don't have too many friends, but I do have one awesome girlfriend. I once told Gabi all I really need is her and maybe one other close friend. I do wish Gabi was here right now though as I am pretty bored. I will see her tomorrow at this football picnic we are going to for the Hitmen, which is a team in an 8 man league I play for. It is the end of the season banquet-like thing for us. Anyway, what to do? I guess I will surf the internet. This is sort of my go to thing when I am alone or bored. I could masturbate, but to me it's less fun while intoxicated, and I am not as horny under the influence either. Yeah, that is the opposite of most people. I am curious about those nude pictures that Gabi mentioned exist on the web. Surely, they won't be easily accessible. What if I go to Bing and turn off "safe-search?" Here I am typing in her name: Gabrielle Tipton. Should I hit enter? What do I want to see when I do? Bam, no turning back now.

Heart pounding, I view the results. Surely, she won't appear here. But what is that first picture? It's a naked woman. Oh No! Holy cow! It's her! There she is, topless, splayed out on a bed, head turned to the side with an oddly confident smirk, and absolutely perfect breasts. I can't believe it. Not only is it her but it is done up like a magazine cover with her name and hometown graphically added to the image. What am I looking at? What have I done? My heart has dropped and my throat is clogged. I quickly shut down my computer and get up and pace. I pace and I pace in utter regret. I did not want to see that. Why did I do it? I am disgusted with myself. Maybe God is punishing me for my impure thoughts. I once thought to myself that it'd be cool to see someone that I knew naked on the internet, maybe an old classmate or something. I guess I got what I wanted, but this is extreme. I don't want it God, I am sorry, please let me go back in time one hour, please. They say, "careful what you wish for." This takes the cake for the meaning of that sentiment. It is horrible. What do I do now? Do I tell Gabi? I lay in bed and I start to cry. Does Gabi even know that it is the first picture that shows up when you type in her name? I am getting very little sleep tonight. I will know what to do in the morning.

Never before had waking up been so scary. I know this day may be uncomfortable, but I know what I need to do. I need to confess to Gabi the atrocity I performed last night. If my mother has instilled anything in me, it is that honesty is of the utmost importance. I also know that if this is the girl that I am to end up with for the long haul, I need to start it off with complete transparency. The reasoning for the truthful words is dignified, and that action will speak louder than the words themself. I want to enjoy the day with her first though and will save the talk for later.

Gabi meets me at my house and we ride up to the football picnic together. I am looking at her and admiring her, savoring the moments I can. I try to act normal but I wonder if she can tell I am distracted. At the pavilion some of the other tough guys are scattered around but not a whole lot of them showed. I introduce Gabi to a few of them and we grab a bite and sit down. The location is in a little park so after we eat, we decide to walk around. We find a curious stone pathway by some neatly groomed shrubbery. We follow the path and it leads to an ornamental bench. This spot is quite romantic with the aroma of flowery love. We sit and hold hands. In complete privacy we are surrounded by beautiful trees. I think to myself that this could be a nice place for a marriage proposal. Next, we find a little monkey gym and hang around for a bit. We catch each other's eyes and I feel like she knows something is amiss. This is the most awkward-feeling day. The picnic is winding down and people are heading out so we decide to as well.

We arrive back at my house and before we pop out of the car, I ask Gabi, "can we talk?" In sort of an odd, quick, and almost excitable manner she replies, "sure let's talk" I say, "okay, so…" then she suggests we get out and have a walk while we talk. So, we are walking up my street and I start my confession. I begin by informing her that I was drinking last night, and wasn't thinking clearly, but was curious. I tell her I did an internet search and I found her picture. I tell her I am very sorry and I hope she won't leave me over it. Then she begins to laugh. I don't understand the reaction and I demand, "Why are you laughing? This is pretty serious." She responds with, "I don't know but this seems like something I just cannot get away from." I proceed to tell her that I feel shame and I was wrong to invade her privacy like that but also that I believe in telling the truth. She agrees with my sentiments. She is keeping a poker face on the subject. She is not one to wear her emotions on her sleeve. I start to realize that she probably laughed earlier as a mechanism to mask the situation's seriousness. I myself frequently turn to humor as a vice to get by uncomfortable situations.

We make it back to my house and we go down into our fort. I am so happy she is not running away from me. We chat some more down here and I give her some more details of how last night went down. I inform her I do not want to be able to see naked pictures of my girlfriend on the internet. I apologize again and we calculate ways to force the image to be taken down. Surely, we can request Bing to take it down. She informs me that it does not show up on Google searches. She says this is giving her some sad thoughts. Understandable. It is about that time for her to head back home and we are just holding each other in the kitchen. I never want to let go. She finally says, "I love you and goodnight." She raised the pitch of her voice at the end of the statement to sound more like a question. So, I answer her: "I love you and goodnight."

The next day I research and discover ways to inform Bing.com of inappropriate and/or illegal content. I then email Gabi links to help her out in getting this deleted from the internet. She responds saying that she put in the request but she is not going to go digging around on the internet for the different places the images could be. She wants to put this behind her. Tuesday, I receive a text from her saying, "Hey, this situation is starting to hit me in a harder way and I need a few days to process, let's meet up Friday evening to talk." I respond, "does this mean I am not allowed to talk to you for three days?" She answers: "I am not telling you what to do but I really need the space right now." I end the text exchange with, "understood, see you Friday." This will be the first time in our entire relationship that we will go without talking. We have texted every day since we initially met. We always exchange good morning and goodnight texts. This will be a real challenge for me.

This dull pain, this lingering fear, this anxiety, I must hide it from my coworkers. I sit in front of a computer all day at work and very few people pass by. I almost feel like breaking down. I am usually amongst the last people to leave work like today. This is good so that no one can see me damn near tear up as I walk out to my car. I have so many feelings to release right now and I have a minimal support system so I will have to write it down in letter form that I may or may not give to Gabi.

Dear Gabrielle,

I have never loved someone the way I do you. I have that deep emotional attachment, I love and respect who you are, and I want to give you my love. I love you fully, full throttle, I am in love with you. That is why this situation is super difficult for me. It's hard for me to understand why I did what I did, and it was super hard for me to tell you because I didn't want to hurt you. I disrespected you when I invaded something you already opened your feelings to me about, and with great trust. I broke that trust and I feel like a giant piece of shit. Excuse my French.

I prayed to God: Dear God, you have sent me an angel, and I have hurt her. Please God if I am just like the past men in Gabi's life, please keep me away from her. Give Gabi the strength to endure the situation. Guide her to happy places. God, give me the strength to cope with my emotions, my demons, and the outcome of this hardship. Amen.

I know I am not like those men in your past! I am better! I am real! I'm sure you noticed I'm a crybaby, but my tears are real. This is not a red flag that you are ignoring. This is just a mistake. This is my confident/angry paragraph.

I want to make you a priority. Because I believe in "I am third" which means God first, loved ones second, and I am third.

I can't take you for granted. You've already shown me more joy than I ever imagined possible. You make me happy with every little thing you do. Even the way you swing your arms makes me smile. You are so thoughtful (in a good way). You give me respect. You are the most cordial girl I have ever met, and so caring too. I can see your efforts. I cannot let you go. As my cousin Preston said "If you find a good girl, hold on." That's exactly what I plan on doing with you. You make me a better person; you make me realize a lot of things. You are helping me get closer to God. I need God, and I feel like I need you.

I hope that you will be able to look at me the same way, the same way you did before with a twinkle in your eye and a gorgeous smile. That smile is infectious. I just want to make you smile. My cry: My error only took one minute. Please don't let that one minute affect our entire future. I am still the same guy I was before, who wants to make you feel good, who loves you, and wants you to be happy. I have plans to do nice things for you, and these thoughts are the only things helping me feel happy and sane right now.

This paragraph does not start with the word "I."

I know what it feels like to have your hopes brought up so high and to just be dropped, let down. I know what it feels like to be broken hearted, and I never want you to feel like that. I hope that if you thought about leaving me that you would first talk to me about it. Please don't make any rash decisions. Maybe you should just go to Spain and enjoy yourself and we can talk more when you return. I feel like I put you in a frame of mind and it will be harder for you to enjoy yourself in Spain, and that makes me sad. I wonder what your "sad thoughts" were that you were having in the fort. It really upsets me to cipher that I may have set you back some steps in your healing process. Reversely you have sent me on a giant leap forward as far as hope goes. I feel awful because I wanted to be the one that helps you forget about your past. After seeing what I saw, I have gained a greater disgust for pornography, and I hereby vow to never look at porn. I might even need to quit drinking. A sober self wouldn't have done this. I wasn't thinking about honor, I wasn't thinking about respect, I wasn't thinking about consequences. It was a split-second decision that is sort of haunting me. I don't know why I looked it up, but I did, and I would not hide anything from you because you deserve that. But that was not you in that picture anymore, that is someone from the past, I don't know that person. I am learning a lot from all of this. I am still growing as a person; there are just a few more pieces of the puzzle.

I don't foresee myself doing anything worse. All this pain I am feeling is pain that I have brought upon myself. Then I think about how your pain must be even worse. It isn't fair, because you have done nothing wrong. It's a horrible feeling to know that you tried your very best to love and respect someone, but then you still hurt them. I think about this often and I break down, going back to the feeling of "I'm not good enough for you," and wondering if I deserve you. I'm struggling with self-confidence and self-worth. I'm feeling like you deserve someone better. I fear this could scar you. I fear losing your respect and admiration. I feel shame. I'm struggling substantially but "I have set the LORD always before me; because he is at my right hand, I shall not be shaken" (Psalm 16:8 ESV). God has always given me everything I needed and in perfect timing, and I know he will here too. We just have to realize God's love and God's Grace!!

"But they who wait for the LORD shall renew their strength; they shall mount up with wings like eagles; they shall run and not be weary; they shall walk and not faint" (Isaiah 40:31 ESV).

Maybe God is testing us? And maybe our relationship will become ever better, stronger, and deeper than before. To know we can keep hanging on after trying times will be a happy victory and a proud accomplishment for us. I'm trying to stay positive, because what we have is a good thing. I want to show you what real love is!

I understand it'll take you time to forgive me as you are still forgiving yourself. I am working on forgiving myself as well. If God can forgive us, why can't we? – Book of Ray

I hope you can think about all the beautiful moments we've shared, the warm embraces, and the awesome connection we have. I want to continue to love you the way I always have, because you have done so much for me that you don't even know about. You are always there for me. You build me up when I am down. You make me laugh like no one has ever done before. I relate to so many of your thoughts. We have so much fun and you make me feel so alive. Thank you for doing all the things you do. I thank God that we met, you are a beautiful blessing. You are the most beautiful and amazing girl in the world! I truly believe this! I thank God that he gave you the strength and the courage to open up to me and start dating again. You have made great strides. With God on your side you can continue to progress your emotions and your wisdom. You are a very strong woman. I see a tremendous light in you.

I don't want you to have this pain, I don't want you to be constantly reminded, and that makes me feel like you'd be better off without me. I bet there is so much going on in your brain right now that I am not aware of. I hope that you can share that with me so I can better understand. Your past is done. I am so sorry that it happened to you. It is a terrible thing, and I am so sorry that you still have to live with it. It's no good to hate. "Let all bitterness and wrath and anger and clamor and slander be put away from you, along with all malice. Be kind to one another, tenderhearted, forgiving one another, as God in Christ forgave you" (Ephesians 4:31-32 ESV). But I have built up a great deal of hate for your ex. I also hate what I have done, because your past doesn't matter to me and shouldn't matter to us. We are new people, and we have built a great new relationship, one with inspiring future prospects.

My feelings have been up and down and I have come up with many conclusions in my head as you may be able to tell by this sporadic letter, but I don't know if any of them are right. What I know is I love you but I am human. I am not magical. I am a regular guy, who tries hard, who wants to walk with God, who wants to be with you, and help you reach your goals as well. I would do ANYTHING for you. First thing I need to do is to earn your trust back. If we can get over this hurdle, I know we can conquer any obstacle. I believe this was meant to be. I believe in you, and I believe in us. Te amo, excuse my Spanish.

Love,
Ray

Wednesday and Thursday the worrisome feeling in my abdomen and the suspense in the waiting tear into me some more. This is the same feeling I get every time a break up happens. I am 50% sure that will be the result here as well. I lay in bed and I pray some more. My mind continues to run like hell.

In this moment as I lie in bed something new is happening. I feel like there is a wave of energy going through me. It is a power I never felt before, and it is completely erasing my fear. Suddenly I am no longer worried, all pain has washed away. I know this is an act from God telling me that everything will be ok. I look forward to seeing Gabi tomorrow!

Friday morning, I immediately receive a text from Gabi saying that she doesn't want to drag it out any longer but she believes that everything will be ok! This to me proves God's existence all over again. I felt the proof last night and this text confirms it! I am not even surprised to see this text; I knew everything would be ok. It did take a couple days of pain and prayer, but God worked his magic!

We meet up outside the Dunkin Donuts in Mt Airy. She has a print out of her thoughts and feelings. As we head over to the picnic area, I whip out my print out. We laugh at the fact that we both did this. We sit down and she initiates conversation. She starts off saying that it's somewhat of an ongoing process but is assuring in her statement, "I forgive you." I squeeze her and kiss her on the forehead. I tell her that I never had that feeling that I had for the past couple days and still ended up with a girlfriend. She proceeds to read off some of the stuff she wrote down but won't share all of it with me. There are a couple of questions she has for me but doesn't want to ask them now. She says that I took away something that could have been enjoyed on our wedding night (seeing her nude body for the first time). She adds, "If we ever get there." She goes on and reveals a good bit of downtrodden feelings but ultimately believes our season isn't over and is still full of joy and wonder. She added Bible scripture to her writing as well. I share that I have Bible scripture in my write up and we share another laugh. We are so similar. I go ahead and just read off my entire letter to her. I have nothing to hide.

- Chapter 14 -
Engagement

Gabi is so beautiful on the inside and just as much on the outside. I have to be better for her, she deserves nothing less than my best. After we conquered what we have, I know we are meant to be together. I understand now why God made me wait so long before. He was saving me for Gabi. The way her story and mine meet together is the epitome of perfect timing, God's timing. I told Gabi I wasn't going to ask her to marry me anytime soon but it's starting to become an idea for me. I need to wait and make sure she is in the same boat. I want to hear her say "I love you" in a more confident manner.

I'm looking at engagement rings now. We have discussed the "pyramid scheme" of relationships: how we get closer to each other as we move up the triangle getting closer to God. I think I'd like to get her a ring that reflects that concept. So, I am thinking three stones: the big one in the middle representing God and the two little ones on either side representing her and I. I know she likes dainty jewelry and doesn't have a gold or silver preference. That is about all I know. I go on to Kay Jewelers website and research up. You can build your own ring on the website. So, I find a band that looks decent and try to pick out a good center rock. The band is a thousand dollars itself and the diamonds have a much higher range. There are many aspects that go into the diamond: clarity, size, cut, and color. I find one that is about 0.8 Karats with decent stats on the other variables. The total cost is about four thousand dollars. I better save up.

I have ordered a universal roof rack that I intend to install on Gabi's car. I also ordered the "J" bars that are designed to carry kayaks or canoes on the roof. She wouldn't have to stuff her boat inside of her tiny car any more. I pay her a visit and install them for her. This is my love language; I am performing an "act of service." I just want to make Gabi's life easier. I am not too sure about the quality of the structure I purchased though. It doesn't exactly seem like it will remain sound on the roof. It simply anchors around the window ledge. I figure we can re-evaluate it when Gabi returns from her trip to Spain.

It is Monday night, August 14, and Gabi is leaving for her two week Spain adventure tomorrow morning. Her parents are out of town and she has invited me over. We have dinner and a movie. We stay up real late as we can't keep our hands off each other. We cuddle and we kiss, sometimes softly, other times more aggressively. I tell her, "The way you touch me and the way you kiss me, it tells me you will probably be really good in bed." She responds with "I could say the same thing," which is something she says time and again. I guess I often take the words right out of her mouth, and I hope I take her breath away like she does mine. My hands continue to caress her all over and hers all over mine. She is reaching her hand up from my hip and across my abs. Her elbow touches my fully erect penis. I don't know if she is doing this on purpose. I don't think she would be one to tease me. My shirt disappears and we move to different areas of the den, mouths still interlocked. We are sitting on the ground, legs wrapped around each other. I pull her hips in closer. Our groins don't conjoin but I want them to so badly. I know I am touching her butt a little bit here and there which is a no-no but I surmise it is ok with today's passion. I say "I want you." She says, "I could conquer." We remain a good girl and boy though, redress, and nap. I feel like we just made love, and even though intercourse didn't happen, it still feels blissful. The sun has risen and It's time for me to leave before her parents arrive and she heads out for her flight.

Gabi made me download an application called WhatsApp so it's easier to communicate from different parts of the world. I can stay updated on her safety and her adventures. I didn't need her to stay in contact with me while she enjoyed her trip but she insisted. She makes me feel important.

The big news today August 17, 2017 is a terrorist attack in Barcelona, Spain. I am at work talking to my boss about it and apparently someone drove a van through the city running over people. I believe that is exactly where Gabi is right now. I must contact her and see if she is ok. Turns out she was very close to the incident, maybe a few blocks away when it happened. When everyone was alerted to the happening, they all scattered and ran for cover into nearby establishments. Gabi and her entourage attempted to talk to the business owner of the place they ducked into using Spanish. Come to find out, the people there spoke English too. They allowed the crew to stay there in safety until the emergency situation was over. It was a very hectic and scary day for her, but I am glad she is alright.

I receive a letter in the mail from Gabi that she mailed before leaving for Spain. It reads as follows:

(paraphrased)

Dear Ray,

There's no doubt in my mind that God brought our lives together for added joys. Every day your steadfastness makes me feel safe. You respect me and are nothing short of a gentleman. You have brought something to life in me in a way that I have never experienced before, something I cannot explain. I know the past has no place in our future. I want to make an effort in preventing it from influencing or placing misconceptions on our relationship. This will be a challenge for me. We are working together to view each other as individuals and it feels real and genuine. I want to continue to see our relationship prosper. All of your effort, everything you've done knowingly and some things perhaps not, has redefined everything I thought I knew about love and life. I want to thank you for being so patient and accepting. I want to thank you for just being you. This foundation we're building is strong because we are seeking God's will. There is so much beauty in this season of our lives. There is so much hope and I want to hold on to these memories and savor them forever. I don't want to take a single moment for granted!

Love,
Gabi

With the letter is also a bunch of Bible scripture about relationships.

-Pray that God will give you wisdom and help you think clearly.
"Teach us to number our days, that we may gain a heart of wisdom" (Psalm 90:12 NIV).

-Pray that God will help you be faithful to your friendship during times of adversity.
"Therefore, as God's chosen people, holy and dearly loved, clothe yourselves with compassion, kindness, humility, gentleness and patience. Bear with each other and forgive one another if any of you has a grievance against someone. Forgive as the Lord forgave you" (Colossians 3:12-13 NIV).

-Pray that God will deepen your relationships.
"Above all, love each other deeply, because love covers over a multitude of sins" (1 Peter 4:8 NIV).

-Pray that God will help you love well.
"Be completely humble and gentle; be patient, bearing with one another in love. Make every effort to keep the unity of the Spirit through the bond of peace" (Ephesians 4:2-3 NIV).

-Pray that God will help you communicate with compassion.
"A gentle answer turns away wrath, but a harsh word stirs up anger" (Proverbs 15:1 NIV).

-In your broken relationships, pray for healing and forgiveness.
"Be kind and compassionate to one another, forgiving each other, just as in Christ God forgave you" (Ephesians 4:32 NIV).

I love the fact that she sent me this. She is so smart and has so much integrity and wisdom. She makes me want to be a better person but at the same time makes me feel accepted and loved.

In a clockwise pattern a rental car full of four Americans visit many of the cities in Spain. Gabi, her best friend Suzanna, Sonja, and Brenden visit the major landmarks in a systematic way. They take pictures at every chance and Gabi has sent some of them to me. They are pretty breathtakingly amazing pictures. I really wish I was on this trip with her. She has been there about a week now and we decide to do a video chat through WhatsApp. I get to see her beautiful face but I also get to meet her best friend for the first time. I am at my home desk and my nieces are here. Ivy had just gotten a bath and runs in wanting to see what I am doing. She is only wearing a towel so I pick her up and say "You're naked! Put on some clothes!" Ivy asks who is that on the screen and I say, "it's my beautiful girlfriend!" Suzanne gets to see her as well. I talk to Suzanne for a bit and tell her I have heard a lot of good things about her and want to thank her for being such a blessing in Gabi's life. It felt awkward but I felt it was necessary to say. Plus, I want to try to make a good first impression on Gabi's best friend. I feel like women value what their friends think immensely. Suzanne tells me that she has never seen Gabi smile so much. This assures me that I really am doing good things for Gabi as well, and that I am affecting her in a positive way.

Finally cleaning out my book bag that I brought along last time I saw Gabi; I notice something unexpected. Gabi had written a note for me and hid it in my bag. It reads as follows:

(paraphrased)

Dear Ray (To my caring, thoughtful, loving, wonderful, funny, talented man)
Our dates 1-12
You know how you said you wrote down what we did? I did too! But I wanted to share it with you and I thout— wow...

can't spell... I haven't slept yet. You're sleeping but I'm awake! It's like 0830. ANYWAY! I thought now would be a good time. Read one a day... or all of them. Up to you.

Love you!! Gabi.

This part is hand written on the outside. Inside is typed on lined notebook paper.

(paraphrased)

To Ray and myself,

My time with Ray has been filled to the brim with hope, spring, and wondrous adventures. The fun-filled happiness of these days makes it hard to imagine life in any other capacity. How long I have been without this joy, this added spice to life. God has been an unfailing and ever-present God, molding me in preparation for His plan.

I don't want these wonderful memories to slip away so here are my thoughts, feelings, and memories of our shared adventures. It can be a way to reminisce and remember where it all began...

Then it proceeds to list out each of our first 12 dates in poetic paragraph form. It warms my heart and moistens my eyes.

Not only do I find this letter in my bag but also scattered around are a bunch of small notes each with simple loving expressions or a quote on them. This is them:

- Thank you for being there to let me vent and process my feelings. (paraphrased)

- "Faith is the art of holding on to things in spite of your changing mood and circumstances." – C.S. Lewis

- Even if I don't appreciate the car world the way you do, I'll always appreciate the time, energy, creativity, and hard work you put in. Thank you for making my car look so awesome! Perhaps we'll even share this interest someday. (paraphrased)

- The bewildered smile you've placed on my face is forever filled with hope. (paraphrased)

- When we kiss my senses are overtaken completely by your warmth. Nothing exists but us and our own music in those moments. (paraphrased)

- "Our weakness is a vessel for it is power and our flaws a canvas for his grace." – Unknown

- "To love at all is to be vulnerable." – C.S. Lewis

- "For the Spirit God gave us does not make us timid, but gives us power, love and self-discipline" (2 Timothy 1:7 NIV).

- "For God is not a God of disorder but of peace—as in all the congregations of the Lord's people" (1 Corinthians 14:33 NIV).

Gabi has landed back home from her trip. She expresses missing me and how the last few days were rough. She claims that she gets annoyed after spending too much time with people, and eventually gets irritated with everyone to some degree. I really hope she won't feel that way about me someday. It doesn't seem like she would, considering she's never really argued or presented irritation with me. She is always full of joy and hugs. She gathered a bunch of little tidbits together as gifts for me. I don't think she realizes how much I appreciate her. So, I am sitting in her room trying strange Spanish candy.

Cobydean was driving Gabi's car around while she was in Spain. The car is technically his, and not hers. The rack that I had installed fell off somewhere along the road. I should have warned about my feelings of that rack being insecure. Liz suggests giving me money for it, but I insist she doesn't. What I do instead, is purchase a higher quality one and Gabi and I install it together in the rain. She couldn't care less that it is raining and says she actually likes washing her car while it is raining. That seems odd but at the same time intuitive because you can use the rain water instead of hose water, and since you are using soap, perhaps rain spots won't appear. I will have to test out the theory some time.

Keeping with my obsession over cars I suggest we perform an oil change on her car together. Gabi has interest in being able to do it herself so I decide to teach her. In my garage we raise the car on jack stands and wrench off the nut for the oil flow. We find the filter and with my special tool we yank it off too. I am content that Gabi is eager to be doing this with me, but in the end, she comes to the conclusion that it may be one thing she cannot do by herself. Her independence lost the battle this time. I do love her independent nature though. I also love her willingness to get down and dirty with me.

I'm meeting more of Gabi's family at the celebration of her father's birth. On the way over I purchase some party horns, primarily for the young cousins that will be in attendance. I meet the kids, their parents, and Gabi's grandmother. I must really be in now that I pretty much met everybody! I play with the kids a little then it's dinner time. I am sitting between Gabi and Grandma. Oops, maybe it would be best if I didn't put my hand on Gabi's leg in this situation. After the meal it's time for cake and I don't want to be rude so I try a piece. I have a distaste for cake and this particular cake doesn't hinder my opinion. Grandma baked it and I don't want her to see me grimacing so I turn away. Why can't I just stand there poker-faced like a normal person?

Pickleball is on the agenda so Cobydean and the posse all head down to the playground tennis court. Cobydean is super into the sport and plays in some kind of league tournaments. Gabi and I team up against the cousins. Cobydean is refereeing.

Team *Rabi* wins! I pick Gabi up and spin her around in celebration in a whimsical manner. It's a lot of fun, and easier with the professional direction Cobydean gives us. We head back to the house and the kids are shooting these helicopter spinning devices into the air. I am glad everyone enjoyed themselves. When it's time for everyone to head out I just stand there awkwardly not knowing how to be normal.

Hanging out in the den on our who-knows-what-number-date-it-is now, some of Gabi's friends join us. Ashley and Tim reappear and a friend I've yet to meet named Shanna joins. She has cute freckles, is a little taller than the others, and seems the shyest and sweetest. She might be my favorite amongst Gabi's friends. We are all just hanging out playing some games. When it's time for the guests to leave each girl gives me a hug. This I did not expect, but hey I don't mind. When Gabi's mom initially hugged me a long time ago, I had the same awkward feeling. I don't think she has ever hugged me since that first time. I wonder if Gabi relayed my comment to her. I didn't mean I didn't want any more hugs. I am probably thinking too much. I do think too much. Gabi and I chill some more and talk about her friends. She mentions that Suzanne was really impressed with me and says that she is "smitten." I respond, "Well then I overshot, I only want her to like me, I want you to be smitten." She says, "I am." I grab her, squeeze her tight and mutter, "mmm, I'm too much for you." I ask if she thinks we could be together forever and she says she thinks so. At night's end I hear the most soothing sound: "I love you," followed by "so much."

I want Gabi in every way imaginable. She shows me how concrete a relationship can be when both parties try. She teaches me so much and I am growing so much because of her. She shows me how happy life can be, and it's at a level I never knew existed. My emotions are out of control. I am writing a poem.

"Desire"

Craving your touch and
Craving your aroma
My senses are tingly
My nerves on fire
I want you so bad
My eyes damp with desire

Fulfilling my dreams and
Fulfilling my persona
My limbs are shaky
Hoping for a better life
I love you so much
Need to make you my wife

Never felt it before
Never knew it could be
A passion so strong
Want to hold you so tight
Must draw you in closer
I could kiss you all night

The sounds of your whisper
The sounds of your laughter
My emotions un-controlled
Chills up my spine
Happiness to last forever
Delights for all time

We have talked about the possibility of learning how to swing
dance together. I think that would be a radical surprise treat for
our wedding guests: showcasing our talents. I didn't mention
the wedding part to her. I have to buy her a ring. I am heading to
the bank for a loan. I want to get a personal loan in the amount
of $10,000. Not only do I want to get a ring but I also want to
purchase a winter car, since it is September already and there's
no possibility of driving the Firebird in the event of snow. It

would be fish-tail and insurance city. There is a Mazda Protege5 hatchback with a roof rack for sale that I could probably get for $4,000. This would be so mondo to get and we could haul kayaks on the roof and just go ahead and take the rack off of Gabi's car. It makes whistling noises as she drives down the road and I think that annoys her. Another expense in the queue is repairing my sidewalk. The City of Hagerstown doesn't make sense, they force you to pay to fix the sidewalk that they own. It is either that or we own the sidewalk but are required to keep it up to code. It's not a battle I can fight, and it will cost me $2,000. So, with a $10,000 loan I could also purchase the $4,000 engagement ring I desire to get Gabi. I am at the bank now and the loan officer reviews my situation. My credit is only at a B tier due to the co-signing I did with Matthew back when he needed help getting a car loan. I can't get one personal loan; they have to structure it as separate loans. They give me a couple options but in total it is only about 75% of what I need. Frustrated, I say "never mind" and walk out. I presume I will have to figure something else out.

It's Labor Day and we are visiting D.C. to see my brother's artwork at the "Fridge Gallery." We are also going to visit the United States Botanic Garden. Zach initially planned on meeting us in D.C. but his plans have changed. We decide to make the drive anyhow. Gabi is always up for anything and never lets anything spoil our fun. We see the botanical garden first and it is nothing less than spectacular. The Corpse Flower or Amorphophallus Titanum has bloomed this year. It only does once every four years. We missed its peak bloom but it is still interesting to see. We take a bunch of pictures and I take a picture of Gabi taking a picture. Next, it's off to Zachery Shawn Thompson's art gallery. Apparently, the entire exhibit is of his work. We are having trouble finding the place, It's back in an alley somewhere. Ah here we go: Fridge Gallery. Hold on a minute the door is locked. I thought it was supposed to be open all day. I contact Zach and he says someone should be there. I bang on the door and there is no answer. I apologize to Gabi for bringing her down here for no reason. She is remaining in a positive spirit. She just has the ability to make everything feel ok. I award her with some *squeezies* and *kissies*.

I have created a list of things to do with my love in the near future. We might visit Frontier Town with my buddy Rich and his girlfriend on Sept 17th. Dicky may be getting a rental cabin on the beach, that would be fun. Gabi and I have scheduled a camping trip September 23rd with My cousin Preston and his wife Stacy. We intend to visit my mom. We want to go kayaking, hike the Appalachian trail, hike the Billy Goat trail, and visit a chlorine infused body of water. I want to dine her at Nick's Airport Inn, which is a fancy restaurant here in Hagerstown, and do the Supreme Buffet. We could do a "Battle of the Sexes" game night, a "Dark Side of Oz" night, and a vinyl record night. We might go to the antique store in Boonsboro. We've talked about doing yoga together and stargazing. I really want to go snowboarding with her. It is something she enjoys as well and it has been many moons since I've been able to have a partner or friend of any type joining me on the mountain. My idea is to possibly do my proposal up there in the snow. I would wait until she falls then I would fall down in front of her accidentally-on-purpose. As I am perfectly positioned on my knees, I would then pull out the ring. I would want no one to be around to see, because in a moment like that I think she'd be most comfortable in privacy. The excitement of the opportunity may be overwhelming but I can't imagine ever wanting to ask anyone else that big question. I frequently fantasize about Gabi walking down the aisle with a big white lacey dress and red flower in her hair. I imagine her giant smile as she stands before me, and I start to tear up. I admire and respect every ounce of her soul with every ounce of mine. I love her so much she'll never know. I imagine us writing our owns vows and me inevitably saying, "Gabrielle Dian Tipton, I will love you forever." I know God has done his work with this relationship and I thank him for sending me an angel.

A corn field is the scenery of the crisp and comfortable Mid-September day. Gabi whimsically finds a divot in the maize maze hidden from society and pulls off the road into it. We proceed to transform her car into an RV by putting the rear seat down and opening the hatch. We lay a blanket down and lie under the stars. We caress and kiss, chatting and snuggling. We take in the beauty of nature and the beauty of love. I don't know how much longer I can't wait without making love to the love of my life. I reach a little too far and she grabs my hand to stop me. Here I just smile at her. I am proud of her. I randomly ask her, "describe your commitment to me." "Commitment?" she replies. I say, "Yeah aren't we in a committed relationship?" She responds with, "Well yeah, that word just threw me off." I then tell her that I am committed to being a great man for her, to help push her along with her schooling and career. I basically tell her I am committed to supporting her every move. I give her a kiss between each comment. Aren't I a sweetie? Gabi expressed starting to have some frustration both with school and work so I wanted to make it clear I am here for her through it. We spend many hours relaxed in the field star gazing; it would have been easier out on the ground but it's actually a little chilly. We finally decide to head back because we are both tired. She comments: "We're just like teenagers." She is funny. I respond, "We are just so magnetic!"

It is September 14 and my dad and I are driving down to a used car dealership in Manassas, VA to buy the Mazda I have been drooling over. It is basically a little wagon with a 5-speed manual transmission, and a 4-cylinder motor. Weighing only 2,600 pounds it should also get good gas mileage. It'll be a good car for me to beat around in for a little while. I am able to swindle them down to $4,000, and with the help of Dad we are able to pay fully in cash. I owe my dad a few dollars but that is better than paying interest on a real loan. I really loathe owing anybody anything, but I am very thankful to have a loving father. He drives his car back home after we stop for a bite and I drive my newly acquired black hatchback with 94,000 miles on it home without an issue.

The Frontier Town idea went under as Rich's plans changed. Gabi and I are going to visit Holly and John in Pittsburgh this weekend instead. The two of them have gotten engaged and it is Holly's birthday this weekend so we are going to take that trip to celebrate. My brother Ralph lives right above Pittsburgh so I suggested to Gabi that we meet up with him too. She agrees so we are saving two birds with one shot of medicine. She also mentions that it will be an excuse to go back again. Gabi insists that she pays for everything this weekend. I don't really ever let her pay for anything but she is very adamant about it. I know Pittsburgh and suggest we stop out at the overlook before meeting at Holly and John's house Saturday morning. We hop in my new old car and head out. I then think and realize that this is supposed to be a weekend for Holly so I tell Gabi we will just drive by without stopping instead. I don't want to waste time. We make it up there around 11:00 am. This is John's house and Holly recently moved in with him. They met online just a few months ago and are already engaged. Holly is previously divorced and so is John. John has a very calm two-year-old daughter from his previous relationship. John seems like a really nice yet taciturn military type of guy. In fact, he is in the military and is going back on duty soon so that is why we made this trip up when we did. Holly wanted the men to meet each other before he goes away for however long it will be.

We all hang out for a little bit getting ready to head into downtown Pittsburgh. I'm putting on a fancy shirt for the occasion and it draws a comment from Holly. She directs the comment to John muttering, "He looks better than you." She said it in a manner that tells me she either didn't expect me to clean up well or she expected John to clean up better. Maybe I am reading too deep. We find a nice restaurant in Station Square which is right by the river. It has a glass wall that oversees said river. I tell them about the mystical ice rink they put up in the winter and this gives us another excuse to come back. At the end of the meal the nervous situation happens where I have to let Gabi pay for me. I don't really want the rest of the gang to know this is happening. As we head out, I suggest we go up onto the mountain and check out the overlook. I think it is the main thing you must do when you are here. They agree and I point the way up a little windy road up the side of the mountain. I point out the Monongahela incline then we stop at the Duquesne incline and overlook. This is one of the most breathtaking cityscapes that exists. It is even more awe inspiring at night. The sun is starting to decline and it'd be cool to stay and hang out but we got to head back and get the toddler to bed.

Back at the house, with the young tucked in, we set up a campfire in the yard. Here we have a few drinks and lull our souls. We get to talking about how we met our significant others and Holly comments that Gabi and I didn't even kiss for like a month. I inform her it was our fourth date and I just wanted to take things slow. Her response is, "Why?" To be honest this question stumps me, but it just felt like the noble thing to do. I feel like Holly is constantly judging me in a way. I honestly don't know how John puts up with her. I'm curious about Holly and John and how quickly it happened for them so I request the story. Holly seemingly happily obliges. The two of them lived three hours apart but Holly knew what she was looking for. She claims that she learned a lot from her previous marriage and that helped her in seeing what she really wants and needs. When they met online, she thought John would be a great match so they did a bunch of video chatting to get to know each other and to make sure all the priorities are in line for the two of them. Once they got to that point, she then decided to spend a weekend with him. I assume they slept together when they initially met in person. I refrain from bringing that up though and just smile and nod.

An ember escapes the fire pit and some flames ignite a small area of the yard. It could easily be stomped out with a foot but Gabi instinctively runs and grabs the hose and starts spraying water everywhere before she even gets back to the fire. She got everything wet and we are all having a hoot. I love this woman so much. It's time for bed and Holly introduces Gabi and I to our room. It is a guest room with two twin size beds. Holly recalls asking Gabi if she should push the beds together. I was there when Gabi responded to the text with, "Yeah in the shape of a 'T' please." Again, Gabi is hilarious. While Holly and John enjoy their king sized bed, Gabi and I snuggle in a twin sized bed for a little while. Eventually we say "I love you," and "good night," as we take to our separate beds. Neither of us enjoy sleeping in entanglement anyway. We'll have to purchase a king size bed of our own someday.

It is morning and we are off to this hay maze adventure thing for some young people's activities. This is mostly for the wee-one but the adults are enjoying it too. We play some tetherball and this is a first for me. It is hot out and I didn't want to become sweaty but here I am. There is a big tire thing you can get into and basically try to roll it down to an end line. It looks quite difficult and I am the last one attempting. I look at my phone and realize Gabi and I better get moving in order to meet with Ralph on time. I feel bad, like I am about to spoil their fun but I inform Gabi and then we say our goodbyes. We sit in the car and I look at Gabi and I feel like telling her she can stay and I will come back later to get her. But then I think that'd be weird so we head off.

We find the restaurant and head up to where my brother Ralph, his wife Amber, and their daughter Christine are. I introduce Gabi to them. She is the first of my girlfriends that they have ever met. I mention I am introducing her to our cousin Preston next weekend and intend to introduce her to our mom soon as well. Amber looks at Gabi and says, "Uh oh, are you ready for that?" Gabi's response is, "yeah," but I am sure she is either blushing or feeling sort of awkward right now. We then talk about the weirdness that is my mother for a little bit. She is so emotional and you simply can't talk to her about politics. I am sure Mom will love Gabi just the way I do. I am very excited to introduce her. Post meal we have some time to waste and are *geocaching*. I have never heard of this before and it is interesting but not something I would do on a regular basis. You use your phone to find little treasures that people have left lying around in public. It is time to head back and we say goodbye to the Thompson crew. I want to give Gabi a little manual transmission driving tutorial in the parking lot before we head out on the road. She is actually pretty good at it. I was not nearly as good when I initially started. The trip back is pretty quiet, we are both pretty tired and I get a little giddy and start giggling for no reason. Gabi is looking at me like I am crazy. She reaches out her hand and I get to hold it with a quiet sense of love warming me. As we cruise on down the misty road, I am one happy man.

Movement C
THE VOLCANO

- Chapter 15 -
Lightning

Stress is getting to Gabi I can tell. She isn't doing great in her class, which means she is probably getting a "B" when she is accustomed to getting all "A's." She is also having some issues at work and with a colleague. I think I will try to brighten up her day or week and get her some flowers. I will prove to her that I believe in us and break the flower curse. I am a godly man and got to stop the superstition. I mentioned the flower curse when we started dating and said I would never give her flowers or else she would leave me like every other girl did immediately after the gesture. I think it will be a pleasant surprise for her. I find this website that delivers to your door, so I will do that. I know she likes daisies so I will pick a cluster with some daisies. To be honest though I am not even sure what a daisy looks like. I figure it out with google and order flowers, type in her address and it should be at her door Wednesday.

Wednesday comes along and I receive an email from the flower company saying the flowers won't be ready until Friday. Now I am frustrated, I intend to see Gabi Thursday, I could have just stopped at a store and hand delivered some to her. I haven't heard much from her lately so I figure I will give her a call and reaffirm that I am all open arms and ears. Us talking on the phone is rare but here I go. She answers and says she is fine but just busy with stuff and wants to push back our meet-up until Friday. I tell her that is cool, and we can gather the necessary things and prepare for our Saturday camping and kayaking trip with my cousins Preston and Stacey. I remind her that she can talk to me anytime she needs to. I tell her I ordered something special, and tease her a little by not telling her what it is. I end the chat with, "goodbye I love you," and she says the same.

It's Friday, September 22nd and I finally get to see my angel after work today. The work day ends and I want to drive up to Gabi's house but she insists we meet at the Dunkin' Donuts in Mt. Airy. Along the way I decide to stop and purchase some flowers at a flower shop. I don't even know if the flowers I sent arrived at her doorstep or not. I also stop in a liquor store and buy some wine. I park at the Dunkin' Donuts and walk up to the patio area where Gabi is sitting, staring down at her phone. She looks rather downtrodden. I sit next to her and wait for her to pick her head up. I tell her I can tell she has been stressed lately. She had a Christian therapist that she really loved named Aubrey. She moved away and Gabi has a new therapist who she doesn't seem to like as much. Gabi proceeds to describe the details of her work struggles and her school struggles and I am actively listening with as much undivided attention as I can trying to be understanding and empathetic. I don't fully comprehend what she just explained but I don't want to make her repeat it because I think that would exasperate her. I don't know what I can do to help but I say, "hey, come to my car, I have some stuff for you."

At my car I pull out the wine and the flowers and I show her the little note I put in the flowers that reads, "I love you with the power of a thousand suns." I request a kiss and she quickly gives me a little peck. I smile at her and say, "So we can break the flower curse, right?" She responds with, "there is no curse." We transfer the items to her car and walk towards the picnic area behind the building. "So..." Gabi starts to converse, "it seems you really want kids." Fear now starts to fill up my core. "Yeah," I mumble. She continues, "and I... may never be at that place. Also, we are *very* different." I think to myself "very different? what the hell is she talking about?" We take a seat on the same concrete picnic table where we read our letters to each other before. This time the tone is different. She mentions not knowing what she wants to do in the future, where she wants to go to school, thinking maybe Colorado or the Carolinas. She also brings up the possibility of joining the Peace Corp, and continuing to do a bunch of traveling while she is still young. She continues to elaborate her feelings. She says she is struggling with multitasking and being able to balance all the factors in her life, that life is hard right now, and that she is irritated and frustrated and doesn't want to drag me down. I ask her, "Gabi, are you thinking about ending our relationship?" As her head suddenly droops a shaky "yes" slips out of her mouth, and a dagger enters my heart. "Is this just a thought or is this really happening?" I cry. With her head still pointed down she responds, "I'm sorry." With moisture in my eyes I finally inform her that I was looking at engagement rings and I bring up all the plans we had. At this point I am squeezing her hands trying to bring her back to life. "Gabi, can you look me in the eyes and tell me you don't want to be with me?" I challenge her with no response. A little kid is playing nearby and interrupts our conversation.

Embarrassed, I get up and walk towards our cars. We get to Gabi's car and I am standing in panic, literally scratching my head as I plead, "can we sit in your car and talk?" She agrees and as soon as we sit down, she cracks the window, I guess out of fear for safety. Here all I do is beg and plead and argue with little response and no resolve. I start to ball a little heavier and wrap my arms around her whispering weakly "I love you so much, please don't leave me." I get the "I love you *and* I care about you... but..." routine. She assures me that I didn't do anything wrong. I thought I did everything right. I really didn't see this coming. I finally realize there isn't much more I can say so I simply give her one last look and mutter, "goodbye." As I open the door and step out, I hear her final words, "I'm sorry." With my tail between my legs and a narrow vision I walk towards my car.

Throat wrenching, lung thumping scream-cries dominate my hour-long drive home. I haven't cried like this since I was a child. It starts raining and I see lightning, but I am already in shock. What just happened? Why God? Why? It doesn't make any sense for the love-of-my-life, the girl-of-my-dreams to throw away my love like this. With a pause of my membrane explosions I manage to inform Matthew via text: "dude, Gabi just ended our relationship, I'm devastated." I also tell Preston that Gabi won't be making the trip tomorrow. My head hurts, my throat hurts, and my chest hurts, but I manage to make it home and find my bed. I pray that this is just a bad dream and I will wake from the nightmare.

Of course, I wake up disappointed. I receive a text from Preston saying that Stacy inquired if I would like this camping trip to just be a guy-thing given the circumstance. I insist she comes along too. I arrive at the campsite, tentless. I guess I will just sleep in my car. I intended to share a tent with Gabi. I must be here early as Preston and Stacy have yet to arrive. They finally arrive in their pick-up truck fully equipped with 2 kayaks. Kayaking is something I've never done before and wanted to share the experience with Gabi. We get some stuff unloaded and start to talk about what happened. I breakdown a little bit but hold my composure. I tell them that Gabi said it's because she doesn't want kids but I do. Preston says, "that would have been one of the initial things I would have confirmed." I respond with, "in the beginning she was open to it." Yeah it is a great reason not to get into a relationship, but it's not a good reason to leave a loving one.

We take a walk along the stream path and it has some beautiful scenery, something Gabi would have really enjoyed. I sit down on a little bridge and stare into the stream. The stillness and tranquility remind me of how alone I am, how things trickle away and change. Why can't one person stay with me?

We return to our site and set up a little gas-powered camping grill for some grub. We also want to set up a campfire but need some firewood. We end up buying some firewood or what was marketed as firewood from a guy down the road. Turns out this box is full of old wicker baskets and some cardboard junk; this is hardly firewood at all. We sit around the fire and I pull out my guitar but hardly feel like playing. I was going to do my classic thing and hand out sheets with lyrics to popular songs and we all could have a good time. Without Gabi so much of me is missing, parts of me that I had before, but that Gabi stole. It's dark anyway now and no one would be able to see the print outs. I occasionally dip my head and proceed to snivel. I do not know if Preston and Stacy can see but it is too hard to keep in. It is sleep time and they have a big tent that could easily accommodate me but I would rather be alone, so I can cry without keeping them awake. I put my back seat down in the Mazda and lay down a bunch of blankets much like Gabi and I did in her car that night we stargazed. It's too small and not flat at all in the back of this stupid Mazda. It's weird how as soon as I no longer had the Saturn, I got Gabi, then as soon as I got this Mazda, Gabi left. This is the most uncomfortable sleep ever. Maybe a few hours of sleep with multiple hours of tears.

Going kayaking for the first time ever is on the agenda for this new morning. There are only two kayaks so Stacy decided to stay back and just read a book. Preston and I throw the kayaks into the water after he gives me a quick run-down or tutorial. This seems nice, just floating in a still lake. It does feel a little weird and wobbly though, I do not feel like falling into the water. Man, all I can think about is how much I wish Gabi was here. We have been wanting to do this for ever-so-long, but so long to that.

Back home, Dad is watching my nieces. I am trying to keep a straight face. I haven't told Dad the news, but when Amili arrives I request her presence in my bedroom. Here I ball on her shoulder and confess my anguish. It's a very unusual thing for us to hug but it is necessary, as there is no one I am closer to. My sister says she is sorry and that she loves me, at least I have that.

- Chapter 16 -
Letters

I am writing Gabi a letter:

Gabrielle,

    I can't believe this happened; I am absolutely devastated. How can we have so much and just drop it? I never loved anyone the way I love you. I never even thought about looking at engagement rings before, but I did with you. I never cried/screamed like I did on the way home after that miserable night. I can't believe the flower curse is still alive. Yes, every time I give flowers, the response is an end to the relationship. And yes, every time I eat chocolate, I get pimples. But this isn't a pimple, it is a huge life decision that I don't like. Everything seemed perfect. I felt God had led us together and everything was right. Every day I was with you felt like the greatest day of my life. And this early fall Sept 22 day feels like the worst.

    I understand you may never want kids; I accept that. I know I honestly would end up trying to convince you though. But right now, I too don't want kids for a while. I thought we would marry and enjoy a few good years of life and love while you study, then think about kids after your career got off. Also, yeah, I am older and if I were to have kids, I would have preferred to have them before I get too old because I would want to still be able to play catch with them when they are teens. So, I was thinking before I turn 40. Then traveling the world with you would be awesome!!! Some early, a lot after retirement! I wanted to see you through your schooling. Yes, I would prefer you went somewhere close, and yes, I believe a long-distance relationship would be a great strain. But I even thought about following you where you go. Maybe I could work from home like a few of my co-workers do. I thought with every ounce of my body that our bond was strong enough to endure life's obstacles. Some people go to school for life. If you aren't a multi-tasker, how can you ever see yourself in a relationship?

I wish I was on someone's priority list. Yes, your schooling and career are important to both you and me. I just don't understand how I can be given up like this. I feel like this kind of love isn't something that happens in everyone's lives. I felt like this was a once in a lifetime opportunity for two people to be in a happy relationship. What is the most important thing to you in your life? I think a job is a way to fund the life we really want. And it is a plus if you enjoy your job. I enjoy being with you more than anything, and thought you enjoyed my company enough too as to at least keep me around as you make your life choices. Is it better to sacrifice some current happiness for the promise of future happiness? Or is it better to have some happiness now with possibility of more happiness? Just a thought I am working on. I was set on guaranteeing your happiness, doing everything I can for you, being your life partner. I suppose it can be complicated but why? Our relationship seemed so easy and natural. It was total bliss.

Perhaps you are thinking too much and jumping to conclusions, perhaps not. But it is something you admitted to doing. I wish you would have talked to me about it first and given it more time. There might have been some things we needed to discuss but didn't. Maybe when Aubrey was around you had that outlet to get things out there. I Wish I could be some sort of help similar to her.

Maybe I will get over this. That is not looking promising but maybe. My buddy Matthew never gets over Becky in their struggles. He expressed similar feelings for his wife who he has loved his whole life. He stated "She is my 'the one,' I'll never feel like that again." I think I can relate right now. It is super weird... and I am not afraid to pour my heart out to you. Sure, I have been broken-hearted before, but I was so sure that you would never make me feel this way. There was no question in my heart that I would be with you forever. Again, it is devastating. I don't understand why, but of course I never do. It never gets easier.

You said I was a great joy in your life. When God shows you something great, why get rid of it? Let God guide you. I believe he brought us together for a reason. You were a godsend for me and I for you I thought as well. This happened so suddenly, why didn't you express your feelings first? You described this as "magical" and said "is this real life?" it can be real life for you and I!

I want you to be happy. I want you to succeed in everything you set out to do. I hope the path you take is the right one, but how can we know? Surely you thought about life and how it will affect relationships. You chose to get back into dating. Did you change your mind and decide that is not what you want? Did you just want a summer/pre-schooling person to date? A fling? I don't believe that is the case. Somewhere inside you want a loving relationship but you are giving up because it seems too difficult and the paths and life choices scare you. This is my life we are talking about too. Is it selfish for me to think I should have a say in this? I thought we were a team. I am so sorry you have to go through the stress and make the decisions you have to make. I want to be able to understand it better. I wanted to know you better and the details of your life. I hope your vision clears up and the path you choose is clear and full of happiness, because you deserve that. You do not deserve the struggles you go through in life. I wanted to show you that someone can treat you right, and I think I did that, but I guess you don't need it. That sucks because a whole lot of me thinks I NEED you. You make me a better person.

We were doing everything right, the way God wanted, I don't see how God's plan has us apart. We were reaching God by way of our pyramid scheme together. I am falling off this pyramid now. It will probably really make me question a lot of things. You got me my Bible; how will I pick it up now? I am sorry I am guilt tripping you... I just have a lot of thoughts too.

I fall easily, but I had no reason not to love you, and I fell way further than I ever imagined possible. If you love me half as much as I do you then that is enough to make it work! Oh boy I am crazy. I don't want to ask this question because I don't want to seem or feel desperate, but under what circumstance would we be able to stay together?? Love is forever, love is kind, and all that jazz. Love is about making sacrifices for someone. I came to understand I would make some sacrifices for you. It doesn't seem you want to make sacrifices for me though. I was accepting possible life changes, because that is where my heart is. But where is yours? I think I got too serious too fast on you. I am sorry.

You were a dream come true for me, and you are literally my dream girl (everything I want and need). I wanted to be a part of your dreams as well. I want your dreams to come true, and I think they will, but I think you need to line up your priorities, and maybe re-evaluate your dreams. I know it is not easy and I am sorry, it is just so hard for me to understand why you wouldn't want my love in your life.

Thank you for showing me a wonderful half of a year and for proving to me that my dream girl actually does exist! (even though I am pissed at you for pissing this relationship away)

Ray

I mailed it to her. I don't want to bother her; I feel like maybe she just needs a few days to reflect and she will change her mind and come to her senses. She always eventually says what I want and need to hear. I know in my heart that we belong together, so maybe it will just take some time.

It's been a few days and I can't take it any longer. I have written another letter and I guess I will send it to her. In the meantime, I will shoot her a quick text. I tap with my thumbs: "Think we could take a break and not break up?" She responds saying she got my letter and was writing me back and hopes it helps me to understand better. We decide to communicate over email even though I just sent the following to her over postage as well as emailed it to her (Sept 25th 2017, 8:25pm).

Why? God why do you allow me to continually suffer so much pain as a result of lost love. Why did I fall so deeply this time? How can I be so sure of something just to be wrong in the end? Why must I try so hard to find love, and why must I love so much when I never get that love in return?

I am starting to understand why you believe this is best. You don't want to waste my time and just disappoint me greater and give me run-arounds. I realize why you think it is best if we are apart. You said you weren't perfect and that you would disappoint, and you are right you definitely did disappoint me. I am finding this hard to cope with, but in the end, I want to forgive you. You taught me the importance of forgiveness, thank you. I may have to seek counseling as a result of this though. I told you multiple times how much I love you, but I don't think you truly understand how strong that love is. It was a love I never experienced before. I don't know, maybe I was mesmerized by the "waiting till marriage" and the fairytale dream-come-true thing. It definitely felt like a dream-come-true to me. I felt like you were definitely the one for me and all the pain I had suffered beforehand had finally come to rest and God brought us together to be in each other's lives forever. It was a beautiful thought. Being able to climb the "pyramid" with someone and to actually have something that feels real in my life made me feel like I was already in heaven. The fact that you spilled your deepest secrets and shared your life with me gave me a sense of closeness and belonging. The bond felt so strong even after our hiccup (my dreaded mistake). Part of me hopes you come to me and say that you think you are making a terrible mistake leaving me. Another part of me thinks it would be hard to trust you not to break my heart again.

I was content before I met you. I never knew I could be so happy while I was with you. I am miserable after you. You have a hard time making up your mind and have a stubborn "do things your own way" mentality. That will be very hard for relationships. I pray that you can have peace of mind one day with your decisions. Nothing is going to go as planned though, and there will always be "what ifs" in the back of your mind. Eliminate those thoughts, ease your mind, and believe in God's ways. You have to work on your outlook first. Got to accept what is given to you, you got to learn how to love. (I think) I thought you were set on studying OT. Then you say you are still thinking about joining the Peace Corp. It doesn't really matter what you do as long as you stay yourself through the process, prioritize, and make solid decisions. You got to think about why you need to do those things. You probably have, I am just thinking out loud. You got to think how it will affect your loved ones too. Be humble.

It bothers me a bit that you allowed us to get so involved just to spring up the possible differences in life that you've yet to fully decide on. It was surprisingly sudden. I wanted us to be able to make some life decisions together. You are so independent it is hard for you to see things that way. But that is what a relationship is about. You said you don't need a marriage or kids and that is ok. That is ok. But if you are going to date, and especially if you are "waiting" what kind of thoughts will you expect men to have? Men pretty much need sex, for reals. It is a beautiful thing to wait. I loved that about our relationship and dreamt about our wedding night multiple times. It made me want you even more.

Right now, I feel like if you said "no kids" I would say "ok no kids, as long as I have you!" Now I don't have you or kids. Can't have kids without my wife. Yes, I could adopt, but I think I have great genes and would love for my blood and name to continue. But I love you so much I would be willing to compromise. Compromise. I would have loved it if we went from my 75% wanting kids and your 25% wanting kids to be 50/50 and for us to make that decision down the road when it is time. Maybe I should have been firmer with that and not let us start a relationship without confirming an agreement on that. But I accepted your undecidedness. I was ok with that.

I guess you finally decided we shouldn't be together since you can't decide on your life. But I ask you this: why can't love prevail? Have you ever had such a good relationship? Has anyone ever treated you as good as me? Maybe you simply don't care and it doesn't matter to you. I guess it is harder for me to accept loneliness, even though I found alone time to be great, and found some contentment in being alone. I hope that I can arrive back to that point, but I doubt I will allow myself to love in that way again. Before you I pretty much refused to say "I love you" and refused to give flowers. I put up walls, I was safe. I tore them walls down for you. And the ultimate happened, I let myself get hurt. I am really hurting bad.

Why can't we talk about this? I want to listen to your thoughts and feelings. Communication is key. I think you would agree. Please talk to me. I feel like you should have talked to me about your feelings towards the different life angles we see in the future. If your final decision is to continue your way without me, I may need a few things. Although it hurts me so much to think about it, I would need you to ignore me for a while. I won't be able to get over you unless I am blocked. I typically always want to still be able to talk to and even stay friends because it's weird to me how you can share so much with someone then have nothing at all ever again. I realize in my experience though that it makes it hard to get over someone if they are still available. Once I am over you, please be my friend. I will always have love for you, but maybe in a different manner. Another request is that you forgive me for some crazy stuff I may say while I am in this state of mind. I might say something mean, I don't want to but I might get a little crazy, it is something I do. I hope to not alienate you with it.

I hope and pray everything will improve for you. I hope the stress levels decrease. I hope you come to peace with everything that is on your mind, and the inevitable decisions you feel you must make. I wish there was something else I can do. All I can do is express my feelings and pray for you. I wish I could be a part of your life, but above all I wish you happiness.

I never met anyone like you. You are so real, honest, kind, raw, fun, spiritual, playful, intelligent, just plain natural beauty. I love everything about you. And have so much respect for you. I never thought I would meet someone so fitting for me, exactly what I wanted. I love our differences too. I love hearing your point of view on things. Man, I just love you *so* much. And the more I mutter it the more I believe it. I feel stupid though, like I am purposely blinding myself from things. Do I in reality need the things I am currently overlooking to be with you? I don't think so but maybe. Man, getting that good morning text every day was just the sweetest feeling, my spirit uplifted every morning. But now it's gone. I didn't even do anything.

I will love you forever, you are a special person. I will forever treasure the memories. I hope this pain doesn't eclipse the greatness that was us.
God help ME, I don't know what to do
God help HER, she doesn't know what to do.

I send her additional thoughts (Sept 25th, 8:35pm):

Here are some thoughts I wrote up while at work today:

If you want to go away to school, fine! Marry me first and when you are done come home to me.
If you want to join the peace corps, fine! Marry me first and when you are done come home to me.
It would be tough but the excitement of your return would be crazy interesting. Or we could marry and we could move together to follow your career. Mine is probably easy to get into around the whole country, I might even be able to keep my job and work from home. These ideas scare me but it will make for a more interesting life!

I want you to be you!
You are who I fell in love with!

Was it too good to be true? Stupid clichés

I know other people have bigger issues/problems and grievances than just a breakup but I am a wreck, I can't even keep my composure at work.

I've had sex with a bunch of girls, many I didn't even have feelings for. I love you most of all and never even got to make love to you. I would trade them in for one night with you. I feel dirty with this crazy thought, I am a sinner. I am sinning more now without you.

I receive an email from Gabi (Sept 25th, 8:37pm):

(paraphrased)

I'm emailing you my letter, then I will read the letter #2 that you just sent me

Ray,

I am truly sorry I hurt you. When you called me and told me something felt off, you weren't wrong. I was struggling with my own emotions and the timing just wasn't right for that conversation. I was still attempting to sort through everything. You told me you were sending me a surprise. I hoped it wasn't flowers. Your intuition sensed something was amiss and then you sent me those flowers and it was like a confirmation of my own feelings. I don't believe in curses as you do, but I do believe in intuition. Listen to yours. There's a deeper level of thought, motive, and perspective that you aren't willing to hear. I'm not trying to criticize you, but to help you understand.

You once commented that you were too much for me, and said you tried to hide it. This made me so sad when I thought about it. God made you special. You are being molded into exactly what God wants you to be. To hide yourself isn't what God wants. He wants you to be completely his and to be wholly you. The right people for you will come and stay in your life. They will embrace everything you are with celebration. I wanted to be that person... but I'm not. I wanted time to prove that our relationship could form a strong foundation. There just isn't enough of me to do that right now. There is too much being demanded of me and there is too much on my plate. I didn't want to take my frustrations out on you, and I am so easily frustrated these days. It's not my place to allow my irritations to ask anyone to change. I have character flaws that I need to work on. I'm not willing to allow my negativity to pull on you when there's already so much negativity in the world. I understand my choices affect others and this makes decision making all the more difficult. I am worn down and can't get a grip, I can't pull myself out or handle my emotions appropriately.

I thought I was ready for a relationship. I thought I could at least grow into a relationship and I know it takes time to build the components of a healthy relationship. You showed me that. You showed me love, hope, and acceptance. I really did need it. I know you love me in a really deep way. Maybe I don't feel the same. I hate to admit that, but it's the truth. It wouldn't be fair to either of us if I weren't completely honest. I'm sorry and it hurts. I am broken and I feel like I don't have enough of myself to give you, or to sacrifice. I can only offer imperfect love, without sacrifice. It's not just about jobs, school, programs, long distance and everything else. You should have everything you want including children and a lifelong love. I don't think I'll ever want children and that's not something you should have to try to let go. It is a big deal and it is time dependent. I know I may never change my mind.

If we're not on the same page about these things, we can't force it. I don't want to do that, and I know you don't either. I really thought I felt the same about you as you do me, and I am so sorry that's not the case. My inability to love you unconditionally shows that there isn't enough love to make it work, and that's not fair.

I pray for your happiness and that God gives you everything you need. I'm proud of you for seeking God. I am proud of your strength. I'm proud of your weakness as well, because humans are weak and need to depend on God. Your link with God doesn't become less because I am no longer a part of that "pyramid." This should make both of us more dependent of God's love, to get us through the rough days and nights ahead. Break-ups are rough, ugly, and painful. I am sorry that I can't help you through that pain. I never wanted to hurt you. I am sorry.

Even though it may not seem like it now, I do care about you. As a sister in Christ, I want you to know that I am praying for you. I want you to continue to be encouraged by God's love. His plan is bigger and better than anything we can devise for ourselves. It may not always feel that way and seems like hope is lost but God knows best.

I can't thank you enough for showing me love, acceptance and making sacrifices. Really, from the depths of my soul, thank you. You kept showing me that there is hope.

I pray for your healing and understanding. It may mean nothing coming from me but don't let God's peace slip from your memories.

Gabi

I email her again:

Dear Gabrielle,

When I first said "te amo" you smiled ear to ear and said "what, in Spanish?" quickly followed by "yo tambien te quiero" you said you thought about saying it yourself for weeks. On a few occasions you assured me you were possibly crazier about me than I you. On the other hand, I feel like you thought we may not be together long. When I mentioned winter activities such as ice skating and snowboarding, I don't remember you expressing a lot of excitement. On the other hand, as far as Pittsburgh goes, you kept saying another excuse to come back. When I mentioned LA next year with me, you shut it down saying you don't know where you'll be at that time. Rightfully so I guess, but on the other hand...

I hope all my thoughts and these letters find you well rather than bombard you and jam you with too many thoughts and more stress. I think this is good for me though and I thank you for responding. I think I was being a bit crazy when I said it would be best to ignore me, so maybe forget that. This letter may start off a little crazy, but I think I am starting to process things better and the latter of the letter will be more concrete. Example (earlier jot): I can't keep doing this to you with the letters and I can't keep doing it to myself, if I want to move on (which I currently don't) I should stop.

I keep repeating in my head that you were the best and how much I miss you. Maybe if I focused on the negative like how you broke my heart, you hurt me, and you don't feel the same way... maybe it will seem easier to let go. Was I everything you could have wanted? Was there anything you wish was different about me? I breakdown at work. If someone sees me, what an embarrassment, a grown man crying. (maybe I am brave enough to be weak?) This only hurts when I think about it. How can I stop thinking about it? How can you stay up half the night making out and not think you love me? I think it is obvious you never been in love, maybe some people don't have that ability. You are not a very emotional person anyway. That is ok though as long as I get love on some level. Respect is more important to me anyway, and you showed me that. It was great.

I think we are both good people deserving of each other if we could get past this.

I am selfish being more concerned with not having you than thinking about your stress and the things you are dealing with. I'd love it if you vented to me. The following is something I wrote many moons ago called "selfish to be sad"

How can one be so SELFISH as to be SAD? How can one not appreciate their life and the world that was given to us for free? Why would one think this gift is imperfect and desire to alter it in some way? What if you gave me a gift and I threw it down and stomped on it? We have an entire world of opportunity at the fleshy end of our fingertips, why waste it? We should be grateful for every breath we take. As I take a deep breath and gaze at the humbling scope of mass clouds in the sky, I realize God's love for me, and I am HAPPY today.

Maybe I shouldn't expect you to love me as deeply as I did you. Maybe one day you will realize love is a choice. IF you ever come to a time in your life when you are ready for a serious relationship and want to choose to love, and IF I am still available, and IF I am willing, perhaps we could give this another go around and perhaps this fairy tale can have a happy ending. As of right now I feel you are the love of my life. I hope if you ever feel foolish for leaving me or you realize or believe I was the one for you too that we could rekindle and grow our love before it is too late. Even though I believe you to be "the one" I can't wait forever. I will eventually try to love again. I hope you never feel the heartbreak I feel, for you have had enough pain in your life, but so have I. I think I am close to forgiving you, but to re-mend my heart may take some time, just as I know you are still healing. I am not saying we are required to heal each other. This is something we will have to work on through our mutual love which is Christ.

You know what? Maybe I think it is incredibly stupid to leave someone who treats you the way I did and selfish to think you "have too much on your plate." Then again maybe it is stupid for me to say something like that to you, and maybe it's stupid for me to expect you to feel the same way I do. But dammit we needed more time. I wanted too much too soon. Marriage?? Before a year into a relationship?? I am crazy because my initial thought was that I should be with someone for 2 years first (which would be a personal milestone) I don't know, guess I just really felt it with you. Also, when I talked to you about it you thought it depended on the persons, so maybe that swayed me into thinking it may be a good idea too. I didn't need you to love me deeply right now but we should have definitely been clear on the emotions so I didn't get you an engagement ring only for you to say you were not ready. I feel foolish for looking and thinking about taking out a loan. I liked how we had little weird conversations outside that church and stuff early on in our relationship. I think the sexual desire started to take over a bit later, starting acting married except not going all the way. It is good we didn't go all the way, but what we were doing was just as sinful. We should have replaced those late nights with the conversations we both know we can have and enjoy.

I feel I am getting a little ridiculous with my desire to dispense all these details with you. I need you. I feel pathetic needing someone, but I really feel that right now. I feel like I am no-one without you. I am feeling like I don't care about my job, or football, or art, or music, or anything I loved. I just feel lost. I was brave loving you; I took a risk; I am proud of that.

"But he said to me, "My grace is sufficient for you, for my power is made perfect in weakness." Therefore, I will boast all the more gladly of my weaknesses, so that the power of Christ may rest upon me. For the sake of Christ, then, I am content with weaknesses, insults, hardships, persecutions, and calamities. For when I am weak, then I am strong" (2 Corinthians 12:9-11 ESV).

I used to think I wanted a big-time job, a huge house, a Rolls-Royce, fame, and all that crap. I have humbled myself a bit, now all I want is a happy life, perhaps a good girl like you by my side.

You ignored God's signs; he brought us together for a reason. One might argue that reason is to learn a lesson to better our future. To alienate your loved ones is not the answer. Leaving me, blocking people out, will not solve your problems. I could tell you were stressed. You weren't saying much when we got back from Pittsburgh. It could have been tiredness, stress, maybe even a little doubt. Doubt is normal, it didn't need to escalate. My intuition kicked in that night I guess, unaware, sorry that makes you sad. Sure, the right people will come along, you can be the right person for me, and I believe I can be the right person for you. I believe it was a sign from God: us meeting, a joy to add to your life, not to complicate your decisions but to help add direction. Sure, relationships can be hard, especially if you don't accept them as a good thing for you. I was good to you, I cared about you. It is not fair to block your loved ones from your life when you feel irritated. That is when these people should be closest and most accepting. It is not fair to not let people be there for you. You are a different type of person, I get it, but still. It is a good trait not to want to drag people down, but you can't do everything on your own. You are just a human. You say there is a lot being demanded of you. Life shouldn't make demands on you; you should make demands on life. I am sorry you feel overwhelmed. Life will continue no matter what you decide. Then you will just have more things to decide on. It will be a never-ending cycle, so why let it tear you up? God is writing this book. Have faith in him and all that is supposed to happen will happen. I guess I could tell myself the same things.

I agree relationships take time to grow into love and to build solid foundations. I am guilty of moving too fast and working off of gut feelings, but I couldn't help it and I expressed that with you. It all seemed like it was working, I had no complaints. This is why the ending surprised me. Maybe we weren't on the same page exactly, but I didn't care. All I wanted was that happiness we shared. I believe that is the most important thing in life - being able to enjoy God's gifts.

All and all you are probably right about everything and spot on. Many of these statements I'm making are still contradicting what you already told me. You may be a better decision maker than you think. I feel like you are much smarter than me, and all these letters I write are simple non-sense. I contemplated not sending them but then I realized this is me, and I got to be myself so I will be appreciated as myself in this life.

Maybe I don't love you the way I thought I did?? Maybe this was just another lesson from God.

I saw happiness in your smile. The way you smiled, the time you gave me, the way you always talked to me, our magnetism, your willingness to hearken, introducing me to and letting me in on family, and all these things show me you love me. You loved me. The deep love thing though, deep love is a CHOICE. It is something you have to GIVE IN to in order to have true happiness. This is what I did with you. I chose to love you because I knew that you were good for me. I knew that you could help improve me as a Christian, and I knew my quality of life could improve. Those things happened instantly. I knew that I could be happy with you and I chose to love you deeply. I thought I demonstrated my worth to you with my willingness, my acceptance, the healthiness, the love, giving you my time but leaving you time for your studies and for yourself, communicating the best I can, my interest in the things you do, the support I gave you, being open as possible, the things I did for you and gave you, the words of affirmation, the non-sexual intimacy, my devotion, and most importantly seeking God with you. I may not be as analytical and articulate as you but I am damn good at living!

So, if you would like to start all over but as friends... maybe we could become pen-pals??

Love,
Ray

Gabi Responds (Oct 2nd, 5:54pm):

(paraphrased)

Dear Ray,

It feels so formal when you address me as Gabrielle, just thought I'd mention that. I'm Gabrielle, Gabi, and Gab. I don't know which layer of me to cling onto anymore. I am so undependable. I won't always be there, no matter how hard I try. That's probably because I feel like there's never enough of me to give any away. I don't think I have the capacity to handle others emotions on top of my own. I've said this time and again. Not to say that I don't still feel emotion because people's stories, their struggles, and vulnerability do touch me.

I was a different person six years ago, more sensitive and emotional, but still as undecided as I am today. Life and my experiences have changed me, not always for the good. I wasn't encouraged to show emotion as a child, and was told, "don't wear your emotions on your sleeve." I am trying to no longer live that way but my callouses make it difficult. For a long time, I couldn't handle anger and pain, I even tried to not feel anything at all. I hated emotion because I was drowning in it. I didn't know how to deal with so much emotion so I didn't, I pushed it away. The feeling left me drained and I still feel that way sometimes. I can't leave the past in the past. I am trying to find the good in it, the "silver lining" or lesson that relates to my relationship with God.

I do not like depending on people, either. I understand what you mean when you say that. Really, I don't even like people, and maybe that's the tarnished side of me speaking. People disappoint. I am still trying to even love myself. I have to live with me and I am my very worst critic. I might still be stuck in "fake it till you make it" mode. When you asked me that late one night I responded with uncertainty and I am still not sure.

You are probably right about me having never been in love. Loving someone and being "in love" are not one in the same. I wanted to be in love and even told myself that I was but I was just being loving and respectful. Respect I understand and can do. I am sorry I hurt you. I am sorry that I didn't feel the same way. Even though I love you in my own way and even though I care about and respect you, it simply wasn't enough to forge on. It would not have been fair for either of us, especially you who loved me so freely. We both had walls. I saw your efforts to tear them down, and I thank you for that. You should be proud of that bravery. I've seen, felt, and given love, but it's never been in my grasp. A relationship should take stress away, not add to it. You are right about that. My approach to relationships is flawed, and I am sorry for that.

I've tried so hard to love myself by reading self-help books, therapy, and seeking advice from those closest to me. I struggled so much before I even considered dating. How can you love someone else when you don't even love yourself? I sought God and in return I received His love and forgiveness. I can see God's hand in everything around me. Immersing myself in a world of faith, listening to Christian radio, crying and singing God's praise… it's all a part of growing. There will be times when we feel distant from God, that is our faith being tested. I have to keep reminding myself of this. Faith isn't based on a feeling but on the word. I still can't show myself that same love and forgiveness. Sometimes I do, but mostly I don't. There is a war raging in my head. God is always calling me back to him, however, and always will. "he refreshes my soul. He guides me along the right paths for his name's sake" (Psalm 23:3 NIV).

We both still need to process everything but you're still you. All of your passions and everything that makes you, you will always be there. Give it time. I know what you're feeling is hard, but we aren't the right people to help each other heal. It's important to have healthy boundaries in order to heal. Let's not let our communication hinder our healing. It is too hard for me to continue receiving your letters. Please respect my decision to move on. Again, I am sorry for hurting you but we need to go our separate ways.

Though we haven't known each other very long, we've had some deep conversations. There is nothing simple about you. Your letters are filled with the many parts of you. They are very articulate and not non-sense at all.

Can people who've been involved in intimate relationships really remain friends? I don't think it should happen. The feelings may fade but they will always be there. Holding on won't let wounds heal. I want us both to be happy and accept that the other has moved on. Staying in contact will not leave room for that acceptance. Wounds can't heal if you keep opening the band-aid and picking at it. We both need a fresh start. We also need boundaries.

I know I am all over the place, and I'm sorry. I now feel so confused about physical affection. I've read that sex can affect a person's spiritual well-being. I was firm in my belief but you are right, even without sex we were still acting on our sinful desires. I now wonder if this matter is, in fact, black or white. Every person has such a different opinion on this. Is it a sin? Is it not? I am not sure I know anymore. We were made as sexual creatures. Maybe that is the world speaking. God's design is to protect us. Things are different now than biblical times. Couples got betrothed so young in the past. I'm not sure what I am trying to say. You said we were still sinning. I suppose in our view of it, we were. Should we even bother kissing? You even said you thought about sex differently in the past.

The idea of sex is all over the place because of the different viewpoints. We showed affection, of course it wasn't always sexual, but we do live in a physical world. We could have spent more time together communicating, connecting, sitting in front of that church. I actually do not want to apologize for us becoming more and more physical towards our latter days. I'm frustrated because even if we tried to change, that physical/emotional attachment is still there. It is deep and it has an effect.

Friendship is a nice thought, but it isn't realistic. I don't want to get in the way of your future relationships. It is hard to let go and move on, but it is the healthy thing to do.

I email her back (Oct, 3rd, 8:57am):

I am sorry the letters in the mail are hard for you, I will stop sending them, I had one more thing I was going to send you, I will email it tonight (it is nice and maybe one day you can look back on it and smile). This email is beautiful, you are a well-constructed human being, full of thoughts, hopes, realness, naturalness, worries, confusion. You were not faking anything though. I believe you enjoyed being with me. you are still healing and the "love" thing doesn't make sense to you yet. It will someday, I just wish I was there with you through it, because I love and respect you more than anything ever in my life. It will be hard for me to come to that point again with someone else, you fulfilled all my hopes and desires, I truly thought you were perfect for me. I feel like in future relationships I would only settle, and that sucks but hopefully I will get over that. SORRY I am crazy. but I will be ok. Please don't worry about me, I will do just fine. (I am all over the place too) Though we can't be friends, I will always hold love for you. you showed me so much about efforts and thoughts and communication, and realness. There is just so much more I want to say but I want to respect your decision and move on.

My fourth writing to Gabi (Oct, 3rd, 6:44pm):

I am sorry all of this happened. Forgive me if some anger presented itself in my letters. I am sorry you are going through so much frustration and irritation with life right now. I am sorry I wasn't able to see it or know what to do to help. I hope everything goes smoother for you. I hope you do well in your physics class. I pray you are not hurting at night over things you can't figure out. You are an amazing person, and you try so hard. I appreciate everything you have done for me. I loved you madly and if you ever wondered why here it is.

I loved how you are a "practicing Christian" and with no compromise
I loved your uniqueness
I loved your interests and talents: how you played piano, ukulele, and cello
I loved how you shared playing with me even though you never do in front of people because it made you nervous
I loved how adventurous you are
I loved how you loved to travel
I loved our long emails on the dating site before we met
I loved how you took interest in the things I said
I loved how you adapted interest in the things I do (like football) and wanted me to explain
I loved how laid back and easy going you are
I loved how you are open to trying new things
I loved how you enjoyed seeing the world
I loved how you wanted to help the world and make an impact
I loved how you always brought up god in our conversations, kept him the focus, and used that to help in daily life issues
I loved how you saw the good in everything
I loved how you were able to see the positive qualities of people and let them shine
I loved how you said "can I borrow your hand"
I loved how when we were kissing you would say "never stop"
I loved how you let me kiss you all over and continuously
I loved how you said I am caring, thoughtful, loving, wonderful, funny, and talented
I loved how you jotted down our dates and shared them with me
I loved how forgiving you are
I love how poetic you are in your letters
I loved how you assured me I was a good person
I loved how you wanted to look up new verses
I loved that you were the one to get me the Bible I always wanted, what a perfect gift

I loved how you accepted my gifts even though you may not want or need them
I loved how you loved my little notes I left you
I loved how long our hugs lasted
I loved how you are seeking getting your Master's
I loved how you wanted to do big things but live in a little house
I loved your positive spirit
I loved how excited you got over small things
I loved how you were open to doing just about anything
I loved how strong you are
I loved how trusting you are
I loved how you took time to think
I loved how respectful you are
I loved how silly you are
I loved the funny faces you make
I loved how you can be yourself
I loved how you dress
I loved how you smell and taste even when sweaty
I loved how you gave me good morning and goodnight texts
I loved how you are aware of your flaws
I loved you lips, your teeth, and your smile
I loved the tones and expressions you made while playing Mad Gab
I loved how you got when you were drinking
I loved your family and their acceptance
I loved how you introduced me to your family and friends
I loved how you stayed active with biking, and hiking, and tennis, and such
I loved how you enjoyed the rain and the mud
I loved how you enjoyed nature and stars
I loved how you wanted tattoos to have meaning or significance to who you are
I loved the outdoor movies and all the creative date night ideas

I loved how you thought of me and got me the root beer and candy
I loved how you listened
I loved how you never complained
I loved how we set boundaries and stuck to them
I loved how you thought kissing was like a conversation
I loved how you openly accepted my secret and never brought it up again
I loved how we weren't too into politics and never argued
I loved how beautiful you look in a summer dress or just in some shorts and a tee
I loved how you appreciated me
I loved your honesty
I loved how you still wanted to talk to me while you were in Spain
I loved how we could go with the flow
I loved how you bring me up
I loved how you don't want to drag anyone down
I loved how you put so much effort into getting A's
I loved how you don't like to take out irritation on others
I loved how you admitted everyone can and will irritate you after too long
I loved the wacky wording you use
I loved the twinkle in your eye
I loved how innocent you are and how staying the night in a hotel was "kinda weird"
I loved your style, not too into what's popular
I loved how you kept long-term friends
I loved climbing a tree with you
I loved picnicking with you
I loved lying on the beach with you
I loved how I could depend on you
I loved how you always try to do what's right
I loved how you do random exploring
I loved how you gabbed it up with my family and friends
I loved how much you try

I loved those little notes you gave me so I could find them and have happy little thoughts of you
I loved hearing you talk about everything
I loved how you had to contemplate our first kiss
I loved how you actively wanted to show interest in the things I enjoy
I loved how you always thought of and brought everything on our trips/dates/adventures
I loved how you were not "high maintenance"
I loved how we could talk about anything
I loved how you were not a phone zombie
I loved how you give so much praise to the people that positively affect you
I loved how you got me, and appreciated my humor
I loved that time when you ran up to me in my car and said "I love you" (you knew I needed a pick-up)
I loved how you laugh at yourself
I loved how you tried extra-hard to be punctual for me
I loved how we could do weird things like build a fort
I loved your collar bones
I loved how you apologize
I loved how you said I don't have to apologize
I loved how you always tried to pay
I loved how thankful you are
I loved how polite you are
I loved how caring you are, always looking for words to help ease my pain
I loved how attentive you are
I loved how comfortable you made me feel
I loved how you returned the gestures I did
I loved how you realize I too would like the same type of things I do for you
I loved how you help and don't ask for help
I loved how humble you are
I loved your flawless flaws
I love you for you
I loved how you appreciate me for me
I loved how you never would leave me hanging

I loved how you had the patience to explain things to me that I did not understand
I loved how you said I was "magical"
I loved how you could always see both sides of every argument
I loved how you posted scripture and reminders on your wall
I loved how you opened up to me
I loved how generous you are
I loved how you expressed longing for my warmth and my hug
I loved how you always tried to find the right words
I loved the weird things you said
I loved how you are a bit nerdy yet a bit classy
I loved how you love Christ
I loved how you appreciate the little things
I loved how strong you are
I loved how you thought about my nieces
I loved how you were shy at times
I loved how you have big dreams
I loved how you had opinions on weird things like using the word "cute" and "baby"
I loved how you were always sure to end the day with "xoxox" or "besitos"
I loved your honesty
I loved how you need alone time
I loved how you weren't afraid to be a kid at heart
I loved how you make a conscious effort to better yourself
I loved how you found it hard to accept the compliments I gave you
I loved how you are not an alcoholic and how you never did drugs
I loved how softly you speak
I loved your movements and mannerisms, the way you nodded your head, the way you walk, the way you swing your arms, and those little hand gestures you make
I loved your desire to be outdoors

I loved how you liked to cuddle but not when it is time to sleep
I loved how you allowed me to eat your leftovers
I loved how you made me feel special
I loved how you love fortune cookie fortunes
I loved your humor and how you enjoyed silly puns
I loved how you balanced time for me
I loved how you knew another language
I loved how you like game night
I loved how you would tackle everything
I loved your calmness
I loved your creativity
I loved your courage
I loved your energy and the fact you enjoyed the power naps
I loved your faithfulness and loyalty
I loved how you were messy yet orderly
I loved how genuine you are
I loved how you are a perfectionist but didn't need me to be
I loved how you take responsibility for your actions
I loved how natural and sexy you are
I love how you are currently denying many of these traits
I loved how respectful you are to others and to yourself
I loved how you love "bodies of water" and always had to take a dip
I loved how you weren't too "girlie"
I loved how we could do things on a whim
I loved how you encouraged me to be me
I loved your kind spirit
I loved how you also don't like babies
I loved how you emphasize communication
I loved how you always said "yes please"
I loved how you thought about us growing old together

I added the "ed" to "loved," as it initially just said "love," a whole bunch of times. I also put that "Desire" poem in there. I receive a response on October 4th:

Dear Ray,

Thank you for all the beautiful letters. I've taken every word, all the encouragement, love, and hard truths to heart. God has blessed us in so many ways with this relationship. I still believe we were brought together in His timing, for His reasons. Unfortunately, it came to a time where it wasn't the right time to continue. The love was real, and all of the thoughts of love were real but there were determining factors regarding the future that could not be ignored. It was my fault for not being clear on decisions revolving around the future: having children, traveling, and careers. I am sorry for that. Everything is so complex and I know I am being confusing. Let's refocus.

Christ's love radiated through you and I didn't expect that. I didn't expect to learn so much about love. Your letter, the reasons why you love me, showed me so much. I am in tears over this incredible love you've shown me, reminding me of how deep Christ's love is for all of us. I can never thank you enough for all the love and respect you've shown me. Words can never express how deeply you've touched me. I'll never forget what you've done for me and how much you've affected my life. Though we unfortunately never made love, we connected on a much deeper level.

My memories of you will always be cherished and I'm so thankful for having had you in my life. We didn't get to have a goodbye kiss but I can imagine it would mean so much. You may never know how much I regret hurting you, but I am so thankful you have forgiven me. Though I can't know exactly what you're going through, I know it must have been hard.

I will continue to pray for you. I'll pray for all your hopes and dreams to come to fruition, exceeding all you have imagined. Trust God, seek Him out, and I know they will.

"And the peace of God, which transcends all understanding, will guard your hearts and your minds in Christ Jesus" (Philippians 4:7 NIV).

With love,
Gabi

I express with Gabi that I want to see her one last time to give her that proper good-bye kiss. She takes a couple days to think about it but ultimately says that it would "mean so much" but she is unwilling to do a second good-bye because it was so hard the first time. I respond saying I would probably just say something stupid to ruin our beautiful letter exchange anyway. I thought my expressions of love for her would draw her back into me, I just don't understand why nothing I say is working.

I have not had any kind of sexual release in several months. Screw it, I can't take it anymore. I look at pictures of Gabi and pull it out but before I am even fully erect, I start oozing all over the place. This is the most abundant amount of stuff I've ever seen come out of me. Meanwhile I am crying and feel the most pathetic I have ever felt.

It's late October and I drove my firebird to work. I can't seem to think straight, but this car gives me some pleasure. When it's time to punch out, I hop in my car and punch it. I am speeding around a slight curve right in front of my company's building. My tires are gripping aggressively in a peculiar way, and the car is pulling to the left. I try to brake but I have no control and slide into a slight ditch or hill-like area. I stop after a loud thump. Angrily, as I believe people at my job could see me, I step back on the gas and manage to get out of the ditch. I drive down the road a little but decide to stop and get out to see the damage. I notice the front end of the car is now a bit slanted. Perhaps the frame is slightly bent. This is not something I will be able to fix on my own. Just more frustration to add to my life.

I am crying every day, mostly while driving, in the shower, and when I lie down at night. I am losing all kinds of weight because all I do when I get home is go for a jog and drink beer. I have not been eating at all. My cupboards are bone dry, and my eyes the opposite. It isn't supposed to be like this; it doesn't make sense. I believe I must keep trying. Gabi however did express that she can't keep going back and forth with me like this, and that I need to respect her decision to move on. This is wrong though, I just know it, I have got to do everything I can to make the story make sense. I am putting together a video with pictures of Gabi and I and of me talking about our dates and relationship. If this won't Grab Gabi's heart, I don't know what will. People have inquired about me needing closure, but it's not closure that I seek.

I email Gabi again (Nov. 5th):

> Here is the link to the video I made for you (and for me), followed by another letter. The video is unlisted so only those with the link can view it.
> (Link)

Gabi,

> Why must I wake up to this nightmare every morning? I kept you on your toes and swept you off of your feet. But now you want nothing to do with me?
> You are a very smart girl but... What makes you think you know everything about relationships, and what makes you think you are making the right decision and why won't you take into consideration all the facts that I present? What makes you think all of a sudden that we are very different? Sure, we have differences but we are very similar and always have been and I have the empirical data to back it up. I don't think you can find someone who can relate to you as well with all the things we've proven early in our relationship.
> We both want to learn more about God and seek Him. We have the same beliefs. We have the same values. Those two are really big deals. We enjoy the same kinds

of activities. We enjoy the outdoors, as well as indoor activities/game nights. We both want to see the world (yes, I would like to travel too). We enjoy similar media, be it music, movies, shows or what have you. We both enjoy playing instruments. We are both thinkers. Neither of us do drugs or smoke. Neither of us drink heavy or are into the bar scene. Neither of us uses foul language. We both appreciate the small things. We are both introverted/shy/quiet/socially awkward. We both like physical affection and kissing. Decisions are tough for each of us. We have a similar sense of humor and love to laugh. We both enjoy alone time. We both admit our mistakes. We both try to humble ourselves. We are both unique individuals, not too swayed by society. We are both educated and want to learn more, having done or plan on attending school for 4 plus years. We are creative, crafty, and talented in our own ways. There is so much more we don't know about each other, there is so much more we could have in common.

Part of me thinks that since you started acting weird when we got back from Pittsburgh that maybe there was something that Holly said that got you thinking. Please don't take offense, Holly is awesome and a great friend to you, but I hope you didn't get bad advice. Holly failed, and most people who divorce once, divorce twice, it is a fact. I don't like to bad mouth people, that is just a thought I had, and I hope the best for her and John. Another thought: maybe I should have let you hang with them more instead of going to see my brother.

Saying "it came to a time where it wasn't the right time to continue" and "we needed to go separate ways" are just robotic sentences developed from an over-thinker and they are complete *bullshivism*. All those doubts you have, are just in your head. Everything was fine and you were a perfectly good girlfriend to me. You used to always see the positives, now it seems you are only seeing the negatives.

You are a perfectionist but relationships will never be perfect, you will have doubts, you may not always feel like you are in love. This is normal. Relationships will never be convenient even if they seem that way at first. My friend Jason who has been married for 20 years even said sometimes he wakes up, looks at his wife and feels like he isn't in love. Relationships are more though, you stay with someone who is good to you, and good for you. I am those things for you, and it is because I want to be those things for you. And that is because I know you can be those things for me. I may not even always feel like I am "in love" with you (as I am pretty angry right now) but I know I love you and want to be with you. I have such strong feelings for you... I feel nobody could love you as much as me. I think that alone is a good enough reason to stay with someone. Our relationship was intense, and all relationships are intense for the initial six months. That initial feeling wears off a bit but doesn't mean there is something wrong. We wouldn't have to keep it so intense if we were to stay together. We wouldn't have to be up each other's butts all the time; we could ease into a more confident relationship and love. Making sacrifices will be necessary but that doesn't mean sacrificing who you are. It doesn't mean sacrificing the end-goal. The process may change a little, the means may be a little different but I wouldn't want to change you. I love you for you, and want to see your dreams come true, if you were to let me in on the fun.

Really the only legit excuse you have is the *kids* thing. If you ever have kids, I will be so mad at you.

Don't you even miss me? If you are missing me right now, I come at you with this question: why choose to hurt yourself and me by forcing us to be apart? We didn't force anything. We didn't force ourselves to be together. We didn't ignore anything. The facts were there and it didn't matter because we were happy. It was a natural and beautiful thing; I enjoyed your company to the utmost and couldn't get enough of your smile and your little comments. With as much connection and happiness we had, and with all the love I gave you, only giving me 6 months feels like an insult. I am obviously still working on forgiving you and I do, but like you said it is an ongoing process. I know this isn't what you meant to happen; I know you care. This is no one's fault.

Truth is I cry every day still (one month out). Lost my appetite and lost 15 lbs. in the first 2 weeks of us being apart. I have a constant empty hole feeling in my chest, a frog in my throat. My nerves are shot. I drove my firebird into a ditch, messed it up a little. Not only do I feel like I lost my girlfriend but I feel like you died because you won't even talk to me now. You were my new best friend, so I also lost my best friend.

As a resolution I am thinking about getting a puppy. I am taking a trip to Mississippi. I have applied to become a big brother for Big Brothers Big Sisters. I am back on internet dating for the distraction. But your memory will always be there, and I can't just block you out all suddenly like this. The following verse helps a bit:

"Beloved, do not be surprised at the fiery trial when it comes upon you to test you, as though something strange were happening to you. But rejoice insofar as you share Christ's sufferings, that you may also rejoice and be glad when his glory is revealed" (1 Peter 4:12-13 ESV).

You are wrong! We did not need to break up. There are other solutions to the problems. I hope you realize so many things, not just for my sake but also for yours. You are afraid of the commitment. Even when I used that word you acted so weird and couldn't describe your commitment to me. I feel I make you feel weird with my neediness or clinginess, but this stems from my being in love with you. Maybe if I didn't love you it would be easier for you to be in a relationship with me and it would last longer, but how is that fair? I love you Gabi...

with all of my heart. Love is all you need. Let me love you.

"If I speak in the tongues of men and of angels, but have not love, I am a noisy gong or a clanging cymbal. And if I have prophetic powers, and understand all mysteries and all knowledge, and if I have all faith, so as to remove mountains, but have not love, I am nothing. If I give away all I have, and if I deliver up my body to be burned, but have not love, I gain nothing.

Love is patient and kind; love does not envy or boast; it is not arrogant or rude. It does not insist on its own way; it is not irritable or resentful; it does not rejoice at wrongdoing, but rejoices with the truth. Love bears all things, believes all things, hopes all things, endures all things.

Love never ends. As for prophecies, they will pass away; as for tongues, they will cease; as for knowledge, it will pass away" (1 Corinthians 13:1-8 ESV).

"So now faith, hope, and love abide, these three; but the greatest of these is love" (1 Corinthian 13:13 ESV).

Put yourself in my shoes. I am in love with you, a feeling I never knew existed. I feel like you were perfect for me and the girl-of-my-dreams. The best days of my life were the days I spent with you. I don't just mutter those things to be cute or sweet, they are the honest truth. Now how would I be able to live with myself if I didn't try my *azz* off to keep you in my life? I know you think it is healthy to have "boundaries" but to be ignored by the person you love does not feel good at all. I want to respect this thought of yours and I am trying but I simply do not agree with your vision on this. It seems immature to me. I am no better though as my emotions make me feel like a teenager. I believe it is important to keep connections with people. Maybe I have attachment issues, whatever. You feel you need me to stay off and respect your space whereas I feel I need you to talk to me and try to work something out with me. I feel I need that. So, we conflict there and I am sorry.

You were literally the best thing that ever came into my life. You meant so much to me, you meant everything to me. You have done so much for me. You lit up my life. You helped me become better. I want to return those feelings to you because I care about you to the utmost. I want to learn how to respect you better. I want to ease your pain. I want to satisfy your needs. I need to discover what it is you need. I want you to feel good. I want you to be happy. I want you to succeed. I want to see you grow. I want to know how you are doing. I want to know how you are feeling. I want you to be comfortable. I want to hear about your day. I want to learn more about you. I want to hear about the complications. I want to know how you feel about all the things in the world. Is it selfish of me to want these things?

I fantasized about our future. I thought about ice skating, snowboarding, camping, kayaking, swimming, seeing comedy shows and going to concerts. I fantasized about taking road trips with you to Alabama, Colorado, LA, seeing the Grand Canyon, sharing driving time, seeing caves and mountains and plains, staying at hotels or hostels or sleeping in cars, seeing other landmarks. I fantasized about getting on my first plane with you and traveling the world, seeing the pyramids, seeing famous art pieces, seeing New Zealand, London, Venice. I fantasized about our wedding, and us living together. I fantasized about making love to you outdoors. I fantasized about waking up to you. I thought about Skyping with you if you were away for long periods of time and how awesomely intense it would be when I finally got to see you in person again. I fantasized about celebrating you receiving your Master's degree. I thought about us living together. I thought about talking and learning more about our pasts and more about your ideas of the future. I fantasized about getting to know your family better and one day calling your parents mom and dad. I fantasized about us volunteering together and making an impact in the world. I thought about how your ambition to study might make me want to go back to school. I thought about us doing more exercise activities like yoga or dancing. I thought about us making songs and other art forms together. I thought about when we got old, who would have to wipe whose butt.

I can hardly breathe without you. You may feel you don't need me but if you saw things my way maybe you would feel you need me for the following reasons. You need the hope I give you. You need my steadfastness and my unconditional love. You need me for how I am grounded. You need me for my honesty. You need my acceptance. We need each other for the smiles and laughter. Our differences make each other better. You always see the gray areas and that could help me with my black and whiteness. I hope my never-give-up attitude rubs off on you and helps you to complete your life tasks. I hope you can see things as I see them.

I am not normally like this. I wish these long letters came to you on the regular when we were good. I don't like the fact that I am only sending you these when it's a desperate attempt to get you back.

I don't want to pressure you or put you in weird spots, but is it really so hard to keep me around? Does life have to be so dramatic? If you are 100% sure this is what you want then I will have to deal with it. But you can take it all back. I have not told my mother that we split yet, it would break her heart. I ask you to please look at our relationship and to please consider keeping me in your life, and giving us more time to let love grow. You wouldn't have to meet my mom yet. You could set the pace, we could even do more of a casual dating type of thing, take our time. I will not trap you; I will not require much. There has got to be something that could sweeten the deal for you. There has got to be something else I could do that would make you want me. Part of who I am is my adaptability. I can prove to you that I am worth it. What is the man of your dreams like? I want to be that man for you. Please Gabi, I have resorted to begging, and I know that's unattractive but please Gabi find the place in your heart that will give us another chance. You can take your time to think about it, but please do, whether it's for a few days or for several months. I will try to make this my last connection, and I am sorry to bug. When I speak to God though, there's no indication our paths are meant to deviate.

Love,
Ray

I get no response this time. I am going to reach out to her parents and let them know that I tried. I am writing a physical letter to them:

Dear Liz and Cobydean,

First of all, I want to thank you guys for your acceptance and welcoming me into your beautiful home. It was a pleasure knowing you for that short amount of time and the memories will remain in my heart forever.
Although I wanted to take things slowly it was just too easy to fall in love with your daughter. She has a beautiful spirit and a gorgeous soul. From the start I did not think I was good enough for her, but she taught me a lot of things. She helped me with my self-worth, proved to me in a biblical manner that I indeed am good enough. She taught me the importance of acceptance, communication, forgiveness, being yourself, and just so many other things I could list. I was a better person because of her. The time I spent with her was the greatest time of my life and I have you guys to thank because you raised this amazing human being. You should be proud of her. I want you to know that we stayed true to our Christian faith and did not get

physical. Truth is I was preparing to ask you (Cobydean) for permission to take your daughter's hand. I am sorry I won't be able to celebrate more birthdays and traditions with you all. I am sorry I won't be able to produce grandchildren for you as I know how much you (Liz) longed for them. It just doesn't seem like Gabi will ever want to do that. I love every ounce of her soul with every ounce of mine but she decided we weren't meant to be. Although it pains me deeply, I am forgiving her as I know she didn't intend to hurt me. I pray both of our confusions subside and hearts heal.

I am sorry if this letter seems out-of-line but I felt the need to let you know how much I appreciate you and how amazing of a woman your daughter is and will become. Gabi will definitely succeed; she is so smart and determined to do bigger things. And I won't be in the way.

Much Love,
Ray

It is November 15th, almost two months after the break up. I remember how Gabi said she ignored the red flags in her previous relationships. Well I am texting her a rebuttal: "This time you ignored the green flags." I follow this text up with, "Since I had no say in us splitting up, you have no choice in us getting back together, see you tomorrow." This is clearly me just being frustrated with a hint of my usual humor, but I receive a response moments later: "Ray just sent that." I am no dummy but Gabi just made a rookie mistake. It is obvious she tried to share my text with someone so I text back, "telling people how crazy I am?" I myself have never said a bad word about Gabi to anyone or ever tried to portray her as the guilty party, and I am a little disturbed by this. Nonetheless nothing will hinder my feelings about her. I get a text from her which seems to finalize it all with a decree: "Look, I am sorry I hurt you, but I don't want kids and we have different priorities. Please respect my decision to move on. You will not show up at my house, and you will not contact me again." Everyday my heart just breaks more and more. I can't believe she is doing this to me. I email her some screenshots of text conversations I had with friends regarding her in an attempt to show her that I never said a bad word and to prove where my heart is. I also text her that I will love her forever. I mean it, but I know I am out of control. I am making it a point to stop though. Maybe she needs more time to think, maybe a few months, or maybe a year?

Chapter 17

Projects

I need a distraction so I dive into projects. My first mechanism is writing and here is a poem:

"The Nerve"

The nerve to shoot a hole in my chest
How dare I be weakened, destructive
Perspiring eyes, unclear perspective
Consuming my heart, my soul, they dissipate
Frogs for breakfast, lunch, and dinner
Blissful dreams, the death of a sinner
Tremors at the wake, shaky days
Everlasting wishes, banished
Wave to the past, goodbye love, you vanished

I have built up the nerve to step foot on my first plane. I am going to go see my "boy" and former coach: Cap. He is coaching football in Mississippi right now in a town very close to Memphis, Tennessee. I got a plane ticket to fly from Baltimore to Memphis where Cap will meet me. After a week we intend to drive back up together as he plans on visiting family and friends back up here.

Dad drives me to BWI Airport in his old rickety 1991 Nissan pickup. The thing seems perpetual. I am in the airport with an empty water bottle as I intend to fill it up somewhere after the security check. Security has been pretty crazy ever since 9-11. I figure out what I am supposed to do and where I am supposed to go pretty easily; the stress over the logistics is always worse than the actual actions. It's time to board so all the folks stand and form a line eventually making our way into the assigned seats on the plane. I am right up against some stranger, shoulder to shoulder, and it's quite uncomfortable. The plane starts to move and I am expecting a takeoff but it takes quite a while before we actually go. When it finally does go it seems powerful but not race car extreme. It actually reminds me a lot of a bus. This is just a giant "Aero-Bus." It seamlessly converts from on-ground to in-air without any evidence except for the visual through window. This isn't so bad at all.

The plane lands and the passengers scurry their way out of the Memphis airport and as soon as I step out, I see my friend: a large man who would need to buy two plane tickets for his body to board. It is quite a sight to see a familiar face in a not so familiar place. This feels like an alternate universe. It is November but feels like a mild summer day. With the sun shining we explore Memphis for a while, taking in the scenery. Home of the blues, and one of my favorite music genres, Memphis is very colorful. We visit the famous Beale street and just walk around, popping into a shop here and there. We stop in a place that serves alcoholic slushies and snow-cone-like treats. This is the proper thing to do mid-day, and mid-week. It is not terribly busy here given those facts. We chill for a bit and later find a restaurant with amazing food, and the friendliest people. Everyone says the word, "hun," making you feel like no stranger.

Cap actually lives in Clarksdale, Mississippi. It is a pretty small, poor, simple town but we arrive at Cap's house which looks like a giant plantation or a mansion of historical nature. He and his parents bought the estate for a quarter of what it would cost back home in Maryland, it's incredible. Morgan Freeman actually lives in this town and also co-owns a blues club called Ground Zero. We decide to visit the club and hope that Mr. Freeman himself makes an unannounced appearance as he apparently occasionally does. The club is located in an old building, not glamorous at all and has a bit of a run-down feel to it, but in a charming and artistic way. There is lots of graffiti everywhere, mismatched chairs, and Christmas lights hanging for illumination inside. A blues band plays most days here and today is no exception. The atmosphere is so laid back, the vibe chill, and the food is inexpensive and delicious. As I take in the bluesy sounds of the attractive blonde singer and guitarist, I realize this may be my favorite "club" I have ever been to. I paid 12 dollars for my meal and my whiskey. I would have paid 30 for it. Even though Morgan Freeman isn't appearing, it is still one of the greatest experiences of my life. I guess I am simple in that way.

Cap and I drive around looking at some of the nearby schools and football facilities, and it is interesting to see how much bigger football is down here.

On our way back we stop in Nashville where my other buddy Steve lives. Steven Upshaw is a country musician trying to become big here in Nashville. We were great friends in elementary school and had gotten reacquainted recently. He has become a handsome man with much talent, I mean he really looks like he could be a country music star. Cap drops me off at Steve's house where he lives with his girlfriend who is gorgeously cute herself. They really are a beautiful couple and could be the poster children for the country music scene complete with an energetic chocolate lab. As we hang around a fire drinking beer, they ask why I am here and I tell them, "forgetting a woman." I don't go into detail but they express condolences. Steve and I then decide to head into town and check out a bar. Music continues as another band is performing live. Before too long Cap says he's coming to get me to take me to the hotel. When we settle in, we start talking about girls and my situation and the frustration comes out and I punch the door. Cap and I have gotten pretty close and I have shared a bunch of stuff with him, but there is so much more inside me that I refuse to dispense.

On the rest of the long drive back we listen to music and are awarded the sight of the Great Smoky Mountains. I conjecture they are called that due to fog that resembles smoke but it looks pretty clear to me at the moment. All in all, I really liked Mississippi, Tennessee, and the trip in general and I feel lucky to have Cap as a friend. I feel like nothing will pick me up out of this heartbroken land though.

My buddy Matthew has been through an intense relationship failure himself. His involves a wife and kids, and how much more emotion could go into all that is beyond me as I am experiencing my limits. He is going through a divorce and lots of arguments over the kids. He is about the only individual I talk to about personal issues and we relate so we either help or enable each other in some way but we are about all we have. Matthew invites me to a new year's party a friend of his is throwing; we are going realizing we each need to blow off some steam. We arrive at the house and just kind of stand around in the kitchen drinking and blabbing as I realize his friend is gay. It must be hard for gay people and all the backlash they get from Christians and traditional views. They start talking about religion without the realization that I am a Christian, and I hear things like, "Oh, Christians are the worst." I refrain from getting into any heated arguments with anyone because I have my own belief issues to work out but the conversation starts to affect me. I start thinking about how it feels like God left me, and I think about my situation with Gabi and I feel like I am near a breakdown. I have to excuse myself to go outside, get a breather, and camouflage these tears. When I return the tone is different and people seem to be approaching me in a friendlier way. I believe Matthew probably mentioned laying off on the religion talk. He is a true friend. Afterwards we ride back and get to talking and I break down and start to cry right in front of him. This is a first, to show my true emotion to a friend like this. We survive the night.

My next project of distraction is to make clear taillights for my Firebird. That is after I submit an insurance claim to straighten out the front end. The car is returned to me and they had repainted my front nose as well as straightened the bent exhaust pipe. I am not mad to pay a few hundred out of pocket to get this car back up to shape, I want it to eventually be a car I can take to car shows. My color theme is navy blue with all white or silver details and the red taillights are screaming to be altered. I learn that you can use a heat gun to melt the silicone and take apart the taillights. After a quick run I realize these particular ones don't have a separate red piece that I can delete. So, I buy a pair of taillights from an LT1 Trans-Am. They are already starting to come apart naturally with age, so I continue the process. I am able to pry them apart and find great joy in it. The difficult part will be grinding off this black grid, and sure enough I slip and cut my thumb. It's not tremendous so I just put some tape around it so particles won't get in there. What I want to do is take off this black grid, and paint a honeycomb pattern on the lens with black paint. This way it will look similar to the newer cars. It will still have the red reflector which I think is required by law. I also will put red bulbs in the brake lights because red illumination surely is mandatory for rear lights. I am able to sand down the lens really smoothly, and I figure clear paint will add shimmer back to it. I have the honeycomb pattern cut from a vinyl paint mask at my workplace and lay it onto the inside of the lens. I paint black first so it will show on the outside, then I paint white to add extra light reflection inside the lens. I discover the glue I bought doesn't react well with the plastic so I proceed forward exclusively with silicone. I paint black trim around the outside and introduce a clear coat; it looks pretty good. I reassemble it, purchase some amber bulbs of which I add red sleeves to, and viola the project is complete. But I have to do it all over again for the other side. It was kind of a cumbersome task but well worth the result.

Maybe something Gabi found unattractive was the fact that I didn't possess a passport. I have never had anyone really to go anywhere with nor have zeal for future traveling. I will have to obtain my passport, as I do have the desire to visit New Zealand, England, and even Germany since my cousin resides there. I go to the library and fill out the form to get a passport. I'm required to mail in my actual birth certificate. That is scary, what if I never get it back? I do get it back but in a separate envelope and on a separate occasion than the passport. That seems weird at first but it makes sense because you wouldn't want both to disappear in the event of a tamper of some sort. But wow here it is, my passport!

It's April and it has been approximately six months since the dreaded breakup. I have lost twenty pounds and gained it all back twice already. On the other hand, I am pretty proud that I haven't tried to contact Gabi since November. It has been really hard but I wonder how she is, what she is thinking, and if she misses me. I have a thought that maybe Gabi has the same thought as me, maybe she will randomly show up at the place we originally met a year prior. It is April 9th, 2018 and I am at the Frederick Café. I have been praying and hoping that God will fix me or fix this story. I wait a little while with patience but decide to shoot Gabi a text. I say, "At this Café a year ago today I met a girl who would ultimately blow me away. This feeling I shall not betray, so for a miracle to reappear I pray." Hours go by and nothing happens. I am wearing a ball cap slanted low on my face to hide my emotions and tears. No answers come to me and I head home embarrassed with myself.

Perhaps if I put up a public posting expressing myself on Facebook, Gabi will discover it one day and decide to contact me. I have written a poem and am posting it June 23rd (Gabi's birthday):

"Dancing in the Rain"

Last summer's story was the single greatest period of my life. Credit given to the fact that I was seein' the absolute girl of my dreams. No one shall enjoy such joy for too long though it seems. As now I am pierced daily in the night like a knife, last summer's breeze was the climatic chapter of my life.
Dear Miss Mystery Girl, thank you for giving me a little taste of heaven. I will love you forever. Happy birthday to you, but a happy death day for me would be just the same. For, when I finally close my eyes, my heaven will be us... dancing in the rain.

Every sentiment in it is authentic to me. The post is complete with a photo of the two of us while we were dancing in the rain up at Delgrosso's Park. You can't really recognize her face and I have been pretty good about not sharing her name or pictures on Facebook for her privacy. Later on, I may hit up a friend of hers on Facebook in hopes that they'll see this post, and hopefully land an extra point for me. I miss Gabi so much.

Since I am contemplating the meaning of life and seeing so much pointlessness, I am feeling the need to give back to society in some manner. Maybe I can leave a lasting mark on someone somehow. After I apply to be a "Big Brother" with Big Brothers-Big Sisters, they run a background check and I am cleared to start the match-making process. I get matched with an eight-year-old fatherless boy. He is a cool dude and I try to impress him. We do artsy things and play sports. I hope I can act like a friend and not like a parent.

Through the organization I get linked up with a mother of one of the little sisters. The 9-year-old kid wrote a story and her mother is looking to get it published but wants illustrations. So, this is adding another project to my catalog. It will be interesting to get some of my work out in a legitimate publication.

I am tired of being hounded by my dad questioning my agenda every single day and not having any clue what is going on in my head or in my life. I just want to be by myself so I request that he vacate my house. I'm putting it simple: "Dad, I love you but I want you to move out." I am giving him until the end of the year, which is approximately six months.

My sister has a special arrangement with her job which provides free therapy sessions for her or an immediate family member. So, this I am taking advantage of. Naturally, the immediate thing they do is suggest medicine. My problem is not about physical feelings, it is about what I believe. I believe I have somehow stumbled into an alternate universe where God is dead. I refuse medication. The therapist herself is really soothing to talk to in a way. She opens up with the commonplace print-out describing the multiple stages of coping with loss. I exit most sessions immediately crying in my car. What is the point? Is it helping?

Maybe another cross-country trip will help. I have bought a kayak at Walmart and am strapping it to the roof of my Mazda. I am driving it all the way to Florida to see my buddy Rich. Along the way I will drop off the old taillights from my firebird that I sold on eBay to their respective destinations. I realized shipping is super expensive so decided to save a buck and add adventure to my trip. I will have to pass through Charlotte, North Carolina and a small town in Georgia. I get to drive past the stadium where the Panthers play after my initial stop. There is substantial traffic in this area. There is minimal traffic as I cross over the Georgia state line. Tons of really tall and skinny trees stand across either side of the road as if this narrow pathway was cut through a thick forest. It's scenic and dreamy, a passageway into the unknown. The sky becomes darker but I have several more hours yet to go. My final destination: Orlando.

Florida is a different place, complete with palm trees and a weird way to turn through big looping streets. Lizards populate the area like birds. I have never seen wild lizards before, and it's engaging. I have a child-like desire to chase one. Rich has two roommates in his apartment including his girlfriend and some dude. Rich has an air mattress for me and a giant padding topper for it. It is a surprisingly comfortable sleep.

Orlando is home of big theme parks, but we don't actually go inside any of them. We do however visit Disney Springs which is a fancy water side shopping area. We also visit the free admission entrance section to Orlando Studios. Lots of stuff to look at here. Tons of people coming in and out of the resort. It is one of the biggest things I've ever attended and I am just at the entrance area. We also hop in the car and travel towards Tampa to visit Clearwater Beach as I get a chance to experience the Gulf of Mexico. The water isn't super clear today but I guess sometimes it is depending on conditions. The water is really warm though! I snap a few photographs but wish Gabi appeared next to me in them.

Another day, another adventure; we are visiting Gator-Land. Here we see a bunch of alligators and other wildlife in a zoological atmosphere. I see two white alligators although only one of them is albino. This place is interesting, you can also do zip lining. Rich doesn't want to join in, I guess he is afraid of heights, but I strap up. I am flying over gator-infested waters. It is pretty fun, but not as much exhilarating fear struck me as I had anticipated.

I brought this kayak so we've got to utilize it. We find a place at a creek that rents out kayaks because this time Rich is going to join in. At the rental place they inform us that there is an alligator named George that lives in the creek. Before setting out, Rich gets a plastic baggy and puts his phone in it so he can bring it along just in case we need it. We get a quick tutorial and head up stream. It is serene, tranquil, and fun. I am glad I'm able to share this moment with Rich even though I wish you-know-who was here. About 45 minutes in we decide to turn around. I basically crossed over this log or branch on the way up and assume I can cross it again coming back down. I seem to get over it fine but suddenly I feel wobbly and try to compensate when it's too late and I capsize. Trying to grab my paddle and my kayak at the same time proves impossible so I just save the paddle. I swim to a log so I can rest, although still very submerged in water. "Well now what?" I mutter to Rich, as my kayak floats away from sight. He remembers he brought his phone so he paddles to the ledge and gives the rental office a call. I wonder how often they receive "rescue me" calls. They said someone will come up and help us. Meanwhile I am sitting here in the water for about a half hour and we finally decide to try to transport my carcass to dry land. We were advised on how to lug a person by kayak without making Rich capsize as well so I grab onto the back of his kayak and just hang on like a literal dead body. He paddles upstream about 15 yards to the concrete area and says that was the biggest upper body workout he ever had to endure. We hang out there for about another half hour and finally the guy arrives and saves the day as he also managed to find my kayak and drag it along. He says it was nearly completely underwater but being bright orange, it was easy to spot out. I don't trust the thing anymore, it seemed way too easy to fall out of. Nonetheless I hop back in it and cruise on back down stream. Rich confirms he really enjoyed the kayaking experience (it was his first time) and believes it could be something he could do on more occasions. Me, on the other hand, I might be giving it up. What if George the alligator was hungry?

I want to try eating some gator. We find a restaurant that sells gator and I can only assume I'm eating a chunk of George's brother. It reminds me of a mixture between chicken and scallops.

I am driving back home and bringing Rich with me as he intends to visit with his family, up in PA, for a while. Along the way up we decide to check out an Atlantic beach near Daytona. There is no one here but me, it is my personal beach party. Exploring the area is fun and we end up spending a night in a motel before we head back to Hagerstown where Rich's dad (Rich Fogart the first) meets him to take him back home to be with his son (with an entirely new name). Even though I clearly have friends, I still feel alone.

My old football buddy Danny Busch just got a job as head football coach at James Buchanan High School and asked me if I would like to coach under him as the defensive coordinator. Of course, I take the opportunity and am grateful for it. This will be good as an additional distraction from my mental state. I am a little nervous initially meeting the rest of the staff (all James Buchanan Alumni), and meeting the kids too isn't easy. Succeeding a few practices, I seem to come into my own groove and feel complacent about the team and situation. We decide to run a 3-3-5 defense which requires 3 linemen, 3 linebackers, and 5 defensive backs. It functions well due to the personnel we have and the fact that I am familiar with it and the simple gap responsibilities. I quickly draw up the defensive playbook and disperse copies to everyone. When I decide to do something, I am typically pretty all-in, and coaching is no exception. We have some talent (three or four of the kids can do backflips) and are full of zeal for the possibility of the first winning season at the school in over a decade. It is a small school so not much is expected of us. Our main battle is the culture around here, with the politics and the traditions that have little to do with football. We just want to win games. I occasionally find myself going through spells of the inability to cope and once in a while the other coaches ask me if I am alright. It's right around the anniversary of the worst day of my life, and it hits me hard. I am not alright but I don't lead on just how severe it is.

I get to talking to my friend Stephanie Manson who is actually an Alumni of James Buchanan as well. I had a bit of a crush on her ever since that day superstar Steve Upshaw brought her to my Halloween party. I look back on our messages and it seems I have asked her out like five times before. Finally, she is available. She tells me her and Steve were only ever just friends, so it's good I am not dating a friend's ex. I have dated a friend's sister which is probably even worse. Stephanie is unique, she is into heavy metal but is girlie too. She has a kid nowadays, a little two-year-old. Stephanie bought her own house in Waynesboro about a year ago and works from home. She is upfront and pretty smart with a little bit of a wild side. She is thin, fair skinned, has long dark hair, sometimes straight, sometimes crimped, and has a few tattoos and a lip piercing. After a date we decide to watch a movie at her house. Afterwards it's time to go and I get up and say, "So, what's up, should we kiss?" We kind of stumble around awkwardly but she eventually says, "oh, I'll just do it." And so, we are sharing a kiss. My first kiss after Gabi, and my first kiss in a year. It feels great but at the same time Gabi is on my mind 24/7 and she is all I can think about on the weirdly surreal ride home.

Stephanie and I start to see each other more and start to really like each other. We become closer and I tell her a bit of my story and how I haven't actually even had sex in about three years. We start to get intimate and she warns me that she gets really wet. "Haha, that sounds like a good thing," I say. She is on top of me and I enter. Oh my gosh it feels so good, I can't believe how amazing it is, it feels like I have never done this before. I express to Stephanie, "you don't know how great it feels to be a man experiencing your vagina right now." It's hot in here and we are sweating like crazy but who cares when you're having so much fun. Afterwards we lie there and turn on the TV. I start thinking about everything and have a little bit of an emotional breakdown right next to her. I hide it though, and questions don't arise. I feel like I am cheating on Gabi though.

The second time we get physical I realize what Stephanie meant by "get really wet." I discover a little squirt. This is exciting. I initially thought she meant that she gets sweaty. The physical is good and we connect pretty well mentally too. I am currently battling God and she has had her battles too. Although she does not consider herself Christian, I am not at a place where I can judge. Something we each value is to not be judgmental.

It is Halloween season and I do my prototypical costume creation to go trick-or-treating with my nieces. Stephanie is into the dressing up thing as an adult too. There is a costume contest at a nearby bar that Stephanie wants to compete in. She is doing this really revealing mermaid costume. She is sure to win out of pure sexiness. Sure-enough she does. I had fun tagging along but the bar allows smoking so the stench is stuck in my clothes and I absolutely loathe it. Social ability seems a lot easier for Stephanie than it is me; she made her rounds and talked to a plethora of people. It's not a problem between us though. After a while we realize there is a real problem, and that is the fact that I am simply not over Gabi. I tried to move on from her but I just don't feel capable, it isn't fair to Stephanie. I still find myself weeping pretty much every day.

I asked Demetrius what the best way to get over a woman is. He responded saying: "get under another woman." Well, that clearly didn't work.

Gabi didn't have a Facebook profile before but I discover that she has created one. Her profile picture features her with another man. Of course, it hurts. I haven't spoken to her in a year and I've decided to send her an email (November 11th, 2018):

> Hey Gabi,
>
> I am sorry I keep contacting you. And I am sorry but I actually tried to contact some of your friends on Facebook. Please understand it's just been hard for me. I knew not contacting you would be an impossible task for me. I tried but it's just not in my blood to completely let go of people like this... especially people that mean so much to me and that I care about so much. It's hard for

me to understand your view on this. I wanted to contact you every day, but most days I succeed in fighting it off. It just annoys you and makes it hard on you, and I am sorry. When I message you and I get no reply it makes me feel worthless, like I don't matter, and it hurts badly, so I guess it would be wise if I stopped. But I am a fighter Gabi, I fight for what I believe in, and so much of me believes we are supposed to be together.

I could tell you I love you until I am blue in the face. I could tell you I need you till I am blue in the face. I could ask you to talk to me until I am blue in the face. I'm coming to realize nothing I say will change your view. The only way you could come around is if you did it on your own.

I hope you are finding your way. I hope all your dreams, hopes, and wishes come true. I hope you come to love yourself. I hope you continue to get closer to God. I hope you feel fulfilled in your life works. I just wish so badly I could be there to witness your growth and to share it with you.

I have been doing a plethora of things, new things, to try to move on. I got my passport, I took vacations, I tried dating, I saw a professional... but I still feel the same. Everything I said was true, I will forever have love for you. Call me crazy, I don't care.

Maybe you didn't feel the same, but you didn't have to. You treated me exactly how I wanted to be treated. To me our relationship really was perfect. How suddenly it ended was shocking and makes me think I didn't get the full truth as to why you left. What you gave me seemed like excuses and not reasons. They might have been good reasons not to start a relationship, but we were already deep into a relationship and they didn't seem like good reasons to leave. If there is a truth that I didn't get, I think I'd prefer to hear it, even if it hurts. Part of me thinks you didn't forgive me for the one mistake I made. Gabi I am so sorry.

It really feels like I need you... I don't want to need someone, but it's how I feel. I need you for emotional stability, for spiritual stability, and for mental stimulation. Almost seems dumb writing it down.

I don't know what to do Gabi. It will be very difficult to ever meet someone as awesome as you again. There is no way I could ever love someone that much again, also there is no way in my eyes anyone else will ever love you as much as I do. You know I would do anything right? You know I would never hurt you right? Do my messages scare you? I am sorry if they do.

Please just tell me you are ok. If that is all you say well then that is all you say, but at least I will feel like you at least care a little. Thank you for everything you beautiful dream.

Love,
Ray

I receive a notice saying the email was not delivered. This demonstrates that she has blocked me. That hurts. Do I deserve to be blocked? Does anyone? Why do people do that? I would never block someone; it doesn't seem right to me. I can't find her Facebook either now, she has blocked me there too.

Football season is over and I need another thing to keep me busy. Every hour of every day needs to be filled or I may go insane and kill myself. I am conceptualizing another car project. I've always been fond of the high-rise spoilers on the Trans Ams. My car has the regular molded spoiler though. My idea is to hand fabricate a spoiler out of fiberglass. The design in essence will look like an extension of the existing spoiler from a side profile, but from the rear you will see the opening for air passage and extra downforce. Every day I arrive home from work and immediately buckle down on this project. Every night I pray to God to give me strength to endure my time away from Gabi. I also pray to help Gabi, and to help each of us get better.

I shape the wing from pink foam, then I seal it with wood glue and proceed to do the fiber glassing process. Next is multiple layers of Bondo followed by sanding to smooth out the surfaces. An electric paint gun turns out to be a failure and a wasted investment so I strip that crap off, apply a heap of primer, and just take it into Maaco. It gets returned to me and looks professional. I debate for a while whether or not I should actually bolt it on to my car. In the end I decide to install it because it's a reflection of who I am and what I do.

I'm making my own Christmas tree this year out of plastic bottles, and my "little brother" is helping. First, we attach a pole to a stand and wrap multi-color lights around it. Then we use hot glue to build up a bunch of clear bottles, bigger ones on the bottom, and smaller ones near the top. The colored light shines and reflects in an interesting way through the bottles. I am satisfied with this one-off idea.

My dad has moved out, he literally milked every day in his allowance and moved out December 31st. I finally have my time alone, my time to cry out loud, to pace back and forth through my house, and I like it. Scenarios pop up in my mind of me being face to face with Gabi, pleading, bleeding internally, and it affects me externally. I experience what could almost be called a flashback or a panic attack daily. I am conscious of it though and I choose to do it, or do I? I have cried almost every day for 463 days now.

I am rejoining the Tigers football team that I had played for many moons ago. I have become aware that one of my favorite coaches is involved with the team: Coach Johnson. I played for him when he was the defensive coordinator with the Chambersburg Cardinals. His defense is basically what I run in my coaching at the high school. Ember, who coaches with me at James Buchanan, is also joining the team. It should be fun. I come out on fire and do really well at the initial practices. There is a heap of hype around my appearance, but that hype diminishes significantly after a scrimmage proves that I am a regular man. I am doing my best but my head of course isn't currently all put together. I do not train like I should, nor prepare like I ought to, and I am simply not as quick as the younger version of myself. I am doing the best I can in maintaining a seemingly normal mental state. The team has a lot of talent and I am just as happy being a back-up. I am glad to add another thing to my list of distractions, but I won't be able to play football forever.

What I can do forever is love Gabi! I am trying to let fate fix it again. If our kindred spirits can reconnect maybe she will show up at the Café this year. So, I do my thing again April 9th, 2019, but again she doesn't show up. I had told Matthew I was busy today but I won't admit why.

I still try to date. I enjoy having someone to talk to, and some physical touch. I want to feel human. Match.com is always good to me and I come across this girl named Autumn. She is actually a local Christian single with no kids and has never been married. My only deterrent is her hideous eyebrows. They have been plucked way too thin. I am not a shallow man though so I message her. She is a little deterred by my long and stringent list of requirements I put on my profile. Nonetheless we chat and decide to meet. I am at the recently fancied up bowling alley in Hagerstown waiting for her. As she appears, I notice she's taller than expected, especially for being half Chinese. She is Approximately 5'-7", super thin, and has long straight black hair. We talk, and bowl, and drink, and flirt. I find out that she actually works for a business located directly right across the street from my job in Frederick. That's a wild coincidence. She is currently doing secretarial work for the company while studying to become a counselor. She has had her personal battles with substance abuse involving pain killers and other pills and so she wants to give back and help others that may have had similar addiction problems. I find it admirable that she has this ambition and has been clean for seven years.

Autumn Green (as I discover her full name to be) invites herself over to my house on our first date, and I invite myself to plunder a kiss. I do this while she is talking mid-sentence. I figure if she is in my house then she must want it. It doesn't progress to sex and I am glad because that is weird for a first date, but she does stay the night. No drinking-and-driving is happening. She will not wreck her blue 2016 Camaro. Yeah, we both drive a blue GM sports car. We relate in many ways and on paper it is a perfect situation for us. We desire similar things.

After a few short months I am supposed to already know that she wants me to peel her eggs in the morning for her. When I see her in a dress I am supposed to say "Holy mackerel Autumn, you are the most beautiful thing in the world in that dress." I don't live up to her expectations and our relationship fades. We keep talking though, I guess a sector of my brain aspires to work something out. She is not allowed pets at her residence but she has a chihuahua that needs a home. I agree to look after "Beamer" for her. The dog is named after a car. Autumn brings him from her ex-boyfriend's house directly to mine. He's a pretty old dog with limited energy so taking care of him is a cinch. I give Autumn a key to my house so she can come and let him out while I am at work during the week (she gets home sooner than I do). About a month in I notice Autumn has left some items at my place accidentally. I see some developed photographs from CVS and I become nosey. I see pictures of her and some guy, is this her brother or a friend? There's a picture with the two of them kissing. Why does this hurt so much? How do people move so quickly from one individual to another? I decide to have Autumn take her dog and cut our ties as I don't need a perpetual reminder of pain and rejection on top of my daily memory of Gabi.

It's an ordinary summer day at my house. I am always on the verge of a breakdown but today it happens in front of my dad and my nieces. A sentence is muttered that sends a wave of pain through my brain and I flop on the ground crying and thumping my fists on the ground. I screech "Someday someone will appreciate me." I calm down and hide in my bedroom for the rest of the day. This "one day at a time" thing is getting old.

It's an ordinary summer day at my work desk. Wasting time, with my phone in my hand, I'm scrolling through Facebook posts. Suddenly I seize a "déjà-vu" feeling. Yet to see it, I envision an image of my friend Charlotte Flutie's dog as I scroll. I take a second and say to myself that if the next thing I see indeed is her dog then that is freaky. I proceed to scroll and sure enough there is her boxer staring at me! I put my phone down and look around in hysteria. Now I envision my co-worker having particular movements as she uses her cell phone. I peek around the corner and see her raise her phone to her ear exactly like I envisioned. Real psychic stuff is happening to me. It lasts about five seconds. What does it all mean? I now have information that could have grave implications on the world and existence as we know it. A "déjà vu" is not what science currently says it is: electrical impulses in the brain making one have a sensation that they have been there before, as if these impulses are randomly firing in memory banks when they shouldn't. I thought I was just experiencing a "déjà vu" as I often do. This time it was greater though. Not only did I feel like I was living a memory but for five seconds I was able to accurately prophesy what was going to happen next. I was able to literally see five seconds into the future. I remembered the future! This is not a joke. More research needs to be conducted. Perhaps the future is indeed already written and we have no free will at all. Perhaps time travel is actually possible. This life episode is affecting me greatly and I don't think it should be ignored. What will people say if I tell them? Will everyone think I am crazy?

I am drawing a flower, delicate and sensual, colorful and innocent. With a light shining under it I flip it over and draw another flower in the exact yet opposite position on the page, this one in different colors. One side I write, "te amo." On the other side I write, "siempre." Those words are Spanish for "I love you," and "always." I am mailing it to Gabi.

I try to hold off on writing Gabi a letter but I feel it might be weird to just send that drawing and this letter might compliment it well. I am lying in this letter and saying that I am recovered and doing well; it is how I should currently feel, and how I would expect myself to feel soon if I were a normal person. (July 2019)

Gabi,

I was worried that I could worship you over God, and that is exactly what I ended up doing. I have the ability to slip into depression, not your fault, it's just part of who I am and I fell very depressed after we broke up. This lasted well over a year, but I finally came to realize that I needed to put God first. I have now put God first and I am telling you I am recovering and I am OK!

This does not mean that I no longer love you. I still love you, I always will. You know you can rely on that. I am ok with this. I Love you abundantly and would do just about anything for you. But I hope one day someone loves you the exact amount you want and the exact way you need to be loved. In the end as much as I wish that person was me, I really just want you to be happy.

Every now and again I will think about something you did or said and it brings a smile to my face. I will forever regard the spring and summer of 2017 as the greatest days of my life. When I was with you, I felt like you were helping me become the man I want to be. Even my sister said that you had brought out the best in me. Thank you! You know how you posted Bible verses up on your wall? Well I have done the same to my cubicle walls at work, and it's helped me get through. My favorites include Romans 5:4, James 1:4, Joshua 1:9, Romans 8:18, Jeremiah 29:11, and 1 Peter 4:12-13.

I am working on separating my love for you from my love for God. I am working on becoming selfless. I have always viewed my life story as me following God and then being rewarded with everything I desired. All those things fell into place with perfect timing including the last brick that I thought was you. I thought you were another proof of God's existence. I see now that this is a selfish way of thinking and it might have put some pressure on you.

I want to confess the only lie I told you during our relationship. Do you remember when that young cat was chasing that young bunny in front of your house? Before we walked into your house, I told you I saw the bunny and it was safe. I did not actually see the bunny, but I didn't want you to be sad.

Since our split I have done so many new things that I wish I could tell you about. One thing I will say is that I got my passport... man would I love to take you to London and see Stonehenge or wherever! I am progressing, making new goals and aspirations, and I am giving back to the world. Wish I could share these things with you. I hope you are finding your way, pressing through your plans. If your plans have changed, I hope you are progressing through them with God by your side. I hope all your dreams, hopes, and wishes come true. I hope you come to love yourself. I hope you continue to get closer to God. I hope you feel fulfilled in your life works. You deserve all of that.

I knew not contacting you would be a task I could not achieve. I know it's hard to understand another person's feelings. I hope this letter or the memory of me doesn't make you cry. I am sorry for any uneasy feelings I gave you through this process. I hope we can forgive each other. I won't expect it but it would mean so much to me to hear from you.

Ray

Summer advances and of course I hear nothing from Gabi. I do still dream though. I dream of Gabi jumping on a pogo stick with a giant smile on her face. I awaken in a weeping state but it gives me an idea. I should buy her a pogo stick and mail it to her. She had told me a story of how she was young and counted how many jumps she could do on a pogo stick. The number was seven hundred or something crazy. Doing this is probably crazy too, but what do I have to lose? I already lost everything when Gabi left. It feels like she passed away and I am a widow (or a *midom*, which is what I would call a male widow). Not only did she abandon me but it feels like God did too. I have been praying so hard for two years now and there's no evidence he's listening. I want this to end. My prayers at night are changing from "give me strength and understanding," to just not wanting to wake up. I pray that God takes my life in my sleep. I don't want to live without Gabi. I see now too that the future is already written, and I do not grasp the point of having to live out this pain for the rest of my life. I keep telling myself to just make it to 2020. Something eminent has got to happen then, it's my favorite number twice, otherwise it'll be the perfect year to kill myself.

Cars always make me happy; I own two cars, but I think I am done with this little Mazda now. It's so light and I feel the struggle as it battles the wind going down the highway. I am ready for a big-boy car. I desire something larger, more powerful, and just as reliable. I do some research and discover the perfect car for my needs and wants might be a Lexus GS350. A used one between the years 2006 and 2012 and with 50-120 thousand miles on it should cost in a range from $10,000-$20,000. They look and feel like a brand-new car with push button start and big navigation screen along with leather and AWD. I do my habitual internet search and hope to locate a red one, as I always wanted a bright red car. I succeed; there's a red 2008 with 105k miles on it for $10,999, but I also see a silver 2007 with 48k miles on it for $12,249. The latter is a better deal so I make the purchase. You can't go wrong with silver, and I've never owned a car with so little miles on it. I practically just bought a brand-new luxury machine with 303 horsepower for only $12,249. Plus, it's a Lexus so it will last forever!

730 days of anguish and more days across from a therapist. The little round scarf bearing man wants to treat me for Post-Traumatic Stress Disorder. He's basically diagnosing me with a plethora of mental illnesses including depression, social anxiety, separation anxiety, and PTSD. He seems cool initially but as time

passes by, I feel like he is more concerned with the "by the book" process than my actual feelings. I am supposed to meet him early in the morning on this particular day, but he is nowhere to be found. I guess no one cares about me, even if I pay them to.

It's been a year since we last hung out but I am talking to Stephanie again. We hang out a few times and I give her a sweet kiss as she leaves my house today. She asks me, "What has happened that makes this different than before?" I respond with, "a year happened." I really like Stephanie, she is real, open, and fun to be with. Later a text alludes to what I would do if Gabi returned to my life. I try to be honest and explain how I never loved anyone the way I loved her so I simply don't know. That was the wrong response. Stephanie affirms she won't settle on being someone's second option. I hate that I do this to people. I am feeling like my honesty is doing nothing but hurting me. What if I never told Gabi that I found her internet nude?

- Chapter 18 -
New News

Every time I search Gabi's name on the internet, it just brings me down, yet I am compelled to do it again. This time I find something about a business partnership with her and some dude named Joseph. It is called Stotler RV service, and it's located in Florida. It's a partnership between Joseph Stotler and Gabrielle Tipton. What the heck is this? Who is this guy? I find him on Facebook and see that he is a thick guy with a dorky smile and nerdy glasses. I see pictures of him and Gabi, and my chest hurts. I continue looking and discover he is engaged. He is engaged to the woman I am supposed to marry. He is going to marry the love-of-my-life. This can't happen. I get up and I pace and I scream-cry again in a convoluted dimension. How can someone get two guys in two years to want to marry them? How is that possible?

 I need to speak to Gabi. I need to inform her that she is all I have been able to think about all day every day for two years now. This can save my life, otherwise I don't see a reason to live. I find the contact to the RV service; there are two numbers for it. I assume the second number might be Gabi's, so I dial it. I do not get an answer so I dial the first listed number. I hear a man's voice answer: "Hello." I say, "Hi, may I speak to Gabrielle please?" He says, "sure hold on." Finally, I am going to be able to talk to my soul mate. I am nervous yet excited because it has been so long. But then Joseph asks me who is speaking. I say, "this is Dave," and he responds, "um, Dave who?" I stumble upon my words; I am unable to keep up the charade and so I just come clean admitting who I am and that I just need to talk to Gabi. He goes to ask Gabi and comes back saying "she says she's good," refusing to talk to me. I go on pleading, and saying that all I think about is talking to her but she has blocked me. He responds with "you think there's probably a reason for that." I tell him I didn't do anything though. I go on saying I am struggling with my faith and I ask if he believes in god. He gives me the "I believe in a higher-power" cliché and I can't believe it. My girl is very religious and she is marrying a guy who says he believes in a "higher-power"? What is going on? Nothing makes sense. Then I admit to Joseph that I am having suicidal thoughts. He tells me to go to a hospital. Finally, he hangs up after telling me to seek help. All the things I have done don't help though; I have done everything I can think of.

I get a phone call a few moments later and I answer hoping it is Gabi. For years now every time my phone makes a buzz, my hearts pounds and I pray that it is Gabi, but it never is. It is the suicide hotline calling me. I talk to them a little and weep a little and tell them the story. They don't reveal who called the hotline for me but it was obviously Gabi so I request that they tell her I love her. At least she cared enough to call the hotline for me.

Screw it I am going to Las Vegas, and maybe I will drive out to the Grand Canyon and jump into it. I never had a desire to go to Vegas but the Canyon is an attraction and I really want to drive out to Los Angeles and witness the car show that they formulate every November. The flights to Vegas are cheaper than LA and so I figure I'll rent a car and do some driving. I purchase some plane tickets and start to work out an itinerary for myself. I have one week of vacation and plan to jam a bunch of activities into my first trip to the west coast. I could effectively do this alone but I get to thinking that maybe my dad who has never been out that way might be interested in joining and checking off a bucket list item. I ask him and he says yes, so I have to get plane tickets for the same exact flights.

We land in Vegas November 20th and I rent a sick brand-new black Camaro convertible. We cruise out to our hotel which is off from the main strip by two blocks. It is a pleasant little calm hotel with ample parking which is always a concern for me when traveling to big cities. I learn that all hotels have a casino within them so I pay a visit and decide to try my luck at roulette. I devise a plan to bet on red every single time since the odds of winning are 50 percent. Each time I lose I simply bet double my last bet and eventually get back what I lost. My starting point is 25 cents, and I am just feeling out my strategy. I end up winning

50 bucks. I must be a genius. I get on my phone and do some research and it turns out my strategy is called "martingale." So, I didn't make it up after all. I never thought of myself as a gambling man but this is exciting, and I can see why it would be addictive.

Day two of west coast adventure sends us eastward through Arizona to see the Grand Canyon, but along the way we stop to see the Hoover Dam. On the pathway walking up to see it there is a memorial of Pat Tillman. He was an NFL player who quit the league to serve the country in the Army and wound up getting killed. It's an amazing story and he deserves such a memorial. We walk across a bridge and see the Hoover. This dam is enormous. Careful not to drop our devices into the dam, we take a few pictures. We hop back into the car and head into the desert looking for cactuses but don't really see any. We do see a bunch of Joshua trees though, which are customary to this area and unique to my eyes. We make it to the park for the Canyon and there is a shuttle that takes you to different overlooks. We get to the Skywalk part and just look over the normal area outside the building.

The canyon is amazing but everything is numbed with the absence of Gabi. There is a hole in my chest with the same magnitude of the vast crack in the land. I would love the bravery to jump in and fly, but I can't with my dad present; I can't leave him stranded in trauma. We spoke to some of the clerks at the "Skywalk" about people falling over the edge and the fact that there is no barrier to prevent such an atrocity. Sure, it happens, but a fence would take away from the beauty of nature. We pay to go on the "Skywalk" itself which is basically a glass floor platform that stretches out over the canyon. I buy my customary shot glass souvenir. This one appears to be bronze and has Road Runner molded on it. We hang out for a while but a chilly mild storm brews so we head back.

Back in Vegas, we go out to see *Blue Man Group*. We find the hotel where the show is by looking for a giant pyramid. Inside the building the ceiling is painted to look like a sky and gives the place a different aura. The show is filled with comedy and mondo music. There is a lot of interaction with the crowd as we are supposed to make something out of this strand of toilet-paper-like stuff. The men with blue painted faces even get up into the audience jumping around on structures and looking awkwardly into some people's faces. They bring an audience member onto the stage and act out a dining experience filled with strange physical humor. They play unconventional instruments. They take a PVC pipe and beat on it while changing the length of it to get different notes. There are sporadic colors and flying paper rolls everywhere. It is an experience everyone should undergo at least once; quite entertaining. We fall back to the hotel and as Dad snoozes, I decide to hit the roulette table again. This time I win 80 dollars, wow.

November 22nd is "travel-to-Los-Angeles day," but my hotel is technically in Glendale, California. The first thing I notice when stopped for a rest in California is the strange signs on the restroom doors. I have to walk through the door with the giant triangle to go pee. Women have giant circles on their doors. We reach Glendale and realize our hotel is really simple and cheap compared to the rest of the neighborhood. We decide to take a walk and explore the area. We discover the serendipity of a lovely, quaint, and decorative shopping area full of spirit, lights, fountains, music, and joy. Christmas is nigh so all the décor is around too. Here I find a Tesla store and the infamous Apple giant glass storefront. The walkway in this center is a converted railway with fancied up hardwood. What a gem for us to stumble on, not even expecting to do anything this evening. I think I like Glendale.

Saturday is completely dedicated to the car show. We drive to L.A., find our designated parking lot, and hop on the shuttle to the convention center. It is directly across from the stadium where the Lakers must play. We enter the lobby of the enormous building and the first thing we see is a Firebird. Technically it is a Camaro that some custom company converted, but it is cool. Then we roam into the main area, an enormous floor full of the latest models of awesome new cars and human models modeling said cars. The main attraction this year is probably the new mid-engine Corvette, and maybe the new all electric Mustang crossover. I take my time gathering in all the new lines and beautiful cars to the point where my old man gets exhausted and needs to sit for a rest. We still have the lower floor to visit too. We eventually do. I enjoy this show but honestly, I was expecting something more, maybe more concepts or something to differentiate this show from the Detroit show that I have been to so many times.

Visiting downtown Hollywood this Saturday night to see the "Stars" and to grab dinner is a mistake, there are just too many people here on the sidewalks, shoulder to shoulder body traffic. This is not enjoyable at all. Maybe a day visit would be better.

It's Sunday, we drop the top on this rental car that I am feeling a bond with, and drive to see the famous "Hollywood" sign. It is actually very hard to find a good spot to see it clearly. We are driving all around these curvy and hilly roads and eventually find a little park area with a decent view. It's nice and sunny out today, perfect for pictures and perfect for the convertible. We then drive through Beverly Hills on our way to the Pacific Ocean. We arrive at Santa Monica beach and experience a new body of water. I get to knock another thing off my bucket list as I am sure my dad is glad that he gets to as well. He is very impressed with my ability to structure this vacation and my ability to navigate. My secret weapon is my cellular communications device, which I just bought a few months ago. I never buy new, it's a used Blackberry "KEYone" with android software and I love it mostly because it has a physical keyboard.

We are going back to Vegas and spending one last night there before we get back on the plane to reality. What happens in Vegas stays in Vegas and I think there is an unwritten law that seeing some breasts is requisite. We already saw the butt cheeks of a pair of performers walking down the street past the Bellagio fountain dressed in these elaborate peacock costumes. Tonight, we are going to see a show called "Crazy Girls." Apparently, it's the last of the classic burlesque shows still running here in Vegas. I don't know what possessed me to purchase tickets to this. That is a lie, I like boobs. Dad and I are getting the real Vegas experience tonight on our last day here. It's admittingly a little strange to do this with my dad but I don't care about anything anymore really.

Looking like a complete bum, my dad falls asleep on the floor at the airport during a layover. I graciously shoot a pic and laugh. We get back home around 2:00 am Wednesday before Thanksgiving. I numb my way through the holidays.

It's now February and I am back online looking up my ex. Gabi is hidden from me but I go on Joseph's Facebook and see his status update. My heart pops out of my chest as I read the two words: "Got married." Up until this point I have been fueled by hope. I hoped that I could get my love back. This hope is gone now. My previous scream-crying may have been a second-degree burn leaving blisters, but I am at a third degree burn now; my heart is scorched.

I heard God's voice telling me that I would marry Gabi one day. Am I just a crazy person? My granddad heard God's voice, was he just a crazy person? Has the very foundation of everything I have ever believed in for the past 20 years just been make-believe?

Years have passed now but what have I learned? I learned it doesn't matter how much I try, or how much I love someone, it doesn't matter what I do or how good I am, no one will ever love me. That's what I learned. Also, it's apparent that I am not my soulmate's soulmate, and that you should trust no one.

My dad stops by on a day that coping has been exceptionally hard. I wind up tearing up and admitting to him that I need help. His exact response is: "The game is on tonight, come watch it," then he leaves. This is something he always says. I finally reach out and I garner no support anyway? What would I expect him to say? No one has told me "come back down to *Earth*," and even if they did, would I want to?

It may appear I have everything; a house, nice automobiles, a job, smarts, good looks, and talents. But what have I without love? I found love and it was a miracle, a perfect partner for me. To be let down like this is unreal or surreal or whatever, please just have me killed. How am I to function if I find peace in nothing?

I climbed the mountain of life only to realize that it's actually a *volcano*. The pyramid scheme I had with Gabi only led to a lava pit, and I fell into the depths of hell. I wouldn't even know how to climb out.

I have multiple reasons to kill myself, and here they are:

> It will end the pain.
> If God isn't real, life is pointless. If God is real, he clearly wants me to kill myself.
> I refuse to love again.
> I want to be famous.
> My family will recognize my love and it could bring them closer.
> I legitimately want to see what's on the other side.
> I'd love to be lost in the memory of Gabi, and I don't want to forget her.
> I can't be myself on earth anymore anyway.
> I am a waste anyway.
> Nobody actually needs me.
> I've always said, "I want to die before I have kids or after they die so that they don't have to mourn me," the latter may be impossible.
> I am just another body to feed.
> I don't want to be the guy I might become.
> I have experienced all the happiness I needed.
> I want to be the author of my life.
> I want to raise mental health/suicide prevention awareness.
> I don't want to get too old to do the things that I enjoy.
> Amili will get a much needed $50,000 check through my life insurance policy.

If I really kill myself it is what is supposed to happen. It'll be what God wants. For every season there is a reason, and we are all merely puppets. I absolutely don't see another resolution. If I continue on, I will just struggle with spirituality and struggle with emotions because I was and always will be so certain of my story, so sure that Gabrielle was "the one." I don't want to become an alcoholic. I don't want to settle with some woman someday just because I want kids. I don't want to be with someone who I don't consider my "number 1." I don't want to be with anyone but Gabi. I don't want to be someone who just seeks sex. Sex is the sole activity I would enjoy succeeding the ability to play football. I've been hooking up with Autumn again, and just a few days afterwards I had sex with someone I met on *Tinder*. My egotistical self is proud that I finally got with a Hispanic woman. I don't want to be this person.

I have researched the most painless ways to die. Google recently has been frequently responding to my searches by giving me the number to the suicide hotline. It's kind of funny. How soon will it be before searches are monitored and the police get called automatically? It's funny that I was a correctional officer considering they have high suicide rates. It's funny that I bumped my head a substantial amount of times playing football, conceivably giving me CTE, a condition that often leads to suicide. It's funny that funny people like Robin Williams commit suicide. Is it funny that I am using the word "funny" to describe something that is tremendously not funny?

- Chapter 19 -
Beautiful Notes

Dear Mom,

From day one you have done everything in your ability to
help me. I love you. Thanks for being a loving mother. You were
always there for a hug, a shoulder to cry on, and never needed
anything in return. I am sorry I had to leave this world so early,
but I have reached my destiny.

Probably your greatest trait and the main thing I learned from
you was the importance of honesty. In my life experience I
honestly think I am the most honest individual I've ever met. It's
a big part of my life story. This story, as in human nature, needs
to make sense to me. Maybe now it finally does.

As a youngster under your care I was frightened of other
people, shy to the core. I had an introverted nature with a desire
to be extroverted. I found solitude and ease in your swallowing.
My brain was confused and undeveloped. By the time I was a
pre-teen our relationship was deteriorating. I can't fully explain
why, but I guess a lot of it had to do with problems between you
and Dad. I had become very depressed and you tried your best
with therapy and medication, but it just made me feel like
something was wrong with me. Maybe I like the idea of "crazy"
as it's always been a theme in my art. At this point I was
diagnosed with social anxiety disorder as well as depression. I
never liked how we as people like to label so many things as
disorders. In reality everyone is different and there are levels on
spectrums of just how different a human can be regarding
particular traits. I am on the lower level of social confidence so I
am labeled to have a disorder. I think this is a disturbing thing
we do to other people that makes them feel as outsiders or not
as complete of a person as others. Whoever dubbed the idea of
Attention Deficit Disorder is also a jerk. Telling Willow that she
has ADD and trying to shove pills down someone's throat

certainly can't help one's psyche. Sorry to rant but there are things I need to get off my chest before my death.

As you remember I attempted suicide once as a youngster, around 11 or 12 years old, I think. You were there to stop me, but had you not been there I may not have even tried. Perhaps it was a bit of a cry for attention. I am so sorry to have put that stress on you but I was a bewildered young kid, and the help I needed eventually came.

Granddad Adams paid a visit on one occasion when I was about 13-14. He had told his now famous story from his war days. The one he had published was awe inspiring, as were the others. I had learned that God is a real power here in our lives. God spoke to Granddad with his voice. God had sent an angel dog to the rescue in a story as well. These stories and this time in my life created a turning point. You made me aware of Christianity but this was the point in my life I had become saved. From here on I kept the faith and foresaw God's grace.

Approximately 20 years passed and everything had come to me with perfect timing. Sure, I struggled some but I kept the faith and prayed and God gave me everything I desired piece by piece perfectly. My faith grew at each step; graduating, getting jobs, home ownership, the last piece would be meeting my woman.

I had struggled mightily with relationships, and ever since my high school sweetheart (Jessy) I haven't been able to hold a relationship steadily for more than a half a year. I had about 9 heartbreaks total. I broke Jessy's heart so perhaps this is my payback or a spell was put on me? I couldn't believe something like that as a Christian so I carry on, rebuilding my wall. I thought I loved a bunch of girls and I learned a lot from those relationships. I dated a girl named Blessica. We had some struggles but I tried hard to make it work. I had to end the relationship because I realized I just couldn't love her. There were multiple reasons but one was that the physical part wasn't satisfying. I knew I was wrong for having that feeling so I decided from then on that I would wait until marriage for sexual relations. After a lot of thought I had become content and happy with myself and my life and didn't need to meet a girl. I thought maybe I was meant to be alone, and I was OK with it. But then God would send me a miracle.

Gabi had come into my life. A spirit of hope and goodness, the epitome of a complement to my life. Instantly I saw signs from God telling me that she was "the one." We had so much in common, and she too wanted to wait until marriage. During our first kiss I heard a voice telling me "This is the last girl you will ever kiss" and "You will marry her one day." We took things slow, God's way. Gabi picked me up with her beautiful words, erasing my doubts, and assured me that I was good enough. Never had I felt love like this. For the first time in my life I knew I was in love. The reasons are deep.

We are all imperfect and I did make one mistake. I snooped and saw something I wasn't supposed to one day. The guilt made me deathly ill, so I confessed to Gabi. I knew I had to do what was right. I had faith in God and our relationship and knew telling the truth was the only way to go. She was upset at the fact but she forgave me. This day was more proof that God was real! I knew that God was there for us and that everything would be alright. Everything was alright for a few more months.

Then she broke up with me out of the blue, and everything I had believed came crashing down and no longer made sense. I tried for 2 years to keep the faith but now she has blocked and ignored me like I am nothing! Nothing makes sense, there are just too many thoughts in my head and I needed it to end.

Suicide is not my decision, but it is the author's decision. This is the only way for my story to make sense. We live our whole lives trying to reach heaven. I found heaven on earth, and it was being with Gabi. Six months of heaven! I thank God for the experience. But is it fair for me to live out many more years of hell? I cry all the time and I know I will never stop. The longer I wait the further away I will be from my memories of heaven. It's my life, it's sort of my decision, it's already written, and it's what God wants.

Let us not be sad now because I am fulfilling my destiny. I am happy my legacy will live on with my art. I did my best in giving people good feelings, good memories, but I just don't feel good being alive anymore. I am excited to see what is on the other side. If it is the Devil I greet, then I will kill him! I love you Mom.

Ray

Dear Amili,

I love you! Our connection and chemistry went deeper than any other. Carrying on with you was the greatest. I am so sorry I had to leave my flesh, but it was my destiny.
Seeing you grow I can tell you I am very proud. You are a fantastic mother and wife to a good man. I am happy for you and your growing family. I will definitely miss our good times. I wish I could be there but I just wouldn't be myself anymore. I've tried to fake it for too long. You had your struggles and conquered them. I look up to you in a way for that accomplishment. I am emotionally delicate, and the thing that always hurt me the most was heartbreak. The last one (Gabi) was obviously just too much for me to bear. Please don't feel anger towards her, she did nothing wrong, it wasn't her fault, and I loved her to the end. You were always the most important person to me, and I fear my death will hurt you the most. Please understand I had some tremendous experiences in life and I am satisfied. I am exuberant to see what's on the other side. I feel the signs were sent from God. My suicide was supposed to happen. Perhaps there will be a great lesson learned by someone out there? Or maybe you will write a book about my story and become an award-winning author? Who knows?
You will be the beneficiary of my life insurance policy worth $50,000. I'd rather be able to just hand you cash like that with a real... big... stupid smile on my face.
Take care of the kids and take care of Dad. He has nothing except you and those kids. With deteriorating health, I can see he is really going to need you.

Love,
Ray

To Willow, Ivy, Lily, and any future kiddos,

I love you girls and wish I could hang around you more and be the best uncle. Just know that I love you. Know that family is important and they all love you, and always will the most. Take care of each other, build each other up, you're all you have.

When you get older be careful with your heart, and be careful with boys' hearts as well. Know that no one is perfect but know how to recognize good in people. Keep the good people around you. Read the Bible, there is so much wisdom in it.

I hope you keep positive memories of me and I hope these jewelry boxes stay in your possession and remind you that I love you. I had each of your names engraved in them. I think they are cool anyways.

Your crazy uncle,
Ray

Dear Dad,

I am sorry I killed myself. I am sorry about all those times I was an asshole. I am sorry I disrespected you so often. I am sorry I didn't show you more love. But let's be positive. I love you. You were the greatest dad for me, always willing and wanting to give a hand. You always wanted to be in my life. Thank you for all the things you have done. Thank you for raising me. It's impossible to show everyone how much I appreciate them, but I just wish I could.

In a way I wish I was more like you. You're simple and you don't let emotions get to you. But I do, I let emotions take over and eat my soul. I wanted to be like you, manly, and not in need of medication.

I struggled as a kid with depression, social anxiety, and all of that. Your relationship deteriorated with Mom and so did mine. I ended up choosing to live with you, as I thought it would help me grow best. The turning point in my life was a result of Granddad paying a visit and sharing his war stories. I attribute this moment to being the time I was "Saved." I accepted Christianity. After attempting suicide prior to this day, it was much needed. From then on, my suicidal thoughts diminished and I saw signs all the time that proved God's existence simply because I believed. I don't think you even fully understand the impacts these things have made on my life.

My relationships with women would continue to struggle whilst everything else was falling into place. I thought I knew Gabi was the final puzzle piece, a great Christian, and an amazing person. She was my one true love much like Malinda was for you. It destroyed me emotionally and spiritually when she left. My entire life story no longer made sense and it's something I cannot accept.

Love,
Ray

Dear Matthew,

You were my best friend. Not by the common definition but you were literally the best friend that I had. Thank you for not just being in my life but being a part of my life story. Thank you for all of your efforts. I "*shoulda-coulda*" learned a lot from you but I am too much of a num-nut thick skull brain. There were so many factors in my life and signs on the wall that made me come to this. I have to follow what I think is my destiny. I am so sorry to leave you, please forgive me. You will be okay; you are a strong man. You learned how to love again, but I couldn't. You've been through way more than me but I am weak, and I believe I was built this way for the story that God is writing to make sense.

I love you brother! Take care of yourself, you semi-genius, and take care of your beautiful offspring.

I really care about you man. I think a personal victory is when you help or do something commendable for someone without expecting recognition or anything in return. I practiced that with you, not just with lending money but the following is something

I was never going to tell you. Do you remember when we were working on your van? I believe it was a Chevy Venture. Something happened and we couldn't get it to run, so it ended up staying overnight in my backyard. It started running the next day "miraculously." What you didn't know is that I stayed up half the night working on that damn thing, and I got it running. I want to be a good person, and I want to prove to myself that I am a good person. It's a personal victory.

Love,
Ray

Dear Robert,

If you are reading this, I have committed suicide, unless of course I am standing before you and just wanted you to read this. Hopefully it is the latter. Either way I am sorry. I love you man. You are like a brother to me. You were my best friend growing up and I appreciate all you have done for me. We have so many vast memories and I hope to take them with me to the afterlife.

I am proud and happy for you for the life you have made for yourself. I am glad that you can pretty much live out your dreams. I hope the positivity continues to pour into your life! I wish as we got older, we could hang out more often. I started getting sad, and I started missing our adventures. I understand though that as you grew with your new life there was less time for friends.

Part of me feared you started holding something against me because of my relationship with Sarah, or maybe even a money thing, since you've paid my way on multiple occasions. I want you to know there is no way I can pay you back for the friendship you provided. I also want you to know that I care deeply about you, and your entire family including Sarah. She was a bright spot in my life and I had love for her. It didn't work out for multiple reasons but I will always remember the good times.

I once told you I never tell girls I love them. It's mostly true I usually don't. I get extremely emotional over relationships and it was my eventual demise. I said it to Sarah once out of desperation after we split but it wasn't meant to be. I eventually found someone whom I thought I was meant to be with. I was at your house the day I was going to meet this girl for the first time after we had been talking a bunch online. I ended up falling desperately in love with her. This was the only relationship where I was the first one to say "I love you." I knew for sure that we would end up married, but I was wrong and she ended up dumping me like they all do. For two years I tried to get her back and be patient and persistent. Amanda once mentioned "just keep trying" or something to that effect regarding a previous woman I had become attached to. Well I found out the love of my life had gotten engaged to someone else. The experience messed up my mind, my self-worth, my spirituality, everything is in question. So, I ended up killing myself over a girl apparently.

I wanted to be one of the other cute couples that come to your house gatherings, but I am alone. I needed to see what's on the other side. I'm sorry.

Love,
Ray

Dear Stephanie,

I am sorry. I was just going to use you. I was going to use you to save my life. I pride myself on being honest and you were right, I would have never been able to make you my number one. Even if I were to try to fake it, you'd catch me sniveling at a romantic commercial or something like that. Anyway, since you are reading this, I guess you know I killed myself.

I want you to know I have love for you, and I have a lot of respect for you. You are a strong woman with a lot of smarts, and the ability to overcome life's struggles. I admire you in so many ways. I am glad I got to make love to you. I wish I could

have been the man you wanted or needed, but I can't and I am
sorry. We had a great connection but my brain is filled with
crap. My best wishes to you and your kiddo and your future.

Love,
Ray

Dear Autumn,

If you are reading this I have passed away by my own doing:
suicide. I am so sorry that so many people you have gotten close
to have died, and I am so sorry to have been added to your list. I
don't really know how it feels to be in your shoes but I am sorry.

I am also sorry that I was unable to provide for you on the
romantic level. My heart was just stuck in one place and that is
why I had to move on to a new world. I don't know if God is
calling me to do this or if the devil has gotten ahold of me but I
am hoping it is the former. You see I have been pretty much
weeping like a little baby nearly every day for over two years
and nothing I tried ever helped.

I want you to continue being strong and pursuing your
passion to help people! I am amazed by you in many ways, to
overcome what you had to in order to become the good human
you are today. Don't give up.

Try to take these concepts with you. A romantic relationship
is a great friendship. It's about loving one another
unconditionally and doing nice things for each other because
you care but not because it is what is expected. The "little
things" is not about getting the details correct but doing the
unexpected. It's not about the give and the take, but accepting
someone for who they are. You will make a great wife and
mother someday if you can understand that. Also, you are
beautiful.

With much love,
Ray

Dear SMI Team,

My choice to leave Earth had nothing to do with my place of work. SMI has treated me far better than my expectation and I actually loved it there. SMI was my happy place during my last days. It was hard to show that with my shyness and depression, but I truly enjoyed everyone at SMI. Thank you all for the opportunity and the kindness.

I hope my departure doesn't have negative effects. I hope the memory of me and my hard work ethic helps strengthen the company and the individuals that knew me. I love you all. Take pride in your work. I am proud to have been on the SMI team.

Sincerely,
Ray Adams

To whom it may concern,

My cell phone lock pattern is in the shape of a giant number 3 in case you want to get on it to inform people of my death, or to get pictures or whatever else you may need. I also have a sheet of paper in my desk with all my internet subscriptions and passwords if needed.

I recently registered to be an organ donor, even though I don't know if my organs will be any good depending on the nature of my death.

I don't want a casket. I want to be buried naked directly in soil. I am an "Adams" and "Adam" means "man of the earth." Let me be a part of the Earth once again.

Thanks,
Ray Diamond Adams

- Chapter 20 -
Bright Light

It's 2020 now, the year I imagined would be the best year of my life, because 20 is my favorite number. Instead of joy there is pain. I still cry a lot, and I am worn out. I am ready to escape. All I do is brood and death is summoning me. 2020 will remain relevant to me personally, because it will be etched on my tombstone. There is already a global pandemic, and I have been forced to work from home, adding to my loneliness.

I have come to terms that this is what God wants. My life wouldn't make sense otherwise. It must be why he made me the way I am. He gave me these feelings and this ability so I can make my mark. If God is real, I know I will enter my version of heaven, which is being with Gabi, forever in the memory. If God isn't real then my life is pointless, and it doesn't matter anyway when I alleviate my pain. If it is the devil doing this then I will find him and kill him. I wish an earthling gave me permission to kill myself, it's what I want. No one will do it for me, no one will understand the "pull the plug" scenario I got in my head. I pray for courage, courage to sacrifice myself.

My plan is to use carbon monoxide. My garage is pretty small and I could run my Firebird to fill the space with poison. I have recently put long-tube headers on "Sweet Lisa" and high flow catalytic converters which surely don't burn off as much pollutant as normal ones would. In addition, I will unscrew the bolts meant for oxygen sensors that are located before the heat makes it to the converters. This will expel more raw carbon monoxide. Breathing in those fumes will be disgusting so I need to configure a way to make myself pass out while all this is going on. Chloroform would do the trick, where the heck can I get some of that? Apparently, it isn't like the movies though and you have to breathe it in heavily for approximately 5 minutes. In my research you can make chloroform by mixing acetone and bleach. I am buying some bleach right now. If this doesn't end up working, I could always try mixing bleach with ammonia which is known to be toxic. Maybe I could make that look like an accident.

I amass some much-needed alcohol in me for preparation. I read old letters from Gabi. I look at pictures of Gabi too. I want these images stuck in me. I should have jumped in that lake with Gabi. I want to release myself off into a happy place: another dimension where I did all the right things. I write a note: "I'm in the garage," and I leave it on my dining room table for whoever to see. I thought about texting Matthew and telling him I need a ride in the AM, and maybe just leaving this note on my door. This way my father, who would most likely be the first one to come to my house otherwise, won't have to be the one discovering my stiff flesh.

I'm skunk as a drunk and head into my garage, fireball in hand. Crying, laughing, and looking at images of Gabi on my phone, I sit in my running car. What a lovely place to die, in my most prized possession. I might lay down on the ground instead so my car doesn't end up smelling of rotten carcass. I have some blankets lying down and a bucket full of mixed bleach and acetone. I drench a towel in the counterfeit chloroform, and start huffing it. All it does is smell weird; I must not have executed it correctly. I never did enjoy nor comprehend chemistry too well. I chug some more cinnamon whisky and have a pretty profound headache. Confusion sets in and my stomach is unsettling. Is the last thing I see going to be the underside of my car? Is this what I really want? I am not ready for this! I try to get up. Where is the exit? I stumble on my car and spew nastiness all around. This utter confusion, is this what hell is like? The garage is spinning and I can't find the door. I trip and fall, but I fall into comfort as it feels a little better down here. Suddenly a stinging on my knee pops me up. What was that? I turn around and I see the door. I sprint to it and flop out in the cold dewy grass. I reach into my pocket, fingers shaky. I text Amili: "Please come help me."

Amili arrives and I am still laying in the grass. I am sniveling and my legs are twitching as Amili lays her hand on my shoulder. She just looks at me and says very little, but at least she is here. At least someone cares enough to come. I eventually get up and we mosey on into my house but I might have been out in my lawn for an hour or two. We chit-chat for a while. I assure her I will be fine tonight and she can go home, so she does.

The next day I take a shower and feel the sting on my knee, for it is bubbling up like a second-degree burn. I go into the garage to discover vomit everywhere, and it has a strange texture being half frozen, it is almost like papier mâché. I find the culprit to my burn; I must have stumbled over the space heater. What a mess.

Some days I manage ok but most days I feel a tightness in my chest. Every day is an interrogation as I get asked, "how are you?" and every day I deceivingly respond with "ok." I arrive home from work and observe many apples on my counter. Some I have gathered from my apple tree and others I have bought. I am not collecting apples but I am after the seeds. In my research I have learned there is a small amount of cyanide in apple seeds. I would have to eat 200 apples in five minutes in order for it to affect me. Cyanide poisoning was popular in war as it can kill you in a matter of minutes. So, I am collecting the seeds.

Meanwhile, I am attempting dehydration as this might be a painless way to go. I have not eaten or drunk anything in three days and I am supposed to go to football practice tomorrow. It is springtime and starting to warm up. Dying on the football field was always kind of a fantasy of mine albeit under different circumstances. Here I am in bed with a headache clearly due to lack of nutrition. My skin is pale, soft, and almost sticky or spongey. My penis has shriveled and I worry about its functionality. This is a very bizarre feeling and it is difficult to sleep.

It is a warm cloudy day at football practice. We carry on with the normal drills and I only feel slightly sluggish. We start running through our team defense. The cornerback on my side starts arguing with me about my responsibility in a cover 2 defense. I am a little disturbed with the lack of respect I get. I have been playing football for many years and I understand these basic principles. Wally the corner raises his voice which is routine for such an alpha and know-it-all. Uncharacteristic of myself I shoot back at him with my vocals as I become tense for the first time in a while. We don't resolve the issue but we move on to something else then we get a water break. Screw it, I will drink some water.

The apple seed idea seems pointless and through research I have discovered a better way to obtain cyanide naturally: raw bitter almonds. There are the sweet almonds that we all enjoy, but the bitter almond is its sinister cousin, scientifically called Prunus dulcis var. amara. Let's see if I can find any raw unprocessed bitter almonds on the internet. I find nothing on eBay which is always my initial go to. I might as well try Amazon. Yup, I see a bag of raw bitter almonds for sale on Amazon, and they are located in South America. The sale of bitter almonds is illegal in the United States apparently. Apparently, these can be really good for you if you eat one or two a day. The body can process small amounts of cyanide with no negative effect. On the other hand, if an adult consumes about thirty of them in a few minutes it could kill them in just a few more. Since I am a little bigger than your average human, I assume it would take a number exceeding fifty of them for fatal results. Their flavor is described as nasty, but I will have the chance to confirm that myself.

I come home from work weeks later and glaring at me between my doors is the bag of raw bitter almonds that have arrived from South America. There it is, I have got my hands on an easy way to die. Nervous and plotting ways to do this thing, I delay a few days before trying one. They do not have a pleasant taste; they remind me of rotten roots, a dirty sock, or a random bad sunflower seed you might get amongst good ones. I understand why this might not be a global scare as no one would want to consume more than one of these unless of course they had a death wish like I do. I set them away and continue to contemplate the end.

Weeks have passed. But time has minimal meaning anymore. I've been told it takes time to heal. Incorrect! Time only produces oblivion as memory fades. But this belief, this feeling, it won't fade, and that is because I refuse to allow it. Almost three years ago Gabi incarcerated my soul, yet it feels like it just happened. Time isn't real! The future already exists and perhaps time travel is possible, but only through death. Death is my calling; it's been calling me for years. Many people aren't privileged with choosing how they die or when. I am dictating my own story, as should be my birthright. I head to the playground to find a four-leaf clover. I search and search until I come across a quad-leaf death curse, this one's for me as I put it in my mouth, chew, and swallow fearlessly. It was fear that prevented my previous suicide attempts. The devil gives us fear, so it was him that kept me alive.

I prepare for my final evening with my personal form of meditation: reading esteemed letters and viewing aged pictures of the greatest period of my life. Heaven was a place on earth and God is calling me back, even if I don't fully understand it. I unload the entire bag of cyanide infused nuts into my blender; there's probably hundreds of almonds awaiting a mince. In with the mix I throw some frozen mango chunks, other fruits, and almond milk as seems fitting. I sip. The resulting product actually is not terrible at all, perhaps the mango obscures the foulness of the bitter almonds. I have dubbed it "Lava."

The giant gulp cup is filled fully as I place it on my bedroom desk with apprehension. It's late and it's dark and I have been bracing for this moment all day. I watch a short video of Gabi and I making multiple silly faces. That is where I want to be. I drink some *lava*. I skim through more photos as the night has gotten to a deeper dark and I drink some more *lava*. My head is throbbing and my stomach is queasy. I take another drink and stumble over to my bed to lie down. This feeling is strange, almost like a numb ache all over. My chest is hurting and I am realizing that this is authentic. I am having a legitimate physical reaction to my *lava* drink. There is a peculiar dizziness as I can't seem to situate myself right in bed, it seems best that I lie still. I need to pee and maybe vomit so I turn on the lamp and it hurts my eyes. As I climb out of bed, I discover the strangest kind of vertigo, more of a weak dizziness than a drunken one. I can barely hold myself up and walk but I make it to the bathroom. I pee and dry heave. I manage my way back to my desk and swallow more poison along with the truth and my pride. I have now drunk the majority of it. I delicately crawl my way back into bed but that lamp is excessively bright so I close my eyes. I pray to God, "If this is really it, take me God, I am ready." I imagine people from my past. I just want to think about Gabi and the good times but my chest has a weird hollow ache, and that light, it just keeps getting brighter... and brighter.

"Sorry Mamma"

Oh Mamma told me there will come a day
Oh Mamma told me hope is on the way
Oh Mamma told me you got to be strong
Got to gather up these pieces you got to carry on
Oh Oh Oh Oh
Dear Mamma, I'm sorry
I never meant to pass this pain to you
And Mamma please forgive me
Just know that there was nothing you could do
Mamma, I'm sorry
Just know that I really loved you
I wish I could be there for one more embrace
And I wish that my prayers revealed God's grace
Everything came together and seemed to make sense
But the glue we knew broke down and
everything is past-tense
When she said that she loved me and I started crying
She didn't know that she was lying
My first and last thought was I got to grab a gun
I'm telling you Mamma that life was no fun
No No No No
Dear Mamma, I'm sorry
I never meant to pass this pain to you
And Mamma please forgive me
Just know that there was nothing you could do
I know that I will never see your smiling face again
Mamma, I'm sorry
Just know that I really loved you
I know that I will never see your smiling face again

– Acknowledgements –
Special thanks to the following people

Stanley Fern Wray
For the impact his stories had on my life.

Aryn McMillan
For being there and helping with paraphrasing.

William Metz
For editorial work and website design.

Jonathan Moser
For illustrations on the flip side of the dust jacket.

You Know Who
For the impact on me and giving me incentive to write this book.

And to everyone else who was "named" in this book, and had an impact on my life stories.

CPSIA information can be obtained
at www.ICGtesting.com
Printed in the USA
LVHW110843030922
727402LV00013B/135/J